# Saving Animals

# Saving Animals

## Multispecies Ecologies of Rescue and Care

Elan Abrell

University of Minnesota Press
Minneapolis
London

Portions of chapter 1 and the Conclusion are adapted from "Lively Sanctuaries: A Shabbat of Animal Sacer," in *Animals, Biopolitics, Law: Lively Legalities*, ed. Irus Braverman, 135–54 (New York: Routledge, 2016); reprinted by permission of Taylor & Francis Group, with permission of the Licensor through PLSclear. Portions of chapters 1, 2, 3, and the Conclusion are adapted from "Animal Sanctuaries," in *The Routledge Handbook of Animal Ethics*, ed. Bob Fischer, 569–77 (New York: Routledge, 2019); reprinted by permission of Taylor & Francis Group, with permission of the Licensor through PLSclear. Portions of chapters 2, 3, and the Conclusion are adapted from "Interrogating Captive Freedom: The Possibilities and Limits of Animal Sanctuaries," *Animal Studies Journal* 6, no. 2 (2017): 1–8.

All photographs, unless otherwise credited, were taken by Jo-Anne McArthur with We Animals or NEAVS, as specified. They were not taken at the author's primary field sites and do not feature any of the animals described in the book.

JO-ANNE MCARTHUR | WE ANIMALS

Published by the University of Minnesota Press
111 Third Avenue South, Suite 290
Minneapolis, MN 55401-2520
http://www.upress.umn.edu

ISBN 978-1-5179-0811-9 (hc)
ISBN 978-1-5179-0812-6 (pb)
Library of Congress record available at https://lccn.loc.gov/2020048325.

Printed in the United States of America on acid-free paper

The University of Minnesota is an equal-opportunity educator and employer.

30 29 28 27 26 25 24 23 22 21          10 9 8 7 6 5 4 3 2 1

*For Niko, Lauren, Lola, Shadow,*
*Owl, and Panza—infinitimitum!*

*And for Adrienne, who fostered my love for animals;*
*Samararose, who shared it; and Freal, who supported it*

*And, of course, for the animals*

I'm truly sorry Man's dominion
Has broken Nature's social union,
An' justifies that ill opinion,
Which makes thee startle,
At me, thy poor, earth-born companion,
An' *fellow-mortal!*

— Robert Burns, "To a Mouse, on Turning Her Up<br>in Her Nest with the Plough, November, 1785"

There is a terrible forest fire. All the animals are fleeing
the conflagration except Hummingbird, who is flying
back and forth, scooping up little slivers of water from
a spring and dumping them on the flames. "What do
you think you're doing, stupid little bird?" the other
animals ask derisively, and Hummingbird says, "I'm
doing what I can."

— Wangari Maathai

Animals also deserve . . . their bread and roses.

— Kendra Coulter, *Animals, Work, and the<br>Promise of Interspecies Solidarity*

Run into the rescue with love and peace will follow.

— River Phoenix

# Contents

A rescued chicken socializing with a rescued pig. We Animals.

# Introduction

## The Story of Bob and Eloise

Bob[1] is a black-and-white Holstein steer, the breed of cattle you might see in milk commercials. Though now a large steer measuring more than six feet at the haunches and weighing almost a ton, he was a diminutive week-old calf when he came to the sanctuary for formerly farmed animals[2] in New York State, where he has spent most of his life. Bob's mother, by contrast, spent her life on the commercial dairy farm where he was born. The farm that owned his mother planned to auction him off to be raised for veal.[3] Before he could be sold at auction, a passing couple saw Bob tied to a tree and decided to rescue him from the miserably confined fate of a veal calf by buying him themselves. According to caregivers at the sanctuary, Bob's rescuers tried to care for him at home but found it too difficult, so they brought him to the sanctuary.

When he first arrived, he slept in a pen inside a barn where dozens of rescued pigs also slept. Because there were no lactating cows at the sanctuary, Bob had to suck milk replacer formula from a bottle, ironically similar to the way he would have been fed as a veal calf, since cows' milk is preserved for sale to humans. As he got older, sanctuary caregivers eventually started supplementing his diet with small portions of grain to help him gain weight.[4] Caregivers spent as much time with him as their daily duties would allow and even slept in the barn with him at night during his first days at the sanctuary, making it easier to give him his regular nighttime bottle feedings. Like a human child, Bob's body and curiosity both grew at a rapid pace that could not be contained by the small pen. When Bob figured out that he could use his nose to knock the lid off the grain storage container next to where he slept, caregivers had to build a gated storage pen to keep Bob away from the grain bags.

One day, while still living in the pigs' barn, Bob encountered Eloise, a calico goat with butterscotch- and licorice-colored spots polka-dotting her shaggy white hair. Eloise was also a new arrival at the sanctuary. Eloise's original human companions abandoned her after their house was damaged in a fire. They left her in their yard with only a few muddy rain puddles for drinking water. She managed to survive in the yard for a few months, until a humane law enforcement officer found her and brought her to the sanctuary. Eloise was malnourished and carrying a large parasite load when she was rescued. She also had difficulty walking. Domestic goats need their hooves to be regularly trimmed since they often do not have access to the kinds of rocky surfaces that continuously wear down the hooves of wild goats. Eloise's hooves were so long that they prevented her from walking properly, affecting the ligaments in her legs. After caregivers trimmed her hooves, gave her antiparasite medication, and helped her regain a healthy weight, Eloise's legs improved.

At first, Eloise showed no interest in socializing with other animals, including the other goats at the sanctuary. Shortly after Bob's arrival, though, they began leaning against each other while separated by the gate between their pens. Since they seemed to want to have physical contact, caregivers opened the gate and allowed them to interact more directly. They became inseparable companions, grazing together throughout the day and sleeping together at night. As Bob grew, however, his playful young calf exuberance became dangerous for the older, more fragile goat. Within a year, he had gained almost 800 pounds. To protect Eloise from injury, caregivers began putting Bob in a pasture during the day with the other steer at the sanctuary, allowing him to sleep with her at night after he had burned off his adolescent energy. Eventually, he had grown too large for even that to be safe, so caregivers decided to keep him full-time with his fellow steer. Nonetheless, spatial segregation could not sever the interspecies bond Eloise and Bob had formed. Despite their separation, Bob and Eloise continue to graze side by side, often sniffing each other's noses or pressing against each other through the wire fencing between them. We may not know what exactly they gain from these interactions—and whatever it is could be different for each animal—but we can at least surmise from their intentional initiation of contact with each other that there is something they value in the interaction.

In many ways, the story of Bob and Eloise typifies the experiences of both human and nonhuman animals in sanctuaries. Built around relationships of care, animal sanctuaries seek to provide spaces where animals can live better lives than their previous circumstances would afford, but they face many challenges in trying to meet that goal. From juggling the medical, dietary, and psychological needs of different animals to the spatial constraints and challenges of housing multiple species together, sanctuary care often requires compromises and sacrifices. Bob and Eloise, for example, were forced to forgo spatial mobility as well as the ability to socialize with each other without the impediment of physical barriers. As this book's analysis of the many potential costs and compromises of sanctuary life will show, this one is relatively minor, especially compared to animals that are required to give their lives for the well-being of others, such as animals that serve as food for other sanctuary denizens. But Bob and Eloise's story is also noteworthy because it provides an example of the kinds of contributions animals make to the greater interspecies community beyond bearing the costs of such compromises. While human caregivers ultimately determine what compromises must be made and who must make them, the outcomes of sanctuary care are not exclusively determined by humans. Through the interspecies relationship they formed, Bob and Eloise provided each other with social enrichment and companionship, an outcome that was neither anticipated nor guided by human caregivers.[5] As they show, sanctuary care is a multispecies collaborative process in which animals like Bob and Eloise can contribute to their own care as well as the care of others.

I run little risk of hyperbole to say that animal rescue stories have a nearly universal positive emotional resonance for people, at least simple ones like an abandoned goat rescued from neglect or a baby calf saved from an early death. However, the more they are fleshed out with the complexities of context and moral nuance that are unique to any given rescue tale, the broader the spectrum of likely affective responses becomes, increasingly mirroring the complex range of attitudes and values that shape the many ways humans interact with other living beings. When we place Bob's rescue in the context of industrialized animal agriculture, for example, we increase the odds that some people may see it as less like a rescue and more like a removal from a food supply chain, with the attendant diminishment in emotional poignancy that such a shift would effect. Animal sanctuaries are concentrated spatial nexuses of such complexity and context. Bob's and Eloise's rescues necessarily critique and challenge the cultural, political, and economic contexts that shaped the conditions from which they were rescued, but the stories of those rescues do not end in a "happily ever after" in their arrivals at sanctuary. The moral choices to rescue each of them were in fact catalysts for cascades of repeated moral choices that must be made about their ongoing care (and mutually influential choices about the care of other animals) for as long as they live in sanctuary.

Exploring how the U.S. animal sanctuary movement functions as a microcosm of human efforts to care for others in the contemporary United States, this book interrogates two separate but inextricably linked meanings of sanctuary: sanctuary as a specific bounded place or state of being and sanctuary as an ideological/ethical mode of being. Bob and Eloise are in the physical space of sanctuary, a specific place where they are protected from the dangers, violence, and deprivations they would have faced if they had not been rescued. Many of the dilemmas of animal care examined in future chapters are a direct result of sanctuaries' material and spatial limitations. The ethical vision of the sanctuary as a space of exception from the typical treatment of animals like Bob and Eloise is an intentionally activist mode of relating to animals that challenges the larger cultural, political, and economic contexts in which they are reducible to living property. This latter sense of sanctuary as an ideological/ethical mode of being influences the realities of care within sanctuary spaces while also being shaped by the realizations of what is possible within those spaces. Moreover, it bridges these efforts to treat other animals better to political movements to treat other humans better. With the hyperxenophobic intensification of U.S. immigration control efforts under the Trump regime, for example, the idea of sanctuary for people is gaining renewed political cachet in the form of sanctuary cities or communities that would provide a physical space of (limited) protection from these efforts. Animal sanctuaries thus provide an opportunity for examining shifting practices of relating to or caring for other species in the contemporary United States as well as for examining how sanctuary as simultaneously spatial and ideological modes of being can counteract a range of different oppressive political projects aimed at humans as well as animals.[6]

## Human–Animal Relations in the Contemporary United States

As illustrated by the different ways Bob and Eloise were treated before and after coming to a sanctuary, there is a deep ambivalence toward animals in the United States. On one hand, the consumption of animals is integral to both its culture and its economy. On the other hand, there is a pervasive and enduring sense of affection for animals throughout U.S. cultural history, as reflected in popular literature, films, television shows, and now endlessly proliferating internet memes and videos. The title of a book about this ambivalence by anthrozoologist Hal Herzog articulates the tension succinctly: *Some We Love, Some We Hate, Some We Eat.* Further complicating matters, these categories are not mutually exclusive. Deer, for example, can be simultaneously loved by children watching *Bambi*,[7] hated by suburban

Rescued goats playing in a pasture. We Animals.

gardeners trying to protect their roses from decimation, and eaten by hunters and their families following deer season each year. Even dogs cannot escape this web of conflicting values. While dogs are arguably the most popular pet species in the United States (rivaled only by cats), cities have passed breed bans against certain types of dogs, such as pit bulls, and cultural conflicts have arisen between different ethnic communities over the consumption of dogs as food.[8] Far from resolving itself, this contradiction has only intensified in the last several decades while the expansion of animal-based industries has fueled the reciprocal growth of animal protection activism.

Some of the most significant effects of postwar production and consumption regimes impact animals.[9] Indeed, everyday human–animal interactions in the United States are embedded in a wide array of shifting cultural and political–economic systems, ranging from food (e.g., factory farms, small-scale organic farms, and hunting)[10] to entertainment (e.g., aquariums, zoos, and circuses)[11] to companionship (e.g., pets and service animals).[12] This vast array of practices and institutions related to the commodification of animals is collectively known as the animal–industrial complex.[13] Building off of Barbara Noske's original formulation of the concept, Richard Twine describes the animal–industrial complex as a "partly opaque and multiple set of networks and relationships between the corporate (agricultural) sector, governments, and public and private science. With economic, cultural, social and affective dimensions it encompasses an extensive range of practices, technologies, images, identities and markets."[14] According to the U.S. Department of Agriculture's (USDA) National Agricultural Statistics Service, the number of farmed animals slaughtered every year for food in the United States doubled between 1980 and 2000, from 4.5 billion to approximately 8.5 billion. That total peaked at approximately 9.5 billion in 2007 and 2008 and since then remained at approximately 9 billion through 2013.[15] Over 90 percent of those animals were chickens, with turkeys, pigs, and cows in a distant second, third, and fourth place, respectively, and ducks and sheep making up the rest. The total annual revenue for U.S. animal agricultural industries (including dairy and eggs) peaked in 2014 at more than $420.1 billion—almost a 32 percent increase from 2010—and has since declined to an average of $370 billion in subsequent years.[16] In addition to this mass consumption of animals as food, approximately 175 million people per year visit zoos and aquariums, generating more than $5 billion in revenue.[17] Nearly 7.6 million cats and dogs enter U.S. animal shelters every year, of which 2.7 million are killed. An estimated 37 percent to 47 percent of U.S. households have a dog, and 30 percent to 37 percent have a cat.[18] In 2014, people in the United States spent $58.04 billion on pets, including $2.5 billion for live animal purchases, $36.01 billion for food and supplies, and $19.88 billion for veterinary care and other services.[19]

These animal-based production and consumption regimes have not gone unchallenged. The U.S. animal protection movement targets these regimes through activism aimed at factory farming, the confinement and mistreatment of animals in zoos and circuses, and large-scale pet breeding, among many other issues. Since New York philanthropist Henry Bergh founded the American Society for the Prevention of Cruelty to Animals in 1866, the United States has become an important center in a global movement to protect, rescue, and rehabilitate animals that are negatively affected by the actions of humans. However, as these consumption regimes have dramatically altered and intensified in recent decades under late-capitalist globalization, they have spurred new forms of animal advocacy distinct from early twentieth-century animal welfare movements, such as humane societies and antivivisection organizations.[20] The extensive range of groups and individual activists that compose what is collectively known as the U.S. animal protection movement are presently engaged in a wide variety of activities, from public advocacy and demonstrations to legal interventions, on behalf of animals. Striving to end what they see as the suffering and exploitation of animals at the hands of humans, these activists are working to reframe the national cultural imaginary as one that recognizes animals as subjective beings with interests worthy of ethical consideration and legal protection rather than objects to be utilized for human benefit.

Activist efforts are bearing fruit. Public attitudes toward animals in particular grow more complex as concerns about animal welfare, environmental impacts of animal-based industries, and new scientific understandings of animal consciousness continue to spread beyond the animal protection movement. Questions about the appropriate treatment of animals and how to balance these concerns against the needs of humans are becoming increasingly relevant to broader segments of the U.S. population. Popular publications by mainstream authors, such as Michael Pollan, Jonathan Safran Foer,

and Eric Schlosser, have contributed to focusing the public's attention in particular on the way animals are treated in the industrial food
system.[21] Public concern over these issues has in turn led to changes
in production practices. For example, in response to a groundswell of
public opposition, several states since 2010 have implemented legislation banning tail-docking of cows,[22] gestation crates for pigs,[23]
and battery cages for hens.[24] Dozens of large meat distributors and
restaurant chains similarly responded to public pressure by implementing corporate policies ensuring that they will only deal with
suppliers who implement these changes. In May 2015, Walmart—the
largest retail chain in the United States—announced its adoption of
the "Five Freedoms Principle," which supports freedom for farmed
animals from hunger and thirst; discomfort; pain, injury, or disease;
and fear and distress and the freedom to express normal behavior.[25]
In practice, this means that, among other policy changes, Walmart no
longer carries products from suppliers that use sow gestation crates,
hen battery cages, or veal crates.

   In another example—this time from the animal entertainment
industry—the documentary *Blackfish* detailed the mistreatment of captive orcas in facilities like the SeaWorld chain of theme parks.[26] This
exposure ignited a public backlash against SeaWorld Entertainment
Inc., resulting in a decline in park attendance, lost profits, and plum-
meting stock prices, which lost half their value between the film's release in 2013 and the end of 2015. In November 2015, SeaWorld seemingly caved to public pressure and announced it would be phasing out
live orca shows at its San Diego theme park (though not at its parks in
Orlando or San Antonio). Five months later, the corporation also announced it would end its orca-breeding program, making the twenty-
four orcas in its three parks the last it will hold in captivity. According to a statement from the company that implicitly acknowledges
the backlash, it is ending the breeding program because "society is
changing[,] and we're changing with it."[27] In a similar capitulation to
broad public opposition to its treatment of elephants, Ringling Bros.
and Barnum & Bailey Circus also announced in 2015 that it would be
phasing out elephant performances in its live shows.[28] In 2017, Feld
Entertainment—the parent company of Ringling Bros.—went even
further when it declared that the 146-year-old circus would come to an
end when it performed its final shows in May 2017.

   Despite their achievements, not all animal activists support these strategies. Debates among animal activists question the value of such efforts, reflecting a tension between the two predominant perspectives in animal activism: animal welfarism and animal rights. Welfarists advocate an incremental improvement in the treatment of animals through legislation and policy reform, whereas animal rights advocates seek an end to the instrumental use of all animals through an extension of basic rights, especially to live free from harm. Abolitionists, a subset of the rights position, extend the logic of this position to its ultimate conclusion, advocating for the complete abolition of the property status of animals.[29] Philosopher Tom Regan summarizes the difference between the rights and the welfare approach as "empty cages, not larger cages."[30] Many animal rights advocates argue that improvements in welfare for animals—such as the ones in agricultural industries described earlier—simply make their exploitation more palatable to consumers and thus more profitable to producers. However, some "humane" farmers explicitly cite caring about the well-being of animals as a major motivating factor in changing farming practices to improve welfare.[31] This trend suggests that concerns about the treatment of animals may even be spreading from the consumption side to the production side of animal-based economies, at least in these limited examples.

In the last three decades, animal advocates have also expanded their strategies by establishing hundreds of rescue facilities across the United States in an attempt to save tens of thousands of animals from factory farms, roadside zoos, and other situations where, they believe, animals are neglected, abused, and exploited. Because it seeks to assist endangered or at-risk animals removed from the various consumption regimes outlined here, this burgeoning animal sanctuary movement—with its focus on the rescue, care, and rehabilitation of animals—provides an ideal context to examine new patterns of human–animal interaction emerging out of shifting cultural attitudes toward animals. In this book, I therefore focus on the U.S. animal sanctuary movement as an increasingly significant component of animal advocacy efforts to influence the ways animals are valued and treated in U.S. society.

At the same time that concern for the well-being of animals is growing, animal advocacy also has its critics. Many people see animal activists as misanthropes who care more about the suffering of animals than about humans. This view is further problematized when animal issues are viewed in contrast to issues like racist oppression and violence. For example, a meme circulating on Facebook following news in 2014 of the contaminated water crisis in Flint, Michigan, showed a picture of a dog being treated by a veterinarian with a caption that read, "The dogs in Flint are testing positive for lead poisoning too; maybe now white people will care." Similarly, when Cecil the lion was killed in 2015 in Zimbabwe, there was widespread condemnation on social media of the U.S. dentist who shot him. But there was also a backlash against the pro-Cecil movement from critics who were upset by what they saw as a disproportionate outpouring of concern for a lion compared to support for the Black Lives Matter movement and Black victims of police violence in the United States.

While it is true that there are animal activists who focus their efforts on the suffering of animals while ignoring the social problems that affect millions of humans around the world, it is also true that there are activists focused on single issues related to human suffering that focus little of their energy on other issues. Moral philosopher Lori Gruen points out that this kind of conflict over which social issues activists focus their energy on is often driven by an unproductive "zero-sum mentality."[32] In fact, many of the activists I have met through my fieldwork care about social justice issues beyond the treatment of animals, while I also know many people who care about social justice issues who give none of their time to activism of any kind. But even if one could make a valid argument that animal activists' time would be better spent on other issues, the work they do now is important and has significant implications for both the future of human–animal relations and, on an even larger scale, the future of humans on the planet.

## Research Design

Every animal has a story about how she came to sanctuary, including the humans who work there. For me, the journey grew out of the simple fact that I have loved animals for as long as I can remember. Not surprisingly, I heard variations of this sentiment expressed by virtually every person I encountered during the course of my research. What it means to love animals, the relationships and obligations that arise from this particularly potent affect, and the spaces created by those relationships are the animating concerns of this ethnography. Love for animals—like the acts of care to which it gives rise—manifests in different ways and means different things for humans and other animals across all my field sites. Much philosophical debate has been devoted to why people should or should not see animals as different or less worthy of moral consideration than humans, but in beginning this research, I could not think of any work that explored why others *do* see animals as worthy of such consideration, much less how and why such attitudes vary in different contexts. It seemed the best sites to explore these questions would be spaces in which people dedicate their time to saving and caring for animals.

Before delving into this story of saving animals, I think it's important to explicitly identify my own ethical and affective orientations toward its subject. I strived to follow the basic anthropological injunction to make the familiar strange in my efforts to understand practices of care and interspecies relationships as much as possible through the perspectives of those engaged in them. Like all researchers, though, I cannot isolate myself from my own values or history. Personally, I support the animal-saving missions of sanctuaries and shelters, even if I do not always fully align with their methods. I tried to see their views, attitudes, and values as separate from my own even when they seemed to closely parallel each other. I tried to suspend my own ethical and political commitments and to see the story of saving animals through the eyes of those who were living it. In practice, this entailed trying to distance myself from my own moral judgments about the ways animals are treated in sanctuaries as well as in the institutions from which the sanctuaries rescue their animals.[33] While trying to understand their critiques of the ways animals are treated in U.S. society without conflating them with my own, I also tried to understand the ways sanctuary caregivers engaged with animals without presuming that those ways were necessarily any better than the practices they opposed. It was not easy, but based on the unexpected insights I gained from my research, it also was not unsuccessful. Still, my positionality no doubt influenced my understandings of and engagements with humans and other animals throughout my research in ways that were not fully apparent to me, so I highlight that positionality here to contextualize what follows.

Sanctuaries must balance their efforts to care for animals against the necessities of captivity, which means they must contend with difficult decisions regarding such factors as the amount of restraint required for potentially dangerous animals, compromises to ideal living conditions and diet due to limited resources, the euthanasia of animals deemed beyond rehabilitation, and the creation of appropriate habitats for captive animals. Equally important are the choices and interpretations of sanctuary workers, volunteers, donors, and detractors in relation to the constraints around resource limitations, new revelations about animal consciousness (born from both scientific research and lay experience), and new challenges related to dealing with animals who themselves are adjusting to new habitats and to novel kinds of contact with humans and other species. Moreover, sanctuary workers must address unique material and ideological concerns according to the types of animals (e.g., farm, exotic, or domestic) and the corresponding political–economic contexts from which they are rescued (e.g., food, entertainment, or companionship). In these highly politicized contexts in which humans tend to be deeply invested in providing animals with the best lives possible, attempts to manage the tensions around improving and regulating the lives of animals encourage new, multiple, and at times conflicting meanings and practices of care to emerge.

Through a comparative study of facilities focused on caring for animals entangled in three different animal consumption regimes—food, entertainment, and companionship—this ethnography explores the politics and ethics of care practices in animal sanctuaries. I treat sanctuaries as laboratories where activists conceive and operationalize new models for ethical relationships with animals—models they hope will influence broader public debates.[34] I spent two years conducting ethnographic fieldwork as a volunteer at a No Kill dog and cat shelter in Texas, an exotic animal sanctuary in Hawai'i, and a farm animal sanctuary in New York. I supplemented this fieldwork with visits to other rescue facilities in New York, Vermont, Texas, Louisiana, and Florida. Through participant observation and in-depth interviews, I collected data on practices of care and rescue as well as the ethical values that inform them. I documented how caregivers structure the living spaces of animals; meet their daily nutritional and sanitation needs; respond to illness and injuries; and address aggressive, destructive, or uncooperative behavior. I particularly focused on the criteria that inform decisions such as which animals are brought into the sanctuary, when to pursue expensive medical procedures, and when euthanasia should be employed. Aside from their physical well-being, I found that care practices also focused on animals' psychological enrichment. To examine how caregivers interpreted animals' psychological needs, I documented their methods for providing animals with social and environmental stimuli, how they explained animal behaviors and characterized individual animals' personalities, the feelings or desires they attributed to animals, and how they spoke to and for them. On the basis of this evidence, I discovered that practices of care and the ethical values that inform them are varied and contested across sites. Specifically, they are influenced by the variety of interrelated ethical dilemmas that arise in determining how best to care for animals.

Focused on the mutually influential roles of ideological and material factors in shaping human–animal relations, this ethnography examines how cultural values—specifically the influence of historical practices of animal advocacy and particular philosophical and scientific understandings of human–animal difference—intersect with the political–economic conditions of captive animal care to influence relationships between humans and other animals in sanctuaries. Importantly, I also focus on the active role animals like Bob and Eloise play in shaping their own conditions of care. This is a direct response to concerns raised by the undercited[35] anthropologist and ecofeminist Barbara Noske, who, in the late 1990s, critiqued much of the previous anthropological work on human–animal interactions for treating animals as objects mediating human relations rather than participants (willing or not) in those relations. On the basis of this critique, she called for a more robust examination of how the subjectivity and agency of animals influence the way humans understand, value, and interact with them.[36] Molly Mullin seconded this call in her *Annual Review* article "Mirrors and Windows: Sociocultural Studies of Human–Animal Relationships."[37]

Research in the relatively new but flourishing area of multispecies ethnography—a name coined by Eben Kirksey and Stefan Helmreich—has responded to these exhortations by focusing an anthropological lens on the increasingly legible "biographical and political lives" of animals (as well as plants, fungi, and microbes)[38] and in the process also "reconceptualizing what it means to be human."[39] Sharing similar concerns about relationships between different species and expanding on the focus of earlier ethnoecology on how different cultures understood their connections to the environment, another body of literature dubbed the "ontological turn" focuses on human–environment interactions within the context of Indigenous cultures. Concerned with Indigenous ontological perspectives, this approach critiques Euro-American epistemology and the foundational distinction between humans and nonhumans "with a call to take seriously a plurality of worlds and not just worldviews," especially those of Indigenous cultures.[40] Literature within this ontological turn thus exposes how "human and animal categories are themselves continuous rather than discrete."[41] Carlos Fausto argues, for example, that Amerindian ontologies "are not predicated upon the divide between nature and culture (or subject and object) that plays a foundational role in the modern Western tradition."[42] Instead, "animals, plants, gods, and spirits are also potentially persons and can occupy subject positions in their dealings with humans."[43] Applying a similar theoretical perspective outside of Indigenous settings, Marc Boglioli's work on Vermont deer hunters examines the hunters' "simultaneously consumptive and respectful" treatment of animals and how it is facilitated by their self-perception as wildlife stewards occupying an essential part of the natural order.[44] Boglioli challenges the assumed dichotomy between Euro-American and Indigenous perspectives toward human–animal relations, calling for further investigation of commonalities as well as differences—a call that was one of the inspirations for this book from its inception.

*Saving Animals* contributes to the growing body of multispecies ethnographic literature while also taking cues from work in the ontological turn. The animal sanctuary movement is important because it serves as a new flash point of contestations around the use and social status of animals in multiple political–economic contexts; specifically, the movement directly challenges practices of relating to animals as property that have shaped much of the Euro-American history of human–animal relations. Focusing on this challenge enables me to examine specific interspecies power dynamics structuring these relations that have as yet not been thoroughly explored in recent approaches to human interactions with other species. This investigation of the cultural and material dimensions of animal rescue efforts provides a deeper understanding of the ongoing transformation of ideas about the roles animals should play in contemporary U.S. society and about what it means to rescue, rehabilitate, and care for animals within the larger context of these enduring power dynamics. Rather than assuming a traditional Euro-American view toward ontological binaries like human–animal, nature–culture, subject–object, and person–property, I adopt the approach of the ontological turn by taking these dialectics and the social relations they produce as questions rather than answers known in advance.

## Unmaking Property, Making Subjects

Of these various ontological categories, perhaps the most central to human–animal relationships in the contemporary United States—including in sanctuaries—is that of property. The animal consumption regimes that sanctuaries oppose both rely on and perpetuate the social, legal, and economic status of animals as living forms of property. In direct opposition to the practice of relating to animals as property, sanctuary caregivers—in some ways similar to the Amerindians described by Fausto—quite literally see animals as persons, or beings who not only can but always do occupy subject positions in their dealings with humans. The ways humans relate to animals in sanctuaries are both predicated on this perspective and intended to encourage its proliferation through the culture at large. In *The Vanishing Hectare*, an ethnography about the transformation of collectivized land into private property in postsocialist Romania, Katherine Verdery describes decollectivization as a "process of unmaking socialist property," reminding us that property itself is a process of "making and unmaking certain kinds of relationships."[45] Following Verdery, I argue that caregivers' practice of relating to animals as subjects is a process of unmaking property-based human–animal relationships. As Verdery also reminds us, though, the end point of these processes of making and unmaking is not known.[46] While the end point of unmaking animal property is likewise unknown, in this book, I map some of its possible trajectories.

Animal activists see broad public recognition of animal subjectivity as one of the most powerful challenges to the hegemonic property-based animal imaginary, but how exactly is animal property unmade, and how are animal subjects made? And what does this human-dominated social movement imagine animal subjectivity to be? Before looking more closely at animal subjectification—the move away from relating to animals as mere objects treated and valued as property and toward engagement with animals as conscious subjects with needs and interests worthy of consideration—it is useful to establish more clearly what I mean when I use the term *property*. *Property* is an eminently multivalent term, especially from an anthropological perspective:

> The concept has been defined in a variety of ways even within western legal tradition—as things, as relations of persons to things, as person-person relations mediated through things, and as a bundle of abstract rights. Extrapolating from Thomas Grey . . . we should probably see most existing definitions of property as specific to a given time period and form of (capital) accumulation rather than as a universally valid conception of it.[47]

Again following Verdery, I understand property "variously as a western 'native category,' a symbol, a set of relations, and a process."[48] As a Western native category, property has certain ideological elements that distinguish it from alternative native categories. The Western native category of property, for example, is grounded in a person–object ontology quite distinct from that found in many other cultures, such as the Indigenous cultures mentioned earlier, who see human relations to land and the environment as much more continuous and mutually constitutive.[49]

One of the most important ideological components of this Western native category for the study of human–animal relations is its subject-making effect. Verdery observes that John Locke "theorized property as a particular relation between state and citizens, a form of subjection to which property entitlements were central."[50] In Lockean political theory "the property–owning citizen is the responsible subject of a democratic polity."[51] In addition to their relationship to the state, people also relate to each other through property. This relational aspect of property is tied to another trait of the Western native category: "it emphasizes rights or entitlements and sees the subjects of property relations as inherently rights-bearing."[52] Property rights simultaneously regulate property relationships between individual citizens and underpin their relation to the state as the citizens whose rights it exists to protect. This web of property relationships and rights in turn reinforces the person–object ontology on which it depends. According to the logic of this particular native theory of property, "if property involves persons, things, and their relations, then those persons and things are clearly bounded, have integrity, and are easily recognizable as separate kinds of entities. That is, standard western property concepts have long presumed an object-relations view of the world."[53] Within this framework, property is one of the primary mediums through which people relate to the state, each other, and the physical world, including other organisms.

Animals trouble this native theory of property because they remain living beings with their own interests even while they are treated as objects. They are incorporated into the democratic polity as property when the property rights of citizens are attached to them, but they do not possess their own rights. Unlike other things to which property rights can attach, however, they share with rights-bearing citizens the capacity for interests that rights *could* protect—rights to life and freedom from harm and restraint, for example. The idea of animals as exploitable resources instead of potential rights-bearers is inextricably linked to "the legal conception of property that confers on legal subjects the right to use and even destroy their property objects."[54] This conception in turn makes rights a determining factor in the relationship between human subjects and animal objects. Legal theorist David Delaney argues that "to the extent that rights are conferred, an entity is subjectified; to the extent that they are withheld, an entity is objectified and rendered (potentially) subordinate to the will of another" (491). As social constructs themselves, however, rights are as determinant of social relations as these relations are of them. And in reality, rights have historically often failed to provide their promised protections to humans, so what extending them to animals would change about their daily lived experiences is unclear. Rather than focusing on extending animal rights in the sense that activists often mean—legal guarantees to protection from certain harms—I focus more narrowly in this ethnography on property rights attached *to* animals and how sanctuaries endeavor to transform them to sanctuary animals' benefit.

Owing to its complete lack of rights, I argue that the animal-as-property is the embodiment par excellence of Giorgio Agamben's concept of bare life. In his analysis of how sovereign power works to exclude certain people (concentration camp internees, for example) from the protection of the law, Agamben uses *homo sacer,* a human who "may be killed but not sacrificed" in ancient Roman law, as a symbol of the state of exception on which sovereignty defines itself through the biopolitical power to determine who can be brought from the realm of *zoë*, bare life, into the realm of *bios*, political existence.[55] *Homo sacer* is excluded from the realms of both civil society and religion. Set "outside human jurisdiction without being brought into the realm of divine law," *homo sacer* has no rights and can literally be killed without it constituting either homicide or sacrifice. Rather than a state of exception, this is the norm for animals to which property rights have attached. While anticruelty provisions in many U.S. jurisdictions do place limited restrictions on a person's property rights in an animal, one could still kill even a perfectly healthy animal without breaking the law. If I simply no longer wanted to care for my dog, for example, I could not legally beat her to death, but I could legally pay a veterinarian to euthanize her for me instead of leaving her at a shelter (presuming I could find a veterinarian who would be willing to accommodate me). Like *homo sacer*, animals as property have no rights, and they can be killed without it constituting a crime. I therefore argue that, as the ultimate and permanent embodiment of bare life, animals as property constitute the category of *bestia sacer*.

Sanctuaries and other animal rescue facilities pose a direct challenge to the treatment of animals as *bestia sacer*, relating to animals instead as thinking subjects with personal interests in not only surviving but thriving. The subject-making practices of caregivers—tending to the physical and psychological needs of animals while seeking to give them the best lives possible—are the means through which caregivers attempt to unmake animal property. However, as I will show, there are at least two related reasons why this unmaking is limited and can perhaps never be fully complete. First, sanctuaries are embedded within many of the same political–economic systems of animal use that they seek to challenge, such as the animal agriculture industry and the animal entertainment industry. Sanctuaries for farmed animals, for example, rely on many of the same animal feed and farm equipment companies and veterinary care providers as for-profit farmers. Many sanctuaries also offer tours to educate the public about the treatment of animals and to generate fund-raising revenue, but in the process, they risk reinscribing animals as objects of exhibitionary consumption even as they seek to treat them as subjects. But even if they were able to fully remove animals from circuits of exchange value and capital accumulation, the animals in their care still retain their legal status as property. It is precisely this property status that makes it possible for sanctuaries to hold them in captivity and care for them in the first place.

Second, while sanctuary animals are arguably gaining new lives based on more egalitarian interspecies power dynamics, dilemmas of captive care also place limits on these lives and raise questions about the extent to which human–animal hierarchies can be subverted. Caregivers across all my field sites share a common goal of providing animals with the best lives possible, but the limits of that possibility are shaped by the material constraints of captivity as well as their own understandings of what constitutes the "best life possible" for different animals. Caregivers regularly contend with difficult decisions, such as how to best serve animals' needs with limited resources and when to euthanize severely ill or injured animals. Especially problematic for their goal of maximizing animal autonomy, they also must often place limits on the exercise of animal agency, such as the use of spaying and neutering to prevent overpopulation or the segregation—or even killing—of animals deemed dangerous to humans and other animals.

Sanctuaries are modeled on ethical visions for more equitable ways of living with animals, but the care practices and physical spaces of sanctuaries may actually limit the full realization of those visions. Owing to both their physical and their ideological separation from the larger U.S. public, these spaces can be understood as not only sanctuaries for animals but also possibly sanctuaries for the ethical ideals they hope to spread. Remaining entangled in larger political–economic contexts of animal capital circulation and still susceptible to constraint and potentially harmful treatment by humans as a result of their legal status, animals are neither fully autonomous subjects nor property. Instead, they can be understood as improperty: living beings within a shifting spectrum between property and subjecthood.

If sanctuary animals cannot be fully unmade as property, they also do not remain entirely rights-less. By recognizing and endeavoring to serve animals' interests in lives free from suffering and control, caregivers extend to animals basic de facto—if not de jure—rights to life, sustenance, and freedom from harm, the exceptions listed earlier notwithstanding. Paradoxically, animals become rights-bearers at the same time that they remain property. In a sense, sanctuary animals arguably gain limited property rights in themselves. Furthermore, by relating to animals as rights-bearing subjects, human caregivers transform the sanctuary space into a sort of polity in which animals operate as citizens. Sanctuary citizenship does not come without its costs, though. If sanctuary animals and humans are forming a new kind of posthuman or nonanthropocentric citizenry, species hierarchies still remain. Postrescue dilemmas impose certain restraints on both humans and animals to meet the larger needs of the interspecies community. However, as the story of Bob and Eloise highlights, animals face costs that humans do not, including restrictions of mobility and association, discomfort when veterinary procedures or constraint is deemed necessary, and at times even death. But as their story also reveals, while multispecies citizenship in sanctuaries comes with costs, it also creates opportunities for animal citizens to participate in their own and each other's care.

As a result of sanctuary efforts to unmake property-based relationships with animals by making intersubjective ones, I argue that animals are moving out of the realm of *bestia sacer* as they become improperty, although a more complete liberation remains elusive and potentially impossible as long as sanctuaries remain bounded spatial sites of protection from the larger ongoing processes of the animal–industrial complex. To understand this transformation, I focus in this ethnography on five main aspects of sanctuary dynamics. Chapter 1, "Coming to Sanctuary," describes the history of the animal sanctuary movement and introduces my three main field sites. This chapter also further explains the concept of *bestia sacer* and how sanctuaries function as zones of exception to the bare life outside their fences. Chapter 2, "Care and Rescue," focuses on the many postrescue dilemmas caregivers face and the limits they impose on efforts to relate to animals as autonomous subjects. Specifically, it examines animal care practices, including how caregivers understand and respond to animals' material and psychological needs, how they address the unique medical needs of different species, and how the spatial organization of sanctuaries facilitates cohabitation between multiple species with occasionally conflicting interests. It also describes the different ways in which animals arrive at sanctuaries, including placement by animal welfare officers, surrender by concerned citizens who cannot care for the animals, and theft from sites of contested animal treatment by activists. Finally, it explains how animals become improperty, suspended between the poles of property and subjecthood. Chapter 3, "Creating and Operating Sanctuaries," examines the political economy of sanctuaries, including funding, governance structures, labor practices, and public relations strategies. Specifically, it highlights the material and economic constraints on sanctuary goals and how caregivers navigate the tensions that arise from using rescued animals as fund-raising mechanisms while simultaneously seeking to challenge the commodification of these animals. It concludes by assessing how sanctuaries can constitute communities of multispecies citizenship as well as provide spaces for the formation of interspecies solidarity.[56] Chapter 4, "Animal Death," examines one of the most glaring contradictions of sanctuary care: saving animal lives also entails sacrificing animal lives. It examines the different ways in which animal death affects sanctuaries, including feeding animals that consume other animals; euthanizing ill, injured, or dangerous animals; and protecting sanctuary animals from external predators. Sanctuaries must make value-based decisions about which animal lives to save and which to sacrifice by designating certain animals as patients of care and others as food, pests, or predators. By making these valuations, sanctuaries engage in practices of necro-care, a form of selective biopolitical intervention that relies on categories of difference similar to those from which they hoped to liberate animals. Finally, in the Conclusion, I examine the possible futures of animal sanctuaries and their significant value to the future of human–animal relations as well. Furthermore, I examine how sanctuary as a form of liberatory political action may contribute to broader social and environmental justice movements.

Animals are gaining recognizable social, biographical, and political lives.[57] But what kind of subjects they may be becoming remains an open and largely unexplored question. A related and equally important question is one that animates much of the recent work in multispecies ethnography. As Kirksey explains, "rather than simply celebrate multispecies mingling, ethnographers have begun to explore a central question: Who benefits, *cui bono*, when species meet?"[58] Through an analysis of how *bestia sacer* is transformed in the context of interspecies relationships in animal sanctuaries, *Saving Animals* illuminates both the possibilities and limits of these efforts to create interspecies ethical praxis.

A rescued steer. We Animals.

# Chapter 1
# Coming to Sanctuary

### Rainbow Haven

"We have to dispose of the testicles," Olivia said, handing me a plastic bucket from the refrigerator in the garage. The bucket was full of approximately a dozen large purplish organs about the size of my fist, snaked with veins of white connective tissue. They sat in a shallow pool of dark blood. Brighter red, clotty globs stuck to the sides of the bucket.

"Whose testicles are these?" I asked.

"They're from some rams we had to castrate the other day," said Seth, one of the veterinary interns. There were three interns: John, who grew up in Hawai'i and had just finished his second year of veterinary school at the University of Washington; Seth, who was from Long Island and had just finished his second year at Cornell's veterinary school; and Kristin, who was from Southern California, had just graduated from UC Davis as a pre-vet major, and was hoping to return to Davis to attend the vet school there. A tenant staying at a property about half a mile farther up the volcano from us had called the sanctuary for help with some sheep that had been abandoned there by the property owner. He moved to Australia without bothering to arrange for anyone to care for his sheep. The tenant felt that it had fallen to her to look after the sheep, even though she knew nothing about caring for them. The males were hard to handle, so Olivia, the sanctuary director, decided castration would help to mellow them out while giving the interns the opportunity to practice the relatively simple surgery.

Seth held a garbage bag for me while I poured the bucket into it with a wet "schlorp!"

"Where are the testicles going?" I asked.

"In the garbage."

Unlike the gradual introduction to volunteer work I would experience at other field sites, my first hour at Rainbow Haven immediately confronted me with the visceral realities of animal care. Rainbow Haven, an exotic animal sanctuary in Hawai'i, is located on several acres of landscaped residential property on a volcanic slope about two miles from the coast. When I arrived, it had dozens of rescued parrots and other tropical birds, flamingos, waterfowl, chickens, owls, a Hawaiian hawk, an American bison, two zebras, a capuchin monkey, two rhesus macaques, two ostriches, five giant African spur-thighed tortoises, three horses, several goats and sheep, three alpacas, a llama, and a peacock. The grounds of the sanctuary are meticulously landscaped despite the fact that weeding is a Sisyphean task in the tropical climate there. Animal areas are cleaned regularly, and the mornings and afternoons are filled with a carefully planned feeding schedule. Olivia often uses the sanctuary's annual USDA inspection as a constant reminder to volunteers to keep the sanctuary clean and the animals well fed and watered, and to report any unsafe conditions to her right away.

After disposing of the ram testicles, I spent the rest of my first day as a volunteer helping the interns repair some of the fencing around the zebra enclosure. The wires in the fence had a tendency to separate from each other when the zebras leaned against it, turning the fence's small square holes into much larger holes, so we tied them back together with more wire. "If we'd left the fence like this, what would Bobby Lynch say?" Olivia asked as we worked, pronouncing the man's name with the thick southern drawl that I assumed was an imitation of his accent. Bobby Lynch, it turned out, was the USDA inspector for the island. Even if she were never subjected to inspection, though, Olivia would run her sanctuary exactly the same way.

When Olivia came to sanctuary, it happened in a flash—literally. Olivia and her husband, Sam, bought the property where Rainbow Haven sits so they could raise horses there, but Olivia was injured when she was struck in the mouth by a bolt of lightning at their wedding. In addition to physical injuries, the lightning caused expressive aphasia, a disorder affecting the speech center in the brain that causes sufferers to utter random words when trying to express themselves. It took her a long time to recover, and she grew very depressed as she struggled to regain her ability to communicate normally again. Seeing how hard she was struggling with her recovery, Sam, a surgeon, came to her and asked, "What do you want? Just name it. Name anything that will help you, and I'll help you get it."

"Giraffe," she replied. She probably meant something like "take me to Paris," she told me later as she relayed the story, but the word "giraffe" is what came out. It was an incredibly fortuitous synaptic misfire, because there happened to be two giraffes on the Hawaiian island of Molokai. Sam had just read about an exotic animal park that was closing there and was trying to find homes for its animals.

"If you can figure out how to get them here, we can build a home for them," he told her. And she did. She put all her time and energy into researching how she could ship the giraffes from the island by boat, what kind of facilities they would need when they got there, and how she would care for them. She credits this all-consuming mission with pulling her out of her depression and giving her the motivation she needed to struggle through rehabilitation therapy.

After she had already made all the arrangements to transport the giraffes, the Honolulu Zoo contacted her. They wanted her to give them the giraffes instead. She was reluctant, but they persuaded her that they were better equipped to care for the animals. Acquiescing to the zoo is her biggest regret; the giraffes were overly sedated and died in transport. Rather than sinking back into a deeper depression, though, Olivia decided that if she could not save the giraffes, she would save other animals. So she turned her home into an exotic animal sanctuary.

"Coming to sanctuary" is a phrase I encountered repeatedly throughout my fieldwork. It refers to the idea that animals usually start somewhere else—somewhere worse—before they end up in a sanctuary. Although, as Olivia's story illustrates, it's also a concept that applies to the experiences of many of the humans who end up working at sanctuaries. Nonhuman animals come to sanctuary in a variety of ways, brought in by good Samaritans (like Bob, the steer from the Introduction) who found them abandoned outside auction yards or running loose on the road, surrendered by owners who can no longer care for them, shipped from shuttered animal parks (when they're not diverted to zoos), or placed there after being seized by animal welfare officers (like Bob's companion, Eloise the goat). And sometimes animals are simply taken by activists without the permission of their legal owners and given to sanctuaries, often with vague cover stories about how they were found wandering loose or abandoned.

As explained in the Introduction, I "came to sanctuary" when this project grew out of a lifelong love for animals. This chapter introduces the sanctuaries I came to—the three primary sites for my fieldwork. It then explains the concept of *bestia sacer*, how it applies to animals in their social status as property, and how sanctuaries provide zones of exception in which animals can escape the realm of *bestia sacer*. First, though, I examine the history of the contemporary animal sanctuary movement and how it has shaped the practice of saving animals.

## The Sanctuary Movement(s)

The modern animal sanctuary movement arguably started with the founding of two sanctuaries in the mid-1980s, one for animals formerly used in entertainment and one for formerly farmed animals. In 1984, Pat Derby and her partner, Ed Stewart, created the Performing Animal Welfare Society (PAWS) to provide permanent homes and lifetime care to captive wildlife rescued from the television and film industry and the exotic pet trade. Derby and Stewart established PAWS's first sanctuary in Galt, California. It is quite possible that Derby may have even been the first person to use the term *sanctuary* to describe such facilities:[1]

> "sanctuary" was my descriptive designation of our attempt
> to properly house and provide care for the hundreds of exotic
> animals who were in need of refuge in the early 1980s. At that
> time, animal shelters were often as bad as roadside zoos, with
> handlers walking young lions and tigers on leashes and breeding
> animals to provide more homeless cubs for display and photo ops.
> I chose "sanctuary" to exemplify our mission which we hoped was
> different.[2]

Then, in 1986, Gene Baur and Lorri Houston used proceeds from selling veggie dogs at Grateful Dead shows to found Farm Sanctuary in Watkins Glen, New York.[3] These innovative experiments in rescued animal care provided models that have been copied hundreds of times as new animal sanctuaries have proliferated across the United States and beyond over the last three decades.[4]

Rather than one cohesive movement, however, it would be more accurate to say the spread of animal sanctuaries across the United States was the synergistic result of multiple intersecting historical social movements related to the way animals are treated by humans. The U.S. animal rescue landscape is composed of a constellation of groups of common intermingling interests with a range of different ideas about who or what animals are and how they should be treated by humans, especially how they should be understood and related to as subjects. U.S. animal sanctuaries can be divided into three basic categories based on the types of animals they rescue: farmed animals, exotic animals, and companion animals. These types in turn correspond to major arenas of everyday human–animal interaction in the United States: food and clothing production, entertainment, and companionship.[5] In practice, these lines are often blurred, especially with smaller farm animals and companion animals living in sanctuaries focused on other types of animals.[6] There is a fourth major arena of human–animal interaction, which is the use of animals for invasive research. Depending on the species of animal used, animals rescued from such circumstances might reside in a sanctuary that specializes in their care, such as rabbits in a facility focused on companion animal or farmed animal care. However, rescued laboratory primates also form a unique category with their own sanctuaries, which can also include primates rescued from the entertainment industry or companion animal context.[7]

One other significant area of human–animal interaction not included in my tripart schema involves human encounters with wild animals in their native ecologies. Unlike the sanctuaries where I conducted my fieldwork, wildlife rehabilitation facilities generally rescue and care for injured animals with the intention of releasing them to the wild and, when possible, minimize human contact and, even more important, social bonding with animals.[8] Although the exotic sanctuaries I visited did have some wild animals that could not be released— for medical or legal reasons (and, in some cases, both)—most animals at these sanctuaries were rescued from other situations of captivity where they had been kept as pets or used for entertainment enterprises. Like primate sanctuaries, other sanctuaries focus their care on a specific species, such as elephants,[9] but these animals are still generally rescued from one of the main arenas of human–animal interaction, such as entertainment.

U.S. sanctuary models are unique from other models of animal care that developed elsewhere. While they have been influential to animal advocacy efforts abroad—and sanctuaries now exist in other countries—U.S. animal sanctuaries generally differ significantly in their goals from wildlife preserves, zoos, and other, more traditional modes of in situ animal care.[10] Unlike efforts to conserve animal species in settings approximating their indigenous environments with minimized human contact, the U.S. sanctuary movement is somewhat unique in its attempt to create environments that actively and regularly foster embodied interactions and socialization between humans and animals. Sanctuary settings thus differ from zoos and other animal-care contexts in that they seek to provide models for spaces in which direct human interactions with animals *as subjects* provide the basis for "interspecies sociality."[11] Unlike the separation of the realms of culture and nature reflected in these older modes of care—in which nature is often presented as a spectacle to be enjoyed at a distance—animal sanctuaries involve care-based interspecies relationships that reflect intentionally subversive ideas about how animals should be situated in human society.[12]

There are important differences in practices of care, ethical values, and aspirational orientations toward the future across sanctuaries. Nonetheless, it is possible to locate the many different strands of the U.S. sanctuary movement between two main historical trends in the larger context of the history of animal advocacy: welfarism and animal rights. As described in the Introduction, welfarism seeks to improve the conditions of animals used by humans by reducing suffering as much as possible. Current broader public debates about the treatment of animals in agricultural and entertainment industries, for example, reflect a welfarist approach to animal ethics. The animal rights approach, on the other hand, seeks to end certain (or all) uses of animals by extending them certain legal rights. In animal activism, and especially when it comes to sanctuaries, it is useful to understand these trends as two ends of a spectrum rather than polar orientations. Many of the people I encountered at sanctuaries support animal rights and the abolition of animal exploitation while also supporting welfarist policies that could reduce animal suffering, while others who see animal rights activism as unrealistically utopian or too militantly radical still share many of the rights approach's critiques of animal use.[13]

Throughout *Saving Animals*, I use the term *sanctuary* to refer generally to the spaces of animal care where I conducted fieldwork. Organizations focused on the rescue of companion animals (mostly cats and dogs, but also other animals commonly kept as pets) are called shelters rather than sanctuaries by those who operate them. There are important differences between companion animal shelters and sanctuaries for other kinds of animals, which I will examine in more depth in later chapters. Most significantly, shelters are structured around a model of rescue driven by the aspiration that the animals will eventually find permanent places to live with human companions in their private homes. The shelter is ideally only a temporary stop in an animal's rescue journey. Sanctuaries, on the other hand, are more often understood as the permanent home for most animals that arrive at them. This is largely the result of the kinds of animals to which different organizations cater. Whereas exotic and farmed species require more resources and experience to care for and are often restricted from living in certain areas by municipal or state ordinances, companion animals are bred to be pets. Adopting common pet species is more culturally normalized and desirable to a much larger portion of the population; the rapid growth of the pet industry in the last century has helped to create an extensive socioeconomic infrastructure to make pet care relatively easy for most people; and millennia of coevolution with humans have made common pet species like cats, dogs, and rodents amenable to living in human habitations. Put simply, a lot more people want to live with a dog than want to live with a tiger or a zebra.

Despite their differences, I have found that shelters and sanctuaries share far more in common in their goals and approaches to animal rescue and care. Including shelters as a part of my research was essential in forming a more complete picture of the culture of animal rescue and care in the United States, both because companion animal interactions are such a significant part of human–animal relations and because the boundaries between the different arenas of animal rescue in this book—companion, exotic, and farmed—are much blurrier in practice than they are in theory.

### Texas Companion Rescue

Located in a large city in central Texas, Texas Companion Rescue began taking in rescued cats and dogs in 2008. The facility is a warren of interlinked medical buildings, offices, and covered dog kennels. Located at the end of a road next to a large parking lot it shares with a few soccer fields, it is easy to walk to from downtown and from a popular recreation trail along a nearby lake. That part of Texas ranges from uncomfortably hot to oppressively hot for about three-quarters of the year, and during the other quarter, it is often surprisingly cold. Owing to this weather, the cats at Texas Companion Rescue are kept indoors. The dogs, however, live year-round in the outdoor kennels. They are given blankets and mats during cold weather, but most of the year, these are unnecessary. The rest of the time, the shaded kennels are kept cool by a series of misting hoses strung above the rows.

A rescued cat. NEAVS.

The kennels themselves are rectangular spaces made of concrete walls and floors with metal gates on the front and back and cyclone fencing along the top—some of the dogs can jump several feet into the air and could escape if the tops were not enclosed. Each kennel has a front and back section divided by a concrete wall. There is a square hole in each of these walls with a wooden, sliding guillotine door on a cable that can be lowered down from outside to close a dog in either the front or back portion. This is especially useful when a volunteer needs to go into one side of a kennel space where a potentially danger-ous dog resides. Most of the time, the doorway between the front and back is kept open to allow the dogs to choose where they want to be.

The kennels run in long rows that form three sides of a large rect-angle with a courtyard in the middle. Each row has thirty to forty indi-vidual kennels running along the front and back sides. The spaces on the outside front and back of each row form the front areas of each kennel, and the rear areas of each kennel face each other across a walkway running through the inside of each row. Sidewalks along the front spaces allow visitors to see dogs, while the walkway between the rear sections of the kennel spaces allows volunteers to see and interact with dogs that choose not to lie in the front portions.

More than a dozen volunteers come throughout the day to walk dogs. And others work indoors cleaning up after, feeding, and pro-viding any needed medical treatments to the cats. Texas Companion Rescue has developed a color-coded collar system that categorizes dogs based on their behavior tendencies. Only volunteers who have gone through multiple trainings can walk the dogs that have been de-termined by the staff dog trainers to have behavioral issues, such as leash aggression, which manifests as barking, growling, or snapping at other people and animals while they are on a leash.

Dog walkers usually take the dogs to fenced-in runs at the rear of the property or to one of the small, fenced-in yards in the central courtyard. The least hyper, most gentle dogs are generally walked the most often because their collar level—blue—is the basic level at which all volunteers begin. Because many volunteers are not qualified above this level, the blue dogs are the only ones they can walk. Generally, the more training a particular collar color requires or the more intimidat-ing a dog is to volunteers, the less often she is walked. Each fenced-in yard has a garbage can and a long-handled scooper for cleaning up dog feces. Volunteers are generally good about cleaning up after dogs when they walk them, and both volunteers and paid staff members clean up after dogs when they notice they have soiled their kennels. It is rare to see droppings left anywhere in the shelter for more than a few minutes. Despite this vigilance, the sheer amount of waste produced by the hundreds of dogs on-site at any given time produces an aroma of ammonia and methane that is often faintly wafting through the air.

My first day at Texas Companion Rescue did not actually involve any work with the animals. The rescue has hundreds of volunteers and has found it necessary to develop a highly organized and somewhat bureaucratic volunteer training system to maximize the efficiency of the time it invests in training. Before you can work with any animals, you must submit a volunteer application online and pay twenty dollars to participate in an hour-long orientation that includes a short video about the history of the organization. Senior volunteers explain all the possible areas in which you can volunteer—from cat or dog care to office work, donor outreach, the media team, and grounds maintenance. During the orientation, I sat in a large conference room in the administrative building with about a hundred other volunteers of varied ages and ethnicities. There seemed to be more teenagers (you have to be at least sixteen to volunteer) and retirement-aged people there than anyone else. Many people were wearing the white T-shirt with a blue Texas Companion Rescue logo that we were given when we paid our registration fees. The air conditioning was not working in the room, so the back doors were propped open and giant fans were running at the back of the room to stir the sweltering, sticky air.

Following the orientation, some people who knew they wanted to work with dogs or cats stayed around for breakout orientations about animal care. I chose a dog breakout group. My orientation leader was Pablo, a retiree from Florida who taught himself how to train dogs. Pablo liked to work with the "problem" dogs that others were afraid to work with. He loved a challenge, and he loved even more the feeling of helping a dog learn the manners that could help her get adopted.

The dog orientation consisted of a demonstration of how to put the different types of leashes and collars on dogs—a body harness that fastened around a dog's shoulders, a gentle lead that fastened around a dog's muzzle, and a choke collar that slipped around a dog's neck. Pablo also explained the procedure for entering a dog's kennel: wait for the dog to sit; open the door enough to slip in and close and latch it behind you; put the leash on the dog and give her a treat if she's calm (plastic boxes with treats hang between most of the kennel doors); wait for the dog to sit before opening the door; walk out ahead of the dog; and leave the gate open so others can tell the kennel is empty. Finally, we learned what to do if a dog gets loose: yell "Dog off leash!" so staff can find the dog and get her back on a leash. You are not supposed to chase the dog, because this may be misinterpreted as a game or a threat and cause the dog to run faster or turn and bite. If you are walking another dog and you hear "Dog off leash!" you are to step into the nearest open kennel with your dog and close the door. Dogs are to be kept apart unless a trainer who is familiar with their temperament is putting them together to play.

After the orientation, my first day was over. It took about two hours. A significant amount of volunteers never return to actually volunteer after the orientation. In addition to bringing in funding, the orientations help to filter out people who are not serious about volunteering, which saves the senior volunteers from investing time in training people who will not come back.

Texas Companion Rescue is a product of the No Kill movement, an animal shelter reform movement that seeks to eliminate the killing of shelter animals as a form of population control. The philosophical origins of the U.S. No Kill movement can be traced back to the creation of the American Society for the Prevention of Cruelty to Animals (ASPCA) by wealthy U.S. philanthropist Henry Bergh on April 10, 1866. Prior to the creation of the ASPCA, animal control practices in New York City were dismal for stray animals. Partly motivated by a fear of rabies and other public health concerns, the city pound's approach was to catch and drown as many dogs as it could. One of the many accomplishments of the ASPCA under Bergh was its opposition to the pound's campaign against dogs. Bergh achieved a series of legislated reforms that, within a year, resulted in an 84 percent reduction in the number of dogs killed.[14] Eventually New York City officials offered to hire the ASPCA to run the pound, but Bergh refused. He replied that the ASPCA "could not stultify its principles so far as to encourage the tortures" that operating the pound entailed.[15] He was adamantly opposed to allowing an organization dedicated to saving animals to take on the task of killing them. The older model of animal control would resurface following Bergh's death, however. The ASPCA did eventually assume responsibility for operating the city pound, and while it employed humane education and adoptions as part of its approach to animal control, it continued killing the vast majority of homeless animals that came in, replacing drowning with a gas chamber, which was perceived to be more humane at the time. Independent but similarly modeled SPCAs and like-minded organizations in other cities adopted the same strategy, which became the national model for animal control.

Over the last century, this strategy has remained essentially unchanged at most animal shelters in the United States. Now many municipalities throughout the country contract animal control tasks to independent humane societies or SPCAs. Although they share similar names and receive advice and support from their large national counterparts, these organizations are not directly affiliated with or operated by the ASPCA or the Humane Society of the United States. Currently between 6 million and 8 million companion animals enter these shelters annually, of which approximately 3 million will be killed.[16] An estimated 80 percent, or 2.4 million, of the shelter animals killed each year are healthy enough to be adopted.[17] This number also includes many lost animals who could potentially be reclaimed by their guardians and feral cats who could potentially be neutered and returned to their habitats, both of which are contested issues within the larger controversy surrounding the killing of shelter animals.

Henry Bergh's philosophy provided the first formulation of the life-preserving approach that underlies the modern No Kill movement in companion animal rescue today. Contemporary companion animal rescue proponents generally fall into two camps. As the name suggests, No Kill proponents advocate a prohibition on killing any adoptable animal. The No Kill movement estimates that up to 90 percent of the total animals entering shelters are savable. It is the vast disparity between the saved and the perceived to be savable—the additional 2.7 million animals who could be saved annually—that smolders at the center of the deeply contested controversy between No Kill advocates and those who believe that the traditional approach is the only way to address what they perceive as a severe animal overpopulation problem. There are many disagreements between the two sides over the efficacy of specific policy reforms and the severity of overpopulation as the primary issue facing shelters. Despite the heated rhetoric from each side of the debate, however, most of the human stakeholders involved share the goal of reducing the suffering of animals, even if they define what constitutes suffering differently.

Shelters that do kill rescued animals refer to themselves as open admission shelters. "Open admission" refers to the fact that these shelters accept all animals that are surrendered by owners or brought in by animal control officers, as opposed to No Kill shelters, which can be more selective about which animals they take in. Advocates for the traditional approach to companion animal rescue often also express an abhorrence for killing animals, but they see it as a necessary evil given the overpopulation of companion animals in the United States. In addition to viewing the killing of homeless animals as compassionate euthanasia that saves them from the suffering inherent to a life outside of a human home or for extended periods of time in a crowded shelter, advocates of this approach emphasize the importance of reducing the reproduction of animals through spaying and neutering as the only effective approach to reducing the number of animals killed in shelters. No Kill advocates agree about the value of spay and neuter programs, though they see them as one component of a wider range of necessary policies geared toward maximizing adoptions.

As with other hotly contested social issues, word choices are politically charged. *Euthanasia* is the preferred term by critics of the No Kill movement. However, I have chosen to use the term *kill* here when referring to the action of ending the lives of shelter animals because I find it to be the most value-neutral option between terms that connote a more critical perspective, such as *slaughter* or *murder*, and terms that connote a more euphemistic sanitization, such as *put down* or *put to sleep*. Despite the argument that the lives of homeless animals constitute a type of suffering, I treat the term *euthanasia* as an example of the latter category since it connotes an act of killing intended to put a physically suffering being out of her misery, while the vast majority of animals who die in U.S. shelters are in relatively good health. The term *kill* is intended neither as an endorsement of the No Kill perspective nor a critique of its opposition; rather, it is an attempt to use the most value-neutral yet still accurate term for this highly controversial practice.[18]

Texas Companion Rescue was founded by a group of No Kill activists who had been lobbying for the city to reduce the kill rate at the city shelter since the late 1990s. At a kill rate of over 50 percent, the

City Animal Center—which, unlike most shelters across the country, is run by the city under its Department of Animal Services—was killing approximately thirteen thousand animals a year. On the basis of their estimates of available homes that would be willing to adopt, these activists were convinced that the city could reduce its kill rate to 10 percent. No Kill advocates define a No Kill shelter as one with a 90 percent live outcome rate, estimating that approximately 10 percent of animals will either be too unhealthy to survive or too aggressive to safely adopt out.

Under the leadership of Dr. Samantha Marshall—a veterinarian who had been converted to the No Kill cause while working in private practice—along with a quickly expanding network of volunteers committed to reducing the city's kill rate, Texas Companion Rescue quickly grew to rival the city shelter in capacity. Texas Companion Rescue's approach was to take as many animals as it could from the kill list each day at the city shelter, thus freeing up more space for taking in new animals there. Texas Companion Rescue does not take in animals directly from the public, instead only taking animals that have already been processed at the city shelter. This strategy, combined with an intense lobbying campaign by Texas Companion Rescue and other activists to get the city council to commit to achieving a No Kill save rate by the year 2011, resulted in the city becoming the largest No Kill city in the country.

In 2018, the city had a 97.5 percent live outcome rate, and in spring 2019, the city council passed a unanimous resolution raising the mandatory live outcome rate for the city shelter to 95 percent. Despite almost a decade of success, however, the pressure is always on. Texas Companion Rescue relieves the city shelter of all its excess animals, preventing the overcrowding that would increase the kill rate, but it is only able to do so through intense adoption marketing campaigns and a large, organized volunteer staff that makes it possible to care for all the rescued animals, some of whom stay in the shelter much longer than they would at a shelter that was regularly killing companion animals to reduce overcrowding. With this increased length of stay in shelter, many new issues related to animal care arise, one of the most important being the need to continuously socialize animals, who run the risk of developing behavioral issues the longer they stay in the relative isolation of the shelter and thus becoming less adoptable.

Texas Companion Rescue is based at the site where the city animal shelter used to be. In fact, at the time I was there, it still shared the facility with the city animal shelter, which used about one-third of the kennels for overflow from its new facilities on the east side of town. Volunteers regularly repaired the worn infrastructure at the decades-old shelter as doors fell off hinges or pieces of fencing rusted through. This ongoing maintenance was primarily motivated by the goal of providing the best conditions possible for the animals there, but concerns about the condition of the shelter were also partially influenced by (and in response to) a major critique of the No Kill movement, which is that refraining from killing animals will lead to the kind of unsanitary, dangerous conditions found in animal hoarding cases. In fact, this issue is one that resonates for sanctuaries in general: not everyone with the desire to rescue animals has the means to do so.

## Roosevelt Farm Sanctuary

My first day at Roosevelt Farm Sanctuary fell somewhere in the middle between the slow introduction at Texas Companion Rescue and the excitement of my first day at Rainbow Haven. I arrived a few minutes after noon. The twenty-three-acre sanctuary for formerly farmed animals sits in a little valley with no cell phone reception in rural New York State. That day, the valley was surrounded by fiery hills of red, yellow, and gold trees on the verge of shedding their foliage for the winter. Sturdy, well-built, new-looking fences lined the dirt drive. Goats roamed in the pasture on the other side, leaning on their front knees to bite at patches of light green grass.

I parked in a small gravel parking lot ("Park snuggly," a cartoon dog on a sign requested) next to a two-story brown, wooden house with a landscaped yard. Another sign stated that the house was a "private residence," while a few others pointed the way to the visitor center, where they suggested I should check in. I learned later that the home belonged to Rita Johnson and Ted Klein, the founders. Following a week she spent filming animal abuse while undercover at stockyards in Texas, Rita decided to go into animal care full-time. After interning at Farm Sanctuary in Watkins Glen so she could learn all the ins and outs of farm animal care, she and Ted bought this property in 2004 to start their own sanctuary.

After I snuggly parked my car between two other cars with bumper stickers extolling the virtues of veganism, I walked down a dirt path through a hinged gate and past two large barns to the visitor center, a freestanding brown, wooden building about half the size of the barns. I passed a woman with pink hair and solarized glasses who was pushing a wheelbarrow. I smiled as we nodded hello at each other. Though I never caught her name, I found out later that she was a volunteer who, like me, had come up for the day from New York City. The visitor center was unlocked, but it looked closed. Nobody was there, and the table was covered in cotton sheets. The email confirmation I received about volunteering gave me the impression there would be more people around, or at least that they'd be expecting me. I went back outside and asked the woman with pink hair where I should go or whom I should talk to. "Talk to Janice," she said.

I turned around and saw another woman wearing a "staff" T-shirt walking out of the large barn next to the visitor center. She had shoulder-length, dark hair and several tattoos on her arms. "Hi, I'm Janice," she said; I picked up how to spell it from the walkie-talkie on her hip that had a strip of yellow tape with her name on it.

She brought me back into the visitor center and had me fill out an electronic waiver of liability form on an iPad mounted on one of the sheet-covered desks. I later learned that the sheets were there to keep the desks clean when chickens from the adjacent medical facility wandered in. I went back outside to find Janice, and she suggested I take a self-guided tour of the sanctuary before starting. While she was explaining where to walk, a donkey strolled over, green water pouring from the corners of her mouth (either from a big gulp of water she had just swallowed or some really juicy grass). She stuck her head in Janice's lap for an ear scratch, emerald rivulets dripping on the caregiver's jeans. Janice smiled and obliged.

I gave the donkey a few scratches, too, and then strolled down to a pasture with several huge grazing steers (one of whom, I would later learn, was Bob). A few goats, turkeys, and roosters wandered free along the paths between fenced-in areas. As I walked beside a chicken enclosure, dozens of hens ran along next to me like they were expecting some kind of treat. I found out later that that is exactly what they were expecting—these birds were what are called "broilers" in the chicken industry. Because of genetic manipulation through selective breeding intended to maximize rapid growth, they are virtually always hungry and will peck at anything that looks like it might be food.

As I walked along the dirt road that made a ring in the center of the sanctuary, I passed five other chicken enclosures, a pig enclosure in the center, and a duck enclosure with its own pond. When I found Janice again, she was crouched by a small fenced area next to the visitor center with three white female turkeys in it. A fourth female stood next to her, pecking at the markings on the back of her hand. "She likes to peck at my tattoos; she thinks they're lice," she said. I put out my hand, and the turkey began pecking at my fingers too. It did not hurt at all because the tip of her beak was missing. The upper part of her beak ended in a jagged line about a quarter of an inch from the tip of the lower part. A tiny bit of pink tongue was visible in the gap where the missing piece should have been. She had been "debeaked" as a chick, a process in which the tip is either cut or burned off with a blade or hot wire. The tip is very sensitive, and the extremely painful procedure is usually conducted with no anesthetic. If there is any concern in the poultry industry for the suffering "debeaking" causes birds,

A rescued goose socializes with a rescued pig. We Animals.

it is apparently outweighed by the financial cost of buying anesthetic or finding an alternate way to house the birds that does not lead to the intense overcrowding and stressed-out pecking behavior they hope to minimize by clipping the beaks. "She also really likes it when you rub her chest," Janice said. I scratched the bird's feathery chest, and she looked at me with dark, potentially pleased eyes.

Janice showed me where I would be working that day: the duck coop, a two-room wooden shed with several inches of wood chips on the floor. While she was there, Janice introduced me to Sasha, a rooster who lived with the ducks instead of the other chickens. He also had a deformed beak, but this seemed to be congenital rather than the result of amputation. The top of his beak curved sharply to the side rather than running parallel to the bottom part. This made it harder for him to defend himself from other roosters that might pick on him, so he lived with the ducks instead. A white duck accompanied him everywhere he went while I was cleaning.

There were a few bowls of clean water sitting among the wood chips in the coop. Piles of duck feces were scattered across the wood chips and stuck in clumps to the bottoms of the walls and door frames. I used a rake, shovel, broom, and paint scraper to clean all the old wood shavings and duck feces from the structure, loading it into a wheelbarrow and dumping several loads into the giant, rusty, yellow scoop on the front of a farm tractor Janice had parked outside the duck fence. It took me most of the afternoon to clean the shed.

At one point, one of the ducks must have taken a bath in one of the clean water bowls I left outside while I was cleaning, because when I came out, it was murky with dirt, and a few feathers floated on the surface. I walked back to the main office to ask Janice where to find water to clean the bowl. She was sitting with another woman, who introduced herself as Monica. They were smoking cigarettes while they stroked a goat's back. The goat, named Bowie, was born a male, but they referred to Bowie as "she" because she "mellowed out and lost her beard" after she was castrated. I asked where I could fill the bowl, and they directed me toward a pump hooked up to a hose.

When I was done with the ducks, I went to see if there was any more work to do. Janice and Monica were feeding the pigs. This was the first time I had witnessed pigs being fed, and in my urbanized ignorance, I found it to be a frightening experience. As soon as they realized they were about to be served, the pigs started screaming. It was a deafening, disconcerting, high-pitched squeal that sounded to me more like they thought they were about to die than that they were about to chow down, though I eventually came to think of it as the sound of joyful excitement as I continued to volunteer at the sanctuary. Three black-spotted pigs isolated by themselves in the large barn for goats, sheep, and cows screamed back in what seemed like a call-and-response pattern. These three were young pigs who had just come to the sanctuary and were only staying temporarily before being transported to a different sanctuary. Pig social groups have complex politics, and caregivers need to be cautious when trying to blend new individuals into a group to avoid violence.

There was nothing left for me to do that day, so I washed my hands at an outdoor sink by the infirmary, which occupied half of the visitor center building. As I was drying my hands, another staff person walked by. She introduced herself as Pattie, the events coordinator. We walked toward the parking lot together and passed a goat named Polk. At fourteen years old, Polk was the oldest goat at the sanctuary. She was wearing a special goat jacket Velcroed around her body to keep her warm. Pattie mentioned that she had been throwing up recently, which might have been due to liver problems. As we approached the pig enclosure, Pattie stopped to scratch the huge floppy ears of a full-grown sow through the fence. "This is Petunia," she said, introducing me to the pig. Petunia was from North Carolina. She escaped from a farm or slaughterhouse when she was young and was found running down the road. She was rescued by a couple who eventually found her a home at the sanctuary. I scratched her chin, and Petunia grunted with a chuckling sound: "huff, huff, huff."

"That's the sound pigs make when they're happy," Pattie explained.

## Protecting and Killing the Sacred

The word *sanctuary* comes from the Latin *sanctuarium*,[19] composed of the noun *sancta* or *sancti* (holy things or holy people) and the suffix *-arium* (which when used together with a noun means a place where that noun is kept): a place where holy or sacred things are kept. The word began to take on its more contemporary meaning as churches in England started granting protection to fugitives fleeing arrest or violence as early as the fourth century, a legally recognized practice that continued into the early seventeenth century.[20] This idea of providing protection or safety to people facing risk of oppression or violence has evolved into multiple contemporary forms, such as the legal practice now employed by many countries of granting political asylum to persecuted individuals.[21] The most recent example is the New Sanctuary Movement, the "present-day revival of the Sanctuary Movement of the eighties in which hundreds of cities around the United States and Canada were declared 'sanctuary cities' where undocumented immigrants (many of whom where fleeing civil wars in Latin America) could be partially shielded from the enforcement of immigration laws."[22] Following the widespread resurgence of xenophobic anti-immigrant sentiment following the U.S. presidential election in 2016 and the draconian immigration policies of the Trump regime, the idea of sanctuary for humans is gaining renewed political support in the form of sanctuary cities or communities, including small towns that could provide a physical space of limited protection from these efforts.[23]

Although the conceptual origins of sanctuary are rooted in the idea of preserving sacred things, the idea of the sacred also plays a central role in the conceptual opposite of the sanctuary: the concentration camp. Philosopher Giorgio Agamben sees the concentration camp, which he calls the "fundamental biopolitical paradigm of the west," as the ultimate spatially localized manifestation of the juridical state of exception that constitutes bare life, a condition in which certain individuals are excluded from the political realm and deprived of its protections.[24] As such, he argues that the camp is "the hidden matrix and nomos of the political space in which we are still living."[25] For Agamben, this state of exception is embodied by *homo sacer*, or "sacred man," a figure from early Roman law who "may be killed and yet not sacrificed."[26] According to Agamben, Jews living under Nazism provide a "flagrant case" of *"homo sacer* in the sense of a life that may be killed but not sacrificed."[27] Their killing constituted "neither capital punishment nor a sacrifice, but simply the actualization of a mere 'capacity to be killed' inherent in the condition of the Jew as such. . . . The Jews were exterminated not in a mad and giant holocaust but exactly as Hitler had announced, 'as lice,' which is to say, as bare life."[28] As this example illustrates, *homo sacer* is confined to the realm of *zoë*, or bare life, by means of a biopolitical exclusion from its opposite realm, *bios*, or political existence.[29]

In *The Open: Man and Animal*, Agamben explicitly links this biopolitical distinction to the categories of human and animal, arguing that "the decisive political conflict, which governs every other conflict, is that between the animality and the humanity of man."[30] He elaborates, "In our culture man has always been the result of a simultaneous division and articulation of the animal and the human, in which one of two terms of the operation was also what was at stake in it."[31] As political theorist Dinesh Wadiwel observes, bare life is "not only a site of indistinction between lawmaking and law-preserving violence, but also the point where a number of fundamental distinctions are blurred, including that between . . . the animal and human."[32] Returning to the model of the camp, in *Remnants of Auschwitz*, Agamben examines the *Muselmänner*, "the term given to the 'walking dead' of the camps, who due to the infliction of continued violence—malnutrition, sleep deprivation, extended work, psychological trauma, etc.—are reduced to a state of fragile indifference to their immediate conditions."[33] Agamben explains, the "*Muselmann* is not only or not so much a limit between life and death; rather, he marks the threshold between the human and the inhuman."[34] This opposition between man and animal or between human and inhuman, in both its modern and earlier forms, is defined by Agamben as the "anthropological machine":

> If, in the machine of the moderns, the outside is produced through the exclusion of an inside and the inhuman produced by animalizing the human, [in the earlier version] the inside is obtained through the inclusion of an outside, and the non-man is produced by the humanization of an animal: the man-ape, the *enfant sauvage* or *Homo ferus*, but also and above all the slave, the barbarian, and the foreigner, as figures of an animal in human form. Both machines are able to function only by establishing a zone of indifference at their centers, within which . . . the articulation between human and animal, man and nonman, speaking being and living being, must take place. . . . What would thus be obtained, however, is neither an animal life nor a human life, but only a life that is separated and excluded from itself—only a bare life.[35]

So, for example, we can see the anthropological machine at work in the extreme of the camp, where "the 'gap' which is assumed to exist between the animal and the human—that between the living being and that between a speaking being, or that which merely has life (*zoë*) and that which also has a cultural or political life (*bios*)—soon eclipses."[36]

Highlighting an inherent problem with the way this formulation affects our understanding of animals, Cary Wolfe (expanding on the work of Dominick LaCapra) argues that it leads to a "flattening of the category of 'the animal' itself" in two senses:

> First, as LaCapra notes, animals in all their diversity "are not figured as complex, differential living beings but instead function as an abstracted philosophical topos" (2009, 166). . . . And second—a consequence of the first—Agamben's position provides no means for a politically focused questioning of "the extent to which certain animals, employed in factory farming or experimentation, may be seen in terms of the concept of bare or naked, unprotected life' (LaCapra 2009, 172). What gets lost, in other words, is our ability to think a highly differentiated and nuanced biopolitical field, and to understand as well that the exercise of violence on the terrain of biopower is not always, or even often, one of highly symbolic or sacrificial ritual in some timeless political theater, but is often—indeed, maybe usually—an affair of power over and of life that is regularized, routinized, and banalized in the services of a strategic, not symbolic, project.[37]

Nicole Shukin argues similarly that in Agamben's theorization of bare life, "animals' relation to capitalist biopower is occluded by his species-specific conflation of *zoë* with a socially stripped-down figure of *Homo sacer* that he traces back to antiquity."[38] Shukin, Wolfe, and LaCapra are correct that an abstract philosophical topos risks flattening important differences and variations among myriad kinds of animals (both human and nonhuman) and that this flattening can in turn obfuscate how biopower, particularly in the form of violence, serves strategic projects of resource extraction and instrumental use of living beings.[39] Wolfe also argues persuasively that understanding the effects of biopower through a Foucauldian lens rather than through Agamben's formalistic topos "has the advantage of making the questions of freedom and power, questions of degrees and not of kind when it comes to the disposition of human and non-human bodies, as those are networked with each other and with technologies, practices, and disciplines which may cluster and co-constitute them regardless of species designation."[40] However, understanding how both humans and other animals are affected similarly—and in certain ways even identically—by biopolitical processes does not preclude also recognizing how the historical construction of human–animal incommensurability has facilitated the contemporary enfolding of nonhuman animals into biopolitical processes in ways that humans admitted into the political sphere are not (e.g., as sources of food). Factory farming and biomedical research on animals may not primarily be strategies employed in service to the symbolic production of the human via the "anthropological machine," but they both contribute to it and are facilitated by it. Going back at least as far as Aristotle—from whom Agamben borrows his categories of *zoë* and *bios*—animals have been excluded from political life, consigned to the category of bare life.[41]

Precisely because Wolfe is right to recognize the value in a politically focused and nuanced interrogation of the ways animals in different political–economic contexts are impacted by this category, I argue that Agamben's abstract philosophical topos is still conceptually useful if we are also careful not to lose sight of the differences it encapsulates. Specifically, *homo sacer*, the embodiment of bare life, is a fitting heuristic for understanding animals as they are impacted by their legal status as property. As Wadiwel argues, the "concept of bare life is directly applicable to the life of the animal, particularly that life which is subject to a biological control which is directed toward power."[42] In the United States, for example, humans have the right to kill—albeit humanely—even a perfectly healthy animal as long as she is their property,[43] with the possible exception of animals that are covered by the Endangered Species Act. This is what enables animal shelters, for example, to kill companion animals, who are technically property of the shelters where they reside. But perhaps there is no greater example of animal bare life than that of an animal caught in the biopolitical gears of modern industrialized agriculture, as Wadiwel illustrates:

> The short life of the veal calf is one which is determined strictly within the coordinates of domination. Calculations made around nutritional and fluid intake, lighting levels, stall size and flooring are directed towards the maximization of market profit from the production of the correctly coloured and textured flesh of the animal. But the priority of the life of the veal calf, no matter how short or painful, is apparent in this process. The life of the calf, maintained in a bare, weak state, is monitored scrupulously

to prevent a premature death; a death that threatens the profitability of that life for the livestock complex. Thus a balance is struck, where life is held at a point that borders upon death itself. We find the same relationship between life and death in the management of battery hens, where maximal profit is achieved through the imposition of the most minimal conditions for life: "on a sloping wire floor (sloping so the eggs roll down, wire so the dung drops through) the birds live for a year or 18 months while artificial lighting and temperature conditions combine with drugs in their food to squeeze the maximum number of eggs out of them."[44]

Firmly in the realm of bare life, the animal as property is arguably the ultimate embodiment of the state of exception: *bestia sacer*.[45]

The category of *bestia sacer* can thus be understood as comprising an alterity that defines and makes possible the liberal subject—it is precisely what personhood is not. Building on Agamben's understanding of biopolitics, Wadiwel sees democratic politics as the process of admitting animal life into the political sphere.[46] He argues that it is this biopolitical distinction that marks "the struggle over the definition of . . . the fully formed human subject," which is reflected in "democratic struggles over the last two hundred years: for example slaves, women, savages, queers and children."[47] But while *homo sacer* has historically been a porous category from which certain groups of humans have been able to escape, even as others have replaced them, the status of fully formed liberal subjects has remained firmly off limits to other-than-human animals. If the concentration camp is the example par excellence of the spatial localization of bare life for *homo sacer*, then the entire world (or at least the parts occupied by human property systems) is spatialized bare life for *bestia sacer*.[48] Animal sanctuaries, on the other hand, invert this dynamic by providing zones of exception *from* bare life, spaces for keeping the sacred safe from its deprivations.

This is not to say that animals outside of sanctuaries are all treated the same. *Bestia sacer* is a heuristic for understanding the general ever-present susceptibility to human violence or instrumentalization to which animals have been subject for centuries, but I do not want to erase the distinctions between the real lived experiences of different animals. There are in fact many kinds of *bestia sacer*. The way a cow in a factory farm experiences her bare life is quite different from the way a neglected dog chained in a backyard does. And animals can also find small zones of exception from bare life outside of sanctuaries. In practice, people regularly form compassionate, care-based relationships with animals outside of sanctuaries, as evidenced by the millions of people with close relationships to their pets. However, as mentioned, these pets are also still subject to that ever-present susceptibility.[49] Writing about her family's relationship with two American spotted asses in their care, artist Karin Bolender describes this enduring contradiction:

> This is the essence of a harrowing truth for me: Aliass and Passenger are killable in the society we live in. If something happened to our family, they would become mere assets without much economic value, and it is likely that they would wind up on a rumbling trailer to the slaughterhouse. More likely (because donkey meat is not much desired in the United States), they would go to a glue factory . . . otherwise known as the local rendering plant. Thousands of unwanted dogs and cats also end up at the rendering plant and so are annihilated and dispersed into products as diverse as makeup and soap and, most horrifically, cheap dog food. . . . However fuzzy the boundary between other species and me may be in my experience and ontology, a stark line is drawn in Western society that renders some of my loved ones killable while others enjoy a full suite of civil and individual rights. Most deeply, I know this to be wrong, wrong, wrong. I know that dog and donkey and horse and cat and every other creature has a unique *bios*, however unwritable or unknowable it may be for human logos. Thus, like so many of us, I find myself in a society with which I am fundamentally at odds.[50]

One of the unique aspects about sanctuaries as institutions is that they seek to provide a space in which that is not the case, in which the norm is that animals are protected from this susceptibility. Although this goal *may* never be fully attainable for actual sanctuaries operating in the larger political–economic system that depends on the existence of *bestia sacer*, it nonetheless remains a broadly shared aspiration among caregivers.

A rescued donkey. We Animals.

## Chapter 2
# Care and Rescue

The primary existential purpose of any animal sanctuary is to care for the animals who live there. But what is care?[1] In its most basic definition, care for another living being can be defined as the act of tending to that being's needs. What care looks like in sanctuaries is the result of particular understandings of what animals need, understandings that are informed by ideas about who animals are and how they should be treated. The very concept of a sanctuary is premised on the idea that the animals who live there were relocated from spaces and situations in which they were previously endangered or at risk of some kind of harm. Eloise, the goat from the Introduction who was abandoned in a small field with little access to water, is an exemplary model of what caregivers have in mind when they talk about rescued animals. They take for granted that animals in sanctuaries have come from contexts worse than the ones in which they now live. It logically follows, then, that the kind of care provided for animals in sanctuaries is intended to be a qualitative improvement over the kind of care they may have received before being rescued.

On the basis of this view of sanctuary animals as rescued animals, care routines at sanctuaries are generally guided by the goal of giving animals better lives than they previously had. Underlying this goal, however, is the even more basic goal of just giving animals life, or as Foucault might put it, making them live.[2] In the course of caring for animals, though, sanctuary workers face many dilemmas, such as how best to serve animals' needs with limited resources, how to treat severely ill or injured animals, and whether and how to limit the exercise of animal agency through such practices as sterilization to prevent overpopulation or the segregation of dangerous or aggressive animals. These decisions often impose certain costs or limitations on the animals for the benefit of the greater sanctuary community of humans and animals. In this chapter, I examine three main types of care. The first part of the chapter focuses on the treatment and care of injured and sick animals; the second focuses on the mundanities of care, including meeting animals' dietary and sanitation needs; and the third section focuses on efforts to foster animals' psychological well-being. Under each of these contexts, sanctuary animals face costs in exchange for the benefits of care, simultaneously creating the conditions of possibility for sanctuaries to operate and limiting the realization of total liberation of animal subjects from their social status as property. The final section explains how sanctuary caregivers transform the relationships that animals have with humans from ones primarily based on their status as property to ones based on a recognition of animals as autonomous subjects worthy of care and respect and how these relationships are nonetheless constrained by the broader social context in which animals remain configured as property (the realm of *bestia sacer*), creating for animals in sanctuaries a new hybrid social status between subject and property I call *improperty*.

## Caring for Injured Animals

One important part of care in sanctuaries is looking out for and treating physical injuries and ailments. Because many animals that come to sanctuaries and shelters have health issues related to the previous conditions in which they lived, veterinary care and physical rehabilitation of animals play central roles in animal care. Sanctuaries, especially those for formerly farmed animals, also encounter health conditions that have not previously been a focus of veterinary intervention. Maximizing the production output of animal bodies, for example, is the primary concern of industrialized agricultural operations, and this can lead to significant physiological problems for animals as a result of selective breeding, artificially accelerated growth cycles, and the densely concentrated warehousing of animals. In the words of one caregiver, "factory farmed animals have it the worst; their whole lives are about dealing with the effects of how they were raised." Joint and foot problems are common for most animals raised for meat, as they are selectively bred for rapid gain but not for the other physiological changes they would need to adequately support that weight. Laying hens experience a range of health problems related to egg production, including egg impactions, infections, and cancer. In addition, many animals come to sanctuary with injuries they sustained in the facilities where they were previously housed. These facilities do not typically have standardized procedures for treating most injuries and health conditions because animal agricultural industries either slaughter animals before these conditions can develop or, from the perspective of profit and efficiency, do not need to treat them because they do not significantly affect output. As a result, sanctuaries' need for new diagnoses and treatments has directly influenced the development of veterinary science, at least for certain kinds of animals.[3] For example, Roosevelt Farm Sanctuary took in a calf named Flower with seriously impaired front legs. As Flower's story illustrates, the fact that farmers have not historically tried to do things like help disabled calves to walk means that the methods for treating Flower and animals with similar conditions are newly refined or still experimental in some cases.

When she came stumbling out of the barn, Flower looked like a cyborg with robotic legs. This was particularly surreal because Flower was a two-year-old female Jersey cow. She was still covered in soft, downy, reddish-brown hair, but she was starting to grow little horns and already weighed a few hundred pounds. Her front legs were encased from hoof to chest in plastic braces held closed with several black Velcro straps. The left one was white and straight like a full-leg plaster cast. The right one was tan and articulated on hinges at her knee joint. Flower walked with a pronounced limp, swinging the left leg out to the side and then stepping forward with the right. The combination of her plastic-clad limbs, her stumbling gait, and her cute, inquisitive calf face give her the air of a Disney character from an animated sci-fi film about farm animals in space.

Flower was born in 2013 at a northeastern dairy farm, where her mother was restrained inside a building with concrete floors.[4] When Flower's mother gave birth to her, she fell onto the concrete and broke her left front leg, tumbling into the manure trough behind the row of chained cows in which her mother stood. A manager at the dairy found the calf with her injured leg already starting to swell. The administration of veterinary care at animal agriculture operations is generally determined by a calculus of costs and benefits, limited to veterinary procedures that will facilitate profit rather than cut into it. Flower's injury would have been much more expensive to treat than any profit she could bring in, so from a business perspective, the obvious choice would be to euthanize rather than treat a calf in her condition. Rather than euthanize her, however, the manager called a woman he knew who had expressed interest in raising a cow as a pet. The woman came to get Flower and drove her home in the back of her car.

The woman, who was named Jennifer (the only detail caregivers knew about her), cared for the calf inside her house, giving her blankets for bedding and feeding her with a bottle. She hired a vet to treat Flower's injured leg. The vet gave her antibiotics but did not treat the fracture in her left knee. Despite the antibiotics, Flower developed an infection in the joint, which never properly healed. Since the leg was too badly injured to support her weight and the uninjured leg also was not strong enough to carry her by itself, Flower taught herself to walk on her front knees. A video of Flower before she received her braces shows her swinging her spindly, crooked legs out to the side and pulling herself forward on her bent knees. When the vet examined her again, he told Jennifer that the calf would never be able to walk and suggested that she be euthanized.

For a second time, Flower was given a reprieve. Jennifer decided to ask for help from Roosevelt Farm Sanctuary. The sanctuary agreed to take Flower in and arranged to get her medical care at the Cornell University Hospital for Animals. Although caregivers at Roosevelt feared Flower's condition would be untreatable, they were pleasantly surprised when the vet staff said they could help her. Because the ligaments in her good leg had become shortened during months of pulling herself around on her front knees, they had to operate on that leg as well as the one with the broken knee. Over several months and multiple return visits to Cornell, a three-hundred-mile round trip in the back of a truck for Flower, her condition gradually improved. Flower received two surgeries at Cornell, one to reset the broken bone and a second to repair the ligaments in the other leg. With the help of the special braces from a company in Florida that specializes in making braces and prosthetics for animals, Flower was now able to wander throughout the sanctuary during the day, using the legs that previously could not support her weight.

Theresa, one of the caregivers at the sanctuary, first introduced me to Flower. Theresa is a white woman in her early thirties who moved to the New York Hudson Valley to work full-time as an animal caregiver at the sanctuary. Originally from a military family in Texas—both her brother and father are veterans—she lived in New York City while working on a degree in early childhood education. While attending a tour during a weekend visit to the sanctuary, she was deeply moved by the animals she met. She had read about the lives of animals in the agricultural industry, but meeting them in person while hearing the tour guide explain the situations from which they had been rescued caused her to empathize with them in a way she never had before. "I couldn't stop thinking about them after I left," she told me. "Shortly after that, I became vegan." Within a few weeks, she decided to give up her plans to be a teacher and applied to work as an intern at the sanctuary, working there for free while learning all the specific skills required for caring for formerly farmed animals. These included various animals' dietary needs and the specific sorts of health problems common to different species and how to treat them. After several months of intern training, she was hired to fill an open animal caregiver position. When I met Theresa, she had been working at the sanctuary for almost two years.

Theresa told me about Flower as we stood together scratching Flower's ears. The calf tilted her head to the side, closed her eyes, and stretched her neck, responding just as my dog does when I scratch behind her ears. It was hard to tell by looking at her if Flower was in any pain, but I wondered if she experienced an improvement in the quality of her life since her rescue and treatments or if her injuries continued to impact her life to the same degree. Theresa felt that there was an improvement. "When I first saw Flower, I really didn't think there was any chance she would make it. It looked *really* bad. But now look at her. Nobody can tell me she's not happy."

Socially, Flower was relatively isolated while I was around her. For her own safety, Flower was kept separate from the other cows at the sanctuary. The full-grown females were bigger, and she was not strong enough to support herself when they bumped into her. Nonetheless, Flower made frequent attempts to interact with the other cows. One day, she managed to climb over a five-foot-high wire fence to join them where they were grazing in a pasture, an impressive feat for a calf with only two fully functional legs.[5] Hearing these stories made

me wonder again about Flower's quality of life. Flower's isolation benefited her by preventing injuries from interacting with the other cows,
but it also benefited the sanctuary more generally because additional
injuries could drain financial resources. It also freed up time for other
sanctuary tasks that caregivers might otherwise have had to spend
supervising her. Flower had to relinquish some of her own already
limited mobility as well as the ability to interact with other cows for
the requirements of the larger sanctuary community, even though her
sacrifice also potentially benefited her by preventing further injuries.

Although Flower's ability to socialize was limited, it was not completely curtailed. Another time, I was helping give the cows, sheep,
and goats in the barn their evening feeding when Theresa asked me
to see if I could lure Flower back to her pen so she could be closed in
for the night. She gave me a large plastic scooper full of alfalfa pellets and a folded-over half of a peanut butter sandwich. "She loves
peanut butter!" Theresa said. "She can be stubborn, but if anything
will work, it should be this. It's also how we get her to take meds—by
hiding pills in the peanut butter." (This may be as close to a universal rule of thumb as there is in the world of animal care—although
there are surely exceptions, I have yet to find an animal that does not
love peanut butter.) Theresa and I found Flower standing outside by
the fence around the pasture where the steers live. Bob, the steer who
befriended Eloise, stood staring at Flower from the other side of the
wooden fence that separated them.

As Theresa and I watched, Bob was making a new acquaintance.
"Oh, wow—this is awesome!" Theresa said excitedly. "This is the first
time Flower has interacted with the boys. I'm so excited to see how
they react!" Bob stretched his neck over the top wooden crossbeam
and breathed in deeply over and over, inhaling Flower's smell. Flower
sniffed back, almost touching his wet nose with hers. Theresa asked
me to take photos with my phone so she could show the other caregivers how interested they looked as they greeted each other for the
first time. I snapped some pictures from different angles, and we
watched silently for several minutes as they continued to sniff each
other and rub their muzzles together. Eventually, Flower seemed to
lose interest and moved away from the fence to sniff at pieces of hay
scattered in the mud next to the fence post.

Sure that I would no longer be interrupting their interaction if
I tried to get Flower's attention, I finally approached her with the

scooper of food. "Flower! Come on, girl!" I called as I held out a handful of pellets. She sniffed at my hand and slurped the pellets out of my palm with a giant, wet tongue, leaving strings of white slobber on my fingers. I took a step back and held out another handful of pellets, and Flower took a stumbling step forward to get another mouthful. We continued like this, step by step, slowly inching closer to the barn. Every time she seemed like she was starting to lose interest in the food and turned to look at something else, I held out a piece of the peanut butter sandwich. She would then immediately flare her nostrils and swing her head back toward me to snatch the sandwich bits from my spittle-glazed fingers. "It's working!" Theresa cheered us on.

After fifteen minutes of slowly walking backward and holding out handfuls of food to Flower, I eventually lured her all the way back to her pen in the barn. Theresa unfastened the Velcro straps that held her braces in place, and Flower lay down in her straw bedding with her front legs bent beneath her. As she munched on fresh hay I had tossed into her pen before luring her in, I asked Theresa about the high cost of her veterinary care—several thousand dollars at this point.

"Do you ever have reservations about how much it costs to care for an animal like Flower when that money could potentially be used to care for multiple other animals that don't have her medical issues?"

"It's true that her care is more expensive than that of a lot of other animals," Theresa told me, "but we don't think about it like that once we take in a rescue. When the sanctuary rescues an animal, we're committing to doing everything we can to give that animal the best life possible, including any vet care needed. Once an animal is here, there's no question that we'll do whatever is necessary to care for her."

Theresa's answer highlights what Flower gets in exchange for her restrictions within the sanctuary: membership in a community that comes with full health care, among other benefits. Flower is arguably not the only animal who faces costs for these benefits, though. My question was motivated by another kind of trade-off that is the basis for some criticism directed at certain sanctuaries by other animal advocates. The argument is that sanctuaries should not spend resources on expensive "special needs" cases like Flower's because they would be better spent on helping more animals whose care is less expensive. The cost this economy of care imposes precedes actual membership in the sanctuary community. The potential animals that could take Flower's place, a vast collective that numbers in the tens of billions at any given time, are denied the very possibility of being members of the sanctuary community, instead remaining consigned to the external world of *bestia sacer*. Furthermore, the same economic logic could actually be applied to any animal in a sanctuary. Not only does every animal have the potential to incur medical costs that another one outside the sanctuary may not have incurred, but even if all the animals remained healthy, every sanctuary denizen occupies a space that could instead belong to another animal that was not so fortunate. On the basis of this logic, the limited nature of sanctuary space and resources means that the animals who reside there are the beneficiaries of a virtually endless stream of sacrifice from the realm of *bestia sacer* outside the sanctuary.

## Mundanity of Care

What does it mean to do what is necessary to care for animals like Flower, Bob, and Eloise? Aside from the importance of veterinary care, Flower's, Bob's, and Eloise's stories reflect other elements of animal care in sanctuaries. In chapter 1, I described how the word *sanctu-*

A rescued steer. We Animals.

*ary* comes from the Latin *sanctuarium*, a place where holy or sacred things are kept. If sanctuaries are places for the sacred, then there is some amusing irony in the fact that everyday practices of care within sanctuaries are largely composed of the mundane, unglamorous tasks related to feeding and cleaning up after animals. All animals need food and water to survive. This sounds obvious, but caring for a variety of different animal species quickly complicates this simple goal, because different species have different nutritional needs. Most animals across all my field sites were fed in the morning and again in the evening. What they ate varied widely, though, and often required specialized knowledge about nutritional requirements and foods that could be dangerous to particular species, such as the danger excessive amounts of grain pose to cattle like Bob.

The animals I encountered that required the least specialized knowledge about their dietary needs were the cats and dogs at Texas Companion Rescue. Caregivers at the shelter feed them regular commercial cat food and dog food and give them fresh water twice a day. Many of the other animals I encountered, including both agricultural animals and exotic animals, can also eat certain commercial food products, like grain or alfalfa pellets that can be purchased from farm suppliers. Many of these animals cannot survive off of these products alone, though, and need their diets supplemented with other foods.

A cattle care guide produced by Farm Sanctuary illustrates the specificity of nutritional knowledge required to properly feed many sanctuary animals. As described in chapter 1, Farm Sanctuary was the first farm animal sanctuary in the United States, founded in 1986 in Watkins Glen, New York. It is also where Roosevelt Farm Sanctuary's cofounder, Rita Johnson, interned in order to learn how to operate a sanctuary. Caregivers at many sanctuaries across the country, including Roosevelt, often contact Farm Sanctuary when they have questions about animal care. These guidelines for cattle care come from materials they have produced for a range of farmed animal species as a resource for other sanctuaries.

Starting with cattle's hydration needs, the guidelines suggest that clean, fresh water always be made available for cattle. Mature cattle generally consume between ten and twenty gallons of water each day, so sanctuaries need containers large enough to hold that quantity. "Consumption is based on weather," the guidelines explain, "so more water should be available in hot weather. If you have animals who have difficulty walking, you must create an area to allow them to get to water easily. Dehydration in cattle can be fatal." The salt and mineral guidelines suggest that salt and mineral licks also always be made available to cattle. "If you are in an area that has selenium-deficient soil," it notes, "a salt block with selenium is recommended." The feed guidelines go into more detail about cattle physiology:

> As ruminants (animals with stomachs that have four chambers), cattle rely mainly on hay or pasture (fiber) to fulfill their dietary needs. Grain is very high in energy and fat, and therefore we do not recommend its use for healthy cattle. If you are caring for older animals who have difficulty keeping weight on due to bad teeth or health issues, however, you may need to supplement their hay or pasture with grain. Altered males can develop bladder and kidney stones when fed grain so other options include hay stretcher pellets, which can be made into a mash for older, thinner animals who have difficulty consuming hay.

Finally, the pasture guidelines suggest that pastureland be plentiful and of good quality because it can provide most of cattle's dietary needs when grass is available. If there is not adequate pastureland, cattle will need their diets supplemented with hay. "Before giving your cattle access to a pasture," they caution, "be sure to remove all plants that are poisonous to them. Contact your County Agricultural Extension agent for a complete listing of poisonous plants in your area." These guidelines reflect the actual provisioning of food, water, and mineral supplements that I observed.

I cite these guidelines to illustrate how the specificity of information about cows' physiological needs is based on knowledge produced through animal agricultural practices. Farm Sanctuary and other sanctuaries draw on nutritional science that was largely developed to improve animal husbandry. The guidelines are tools of biopower for fostering the lives of cattle developed within the biopolitical regime of the animal–industrial complex.[6] Roosevelt Farm Sanctuary's care-givers knew to prevent Bob from eating too much grain because of the knowledge produced by this regime. Sanctuaries have adapted this knowledge to their own needs, however, producing new kinds of care knowledge in the process. Consider the advice about creating an area to allow animals that have difficulty walking to access water more easily or the advice about making a mash from hay pellets for older, thinner animals who have difficulty consuming hay. These insights are based on concerns that agricultural facilities do not generally share. Animals do not usually live long enough at agricultural operations to develop chronic mobility issues or to need their food altered to assist digestion. And animals that do develop problems, like Flower, are not generally kept around to accommodate their needs. As artist and disability and animal rights scholar Sunaura Taylor observes,

> There are many examples . . . of animals who need simple accommodations to survive. Perhaps they need to eat their meals away from the group or be put in a living space with less dominant animals (even of another species), or perhaps they need to be fitted for some sort of mobility device. . . . Yet in an anthropocentric world, accommodating farmed animals takes on a whole other meaning. [A sanctuary] is in many ways an accommodation in and of itself, as the vast majority of farmed animals don't have access to environments in which they can go about their lives in species-typical ways, let alone thrive—regardless of disability. Instead they are forced into environments that limit and harm them.[7]

While many sanctuaries draw on agricultural knowledge to care for these animals, they also apply it in new ways to provide care to animals for reasons beyond the interests of the original knowledge regime. And, rather than applying this knowledge to the management of large populations of particular species, as industrial farms do, sanctuaries adapt it to address the interests of particular individuals with unique needs, like Flower. While industrialized animal farming has made farm animal sanctuaries necessary—at least from the perspective of human caregivers—it has also shaped the conditions that make it possible for those sanctuaries to provide care to rescued agricultural animals. In other words, the cause of the need for accommodation indirectly supplies some of the resources for providing it.

For animals that are not from agricultural industries, however, veterinary knowledge may be even more limited. In these cases, sanctuaries develop new care knowledge on their own, responding to and learning from problems as they arise. At Rainbow Haven, for example, caregivers collect hundreds of pounds of long brown seedpods from around the monkey cages every summer. These pods fall from several large monkey pod trees, a tropical tree in the pea family that grows up to eighty feet and produces seedpods similar in appearance to tamarind pods. The monkeys like to eat the monkey pods, but as the caregivers quickly learned, this makes them ill. One day, while helping to pick up monkey pods, Olivia, the sanctuary cofounder, observed with a smile, "It's ironic that monkey pods make monkeys sick."

Sanctuaries also develop preventative strategies to avoid problems before they occur. When bringing these same monkeys food bowls, caregivers dip the bottom of their shoes in a puddle of chlorhexidine, an antiseptic chemical, before entering the outer-cage area. They also put disinfectant gel on their hands before coming into contact with the monkeys and wash the monkeys' empty food bowls with chlorhex before placing them in the sun to dry. These precautions are designed to prevent the monkeys from contracting bacterial or viral infections from humans. If someone is sick with a cold or the flu, Olivia won't let them go near the monkeys, and she requires any visitor to the sanctuary who just flew into the island to wait three days before going near the monkeys to make sure the visitor is not sick with something he can pass to the monkeys.

Aside from the different issues that arise in relation to what animals consume, there is one aspect of animal care with which all sanctuaries and shelters must contend equally: what happens after the animals eat. Waste disposal is a never-ending task at any facility that cares for animals. The bulk of my actual work time volunteering at each of my field sites was spent helping to feed and clean up after animals, and a significant portion of that time was spent cleaning up feces.

At Roosevelt Farm Sanctuary, it was not uncommon for me to spend hours each day using a small, long-handled spade to scoop up pig feces from the muddy pasture adjacent to the pig barn. Pigs are generally very clean and usually go outside to defecate and urinate, but they did occasionally urinate inside the large barn where they slept. It was therefore also necessary to clean out urine-soaked straw that lined the barn floor and replace it with fresh straw. On other days, I spent hours cleaning woodchips and straw caked with chicken or duck feces out of the various bird coops. I also occasionally cleaned cow pies from the pastures where the cows grazed, but because of their larger size, these were actually the easiest to scoop up. One of the caregivers would park a tractor near the area I was cleaning with the large scoop on the front lowered to the ground so I could dump wheelbarrow loads of feces and soiled hay and wood chips into it. After the scoop was full, one of the caregivers would drive the tractor to a clearing in some trees on the southeastern corner of the sanctuary. There they dumped the tractor load onto the freshest heap of several large mounds of compost that sat in various states of fermentation. After cleaning out a coop or barn, I would spread fresh wood chips or hay across the floor so the process could start all over again.

At Texas Companion Rescue, waste disposal was folded into socializing for the dogs. Cats used litter boxes that needed to be scooped, but dogs would often defecate while volunteers were walking them or throwing a ball for them in one of the fenced-in dog runs. Garbage cans with poop scoopers sat near each dog run. When I walked dogs outside of the runs, I also took plastic poop bags with me to clean up any messes left on sidewalks. Paid cleaning staff emptied the garbage cans daily and tossed the full bags in a large metal dumpster in the parking lot behind the shelter building. They also checked dog kennels throughout the day and cleaned out any dog feces they found inside kennels. Despite all this cleaning, the pungent odor of dog feces and urine lingered around various spots throughout the shelter grounds. If you were there for a few hours, you stopped noticing it, but it never actually went away.

After doing so much waste disposal at the other sites, I was surprised to find that many of the animals at Rainbow Haven did not need to be cleaned up after. For example, feces disposal was not an issue for the zebras. The hot, wet climate and lush vegetation that covered the ground in a large part of their paddock perhaps also helped the zebra feces to break down before it could accumulate. The rodents, most of whom were there as food sources for the birds of prey at the sanctuary, did need their cages cleaned regularly, and some of the smaller exotic birds that reside at the sanctuary also lived in cages with bottoms that slid out. Each day, one of the caregivers changed the newspaper lining the bottom of these cages. The bottoms of the large birdcages surrounding the landscaped area of the sanctuary that caregivers called "the lawn" were just grass-covered dirt and, like the zebras' area, never seemed to need cleaning. The only place where animals defecated directly on the ground that actually needed regular cleaning was the monkey cage complex. This was to ensure that the monkeys did not become sick. Like the large birdcages, the bottom of the monkey complex was just exposed earth. One caregiver would lock an internal sliding gate inside the enclosure to keep the monkeys in one half of the cage, while a second caregiver went inside the cage and used a scooper to pick up monkey feces. The cleaner also used a brush and disinfectant to scrub the foot-high stone and concrete barrier that ran along the base of the outer cage walls. Then the monkeys were allowed to go into the clean part of the cage, and the caregivers repeated the cleaning routine in the other part of the cage.

The mundane aspects of care tend to impose little to no cost on sanctuary animals. Instead, they make up the bulk of quotidian benefits that animals receive as members of the interspecies sanctuary community, benefits in exchange for which animals must bear other constraints. Many of the limitations I have identified so far relate to animals' freedom to move through the sanctuary space and interact—or refrain from interacting—with other animals, including humans. Flower, Bob, and Eloise all must accept the limits placed on their ability to move around freely and socialize with other animals. In addition to constraints on the ability to socialize, many of the animals at my field sites—and at most sanctuaries in general—also face constraints on their ability to avoid unwanted human interactions.[8] This, of course, includes interactions with human caregivers but also can include human visitors at sanctuaries that offer tours or are otherwise open to the public, a topic I examine further in the next chapter. Caregivers are aware of the costs these constraints can impose on animals, however, especially the potential psychological effects of captivity and forced interactions with humans.

## Keeping Animals Happy

For sanctuaries, caring for animals is about more than just keeping them alive and healthy. Providing the basic necessities for life—such as food and water and a living space clean enough to avoid illness—are the minimum elements of care required in any context in which an animal is to be kept alive. Animal farms, such as the dairy farm where Flower was born, must provide basic sustenance to their animals as well, at least enough to keep their animals alive and physiologically healthy enough to produce milk or eggs or grow big enough to be slaughtered. To the extent that they both seek to foster life to some extent, sanctuaries and farms share a major care goal: animals *need* things like food and water.[9] Unlike many agricultural operations, however, sanctuaries also identify needs beyond the basic ones required for life. These interrelated needs include socialization, mental enrichment, and freedom to move through and interact with or refrain from interacting with their environment.

Flower's care reflects this concern for needs beyond basic sustenance and veterinary care. Roosevelt's cofounder, Rita, explains the rationale behind the decision to get Flower surgeries and leg braces in a video posted on the sanctuary's website: "What matters is that she is happy; her life matters to her and to us." In addition to food, water, and the medical procedures necessary to make it possible for her to walk, Flower's care is shaped by this goal of making her happy. What happiness means for a cow with two disabled front legs is, of course, open to interpretation. But as Taylor observes in explaining her coining of the term *animal crips*,

> to call an animal a crip is no doubt human projection, but it is also a way of identifying nonhuman animals as subjects who have been oppressed by ableism. Naming animals as crips is a way of challenging us to question our ideas about how bodies move, think, and feel and what makes a body valuable, exploitable, useful, or disposable. It means questioning our assumptions about what a cow or a chicken is capable of experiencing. And it means stopping to consider that the limping fox you see through the barrel of your rifle may actually be enjoying his animal crip life. Animal crips challenge us to consider what is valuable about living and what is valuable about the variety of life.[10]

The idea that animal happiness should be a goal in Flower's care is premised on the recognition or understanding that it can be—that Flower can have a happy, fulfilled life despite her unique mobility limitations. Granted, how her emotional state is assessed is also shaped by the way she is understood by her caregivers and thus subject to potential misinterpretation. Nonetheless, this concern for the affective and psychological experience of animals and the resulting recognition of an expanded pool of needs and benefits is an extension of caregiver efforts to engage with animals as fellow subjects rather than the living means of production they are as *bestia sacer*.

Rita's statement about Flower's life mattering to her human caregivers as well as herself reveals a second way in which meanings of care can diverge in accordance with different purposes in applying that care. One can think of the practices of care described in the first part of this chapter as caring *for*, but to care can also mean to feel concern about someone or to assign importance to that someone. Rita's statement about Flower mattering explicitly invokes this second meaning of care, caring *about*: the humans at Roosevelt Farm Sanctuary are concerned with Flower's physical and emotional well-being because they see her as important in and of herself. This care about animals and their well-being conflicts with a more instrumental caring about animals in other contexts. Industrialized dairy operators, for example, may care about the well-being of their cows because they want to maintain a certain level of milk production that would be impossible if their cows were too malnourished, but that type of care is tied to external outcomes separate from the cows rather than to the intrinsic value of their well-being to the cows themselves.

Caring about animals obviously does not only happen within sanctuaries. The dairy farm worker who found Flower, for example, cared about her well-being enough to call the woman who rescued her rather than just euthanizing her. Although we do not know how he may have understood and valued Flower as more than an instrument for profit, the fact that he felt concern for her well-being and assigned her some importance beyond production value suggests that he did to some extent care about her in a way similar to the kind of caring Rita describes. At an institutional scale, however, facilities like dairy farms—where animals are reduced to the status of *bestia sacer*—are shaped by an instrumental approach to animal care, while sanctuaries are guided by an ethos of care that treats the well-being of the subject for the subject's own sake as its primary goal.

One of the primary problems sanctuaries face in trying to foster psychological well-being for animals is that, like the places from which many of them were rescued, sanctuaries are still a form of forced captivity that constrains animals' ability to move freely through the world as they may otherwise choose to. Even though animals may notice that the quality of their living conditions has improved in sanctuaries, we cannot assume that they see their captivity as part of a reasonable exchange for those improvements. Ecofeminist philosopher and ethicist Lori Gruen describes captivity as "a condition in which a being is confined and controlled and is reliant on those in control to satisfy her basic needs."[11] Sanctuaries, although largely committed to minimizing control and confinement, nonetheless still fit this definition of captivity. As Gruen notes, the goals of "sanctuaries are to rehabilitate abused animals, nurture orphaned animals, provide companionship and enriched environments in which animals can express species-typical behavior, and to respect each animal,"[12] but sometimes expressing species-typical behavior conflicts with the other goals of a sanctuary.

For example, most sanctuaries are opposed to captive breeding, both because there are already countless living animals that could fill very limited sanctuary space and because allowing captive breeding would subject future generations of animals to the same restrictions on their freedom that their parents already face.[13] As Gruen argues,

> the freedom to reproduce and to care for young is central in the development of important affiliative social skills that are necessary to build meaningful bonds with conspecifics and to enhance group stability. Denying captive animals the possibility to reproduce strips them of the chance to engage fully in species-typical behaviors, and this is particularly detrimental to females who are, in most species, primarily responsible for rearing young. Having infants born in captivity allows individuals to experience a full range of social relations, and it serves as enrichment for captive groups. Yet, allowing captive breeding perpetuates the wrongs that captivity poses.[14]

Relatedly, philosophers Will Kymlicka and Sue Donaldson argue that, while domesticated animals would ideally be afforded the agency to engage in sexual reproduction "to the extent that autonomous control over their sexual and reproductive lives is possible for such animals," in situations in which "animals do not or cannot self-regulate their reproduction, the costs to others of having to care for and maintain their offspring could become prohibitive,"[15] as would be true in sanctuaries, especially in the case of industrial laying hens who could potentially produce rapidly overwhelming numbers of baby chicks.

Both Roosevelt Farm Sanctuary and Rainbow Haven regularly confronted this specific issue with rescued birds. Based on their experiences with chickens, duck, geese, and parrots at these sites, several caregivers informed me, and I observed myself, that not all female birds seem to have a desire to nest. Some lay eggs and immediately abandon them, while others will brood on their eggs until they are eventually taken away.[16] On the other hand, one small Hawaiian chicken named Mama was so attracted to brooding that caregivers at Rainbow Haven provided her with golf balls to sit on since she rarely laid her own eggs but would brood on other birds' eggs whenever the opportunity arose.

Because caregivers do not segregate male and female birds to allow them to form as much as possible their own preferred social groupings, it is often necessary to take away eggs to avoid a proliferation of baby chicks. I witnessed exactly this outcome at a sanctuary for formerly farmed animals that I toured in Texas, where a mother hen led around five peeping chicks who had hatched from eggs that had been overlooked by caregivers. With industrial laying hens, whose bodies have been altered through generations of selective breeding to maximize their laying output, recycling the eggs into a mash that is fed back to the hens also helps them gain back some of the nutrients—such as calcium—that constant laying rapidly depletes from their bodies. Many caregivers I worked with expressed feelings of guilt about taking away the eggs from brooding hens, but they also felt there was no alternative. While cleaning bird enclosures, I too felt bad about having to take eggs out from under squawking, agitated hens. Although probably relatively small in comparison to the violence and neglect they experienced in their previous lives, I felt as though I was inflicting a subtle but significant emotional harm on these hens by ignoring their protests and stealing their eggs.

The challenge of trying to foster animals' psychological well-being within conditions of captivity that can simultaneously have deleterious effects on that well-being reflects a paradox at the center of the sanctuary project. As mentioned in the Introduction, philosopher Tom Regan summarizes the difference between the rights and the welfare approach to animal advocacy as "empty cages, not larger cages."[17] Paradoxically, although they seek to liberate animals from cages, one could argue that in the end, sanctuaries themselves are ultimately larger cages. One way caregivers try to navigate through this paradox and mitigate the negative impacts of captivity as much as possible is by avoiding stimuli that they think may cause animals stress. They often accomplish this through either minimizing human contact with them or trying to provide social or psychological enrichment, such as toys to play with or opportunities to play or otherwise interact with other animals. In addition to trying to counter the psychological effects of captivity, these efforts can help to soften the captivity paradox as well by giving animals more autonomy and control over their own spaces. If sanctuaries are larger cages, they are qualitatively different cages in which animals are related to as subjects rather than *bestia sacer*, and the limits imposed on them are the result of efforts to foster and respect their subjectivity while maintaining the functional stability of the sanctuary for all its denizens.

At Rainbow Haven, for example, Olivia designed many of her methods for approaching or interacting with animals with the specific goal of minimizing any anxiety or stress she might cause. Maui, a female cockatoo, was one of the most prominent beneficiaries of this approach at the sanctuary. Olivia actually purchased Maui as a pet, but when she learned more about exotic birds as they started coming into the sanctuary as rescues, she came to the conclusion that exotic birds should not be pets. She felt that their psychological and emotional lives were too complex for them to live happily in most pet situations because they became too dependent on emotional support that humans could not reliably provide. She explained to me, "What people don't understand is that exotic birds like cockatoos and parrots are highly intelligent birds, and they bond for life. People get them when they're babies and form close bonds with them, and then if their personalities change as they get older and they get more difficult to care for or they outlive their owner, people just get rid of them. And they're totally heartbroken and depressed. Exotic birds in particular will resort to self-abuse when they're upset, doing things like pulling out their feathers compulsively."

There were examples of this behavior in other birds at the sanctuary. Magma, for example, is an eclectus parrot that lives in a cage near Maui's. She was given to the sanctuary by relatives of her owner after her owner died. Native to parts of Melanesia, Australia, and Indonesia, eclectus parrots have striking sexually dimorphic plumage, which is rare among parrot species. The males are usually a vibrant green, and the females are scarlet with a bright indigo chest. Magma, however, had pulled out most of her feathers prior to coming to the sanctuary. The only parts of her that really looked like an eclectus anymore were her yellow beak and red head and wings; the rest of her body was covered in wrinkly bluish skin, like a hatchling. Magma got excited when people walked near her cage, prancing back and forth on one of her perches and saying "hello!" in that high-pitched voice all birds seem to share when speaking human languages. According to Olivia, she preferred the company of men and would get particularly excited when certain male volunteers were nearby. Sometimes Magma would even break out in the chorus of "I Left My Heart in San Francisco." She carried the tune well—Olivia claimed that she had perfect pitch—though she usually trailed off after "I left my heart."

Aside from the feather pulling, Magma exhibited other behavior that caregivers interpreted as signs of stress or anxiety. Maternal nesting behavior is another common trait in eclectus hens, and they will often lay and brood on infertile eggs even when living alone. Eclectus parrots are sometimes used to incubate other parrots' eggs. Magma had one such egg in her cage with her. It was there before I arrived at the sanctuary and remained in the cage for months. Caregivers left it there as a calming mechanism, a sort of security blanket that allowed her to engage in species-typical behavior that could alleviate some of the stress of captivity. One day, Olivia had the idea to give her a baby chicken she could foster as her own offspring, hoping that this would provide an even better opportunity than the infertile egg to engage

A rescued parrot. NEAVS.

in species-typical behavior that could provide social and psychological enrichment. Olivia was not sure how Magma would respond to the chick, but she was definitely not expecting what followed when she placed the chick in Magma's cage. Rather than indulge her broody tendencies, Magma displayed a different tendency of eclectus parrots. In certain circumstances, wild eclectus hens have been observed committing infanticide against their male offspring when they have both a male and a female hatchling. Olivia did not know the sex of the young bird, but even though Magma was not wild, and she did not have two hatchlings, she "immediately shredded the baby chick," a caregiver later told me.

Feeling extra responsibility because she had purchased the bird herself, Olivia was determined to minimize Maui's stress as much as possible and prevent her from becoming more like Magma and some of the other birds at the sanctuary. As a result, Maui quite literally ruled her roost. During the day, she sat atop a cage in an open barn area. Caregivers turned on the radio during the day for Maui because she seemed to like music. Sometimes she would even bounce up and down and fan her head feathers, dancing to songs with a good beat. Dancing to music is not uncommon for cockatoos, as a YouTube search will quite entertainingly illustrate. Maui also had a bell she could ring whenever she wanted a treat. Although she seemed to really like some caregivers, perching on their hands and saying "hello" or "Maui's a good bird," others (including me) could not get too close to her cage or she would try to bite them. Occasionally, if she made her way to the floor, she would even chase the people she did not seem to like out of the barn, nipping at their ankles and flapping her wings. The primary rule in interacting with Maui, as established by Olivia, was to avoid agitating her whenever possible.

To avoid upsetting Maui, caregivers were instructed to open the door to Maui's room first thing in the morning before anybody spoke a word, otherwise she might hear the voices outside and could become agitated and hurt herself in the cage where she slept at night. Sanctuary workers, particularly the ones she seemed not to like, were also supposed to generally avoid bothering her to prevent her from getting too agitated. More than one caregiver privately expressed frustration with her since her daytime location in the center of the barn made it difficult to do daily cleanings if she was acting excited.

Cammie, for example, had been volunteering at the sanctuary since Olivia first started taking in animals. She was a retired accountant and started working at the sanctuary after her husband died. She loved her work there and relished the opportunity to be around all the other animals, but she told me she could not stand Maui. "She bit my wrist one time pretty bad, so I generally stay away from her. I don't know why, but she really doesn't like me. I swear, one time, she called me a bitch out of the blue. I've never heard her say it before or since, but I was sweeping near her cage, and my hand got too close, and she stuck her head out and tried to bite me. I pulled my hand away, and she clearly said, 'Bitch'!"

Maui was able to shape the conditions of her environment and daily care through a combination of her assertive behavior and caregivers' willingness to respond in a way that was intended to minimize her stress, not to mention theirs. In this particular dynamic, the caregivers' accommodating responses to Maui afforded her the opportunity to shape the conditions of her care to a greater degree than many of the other animals at the sanctuary could. They went out of their way to avoid bothering her, working more quickly when they had to clean near her, talking quietly around her, and taking indirect routes to avoid walking through the barn when possible. These compromises may be relatively minor compared to the fact that Maui had to spend most of her life in or on top of her cage, but her relationship with caregivers stands out among all the ones I witnessed as being the most clear example of an animal so regularly inverting the power dynamic between herself and humans.

While starting from the same goal of trying to minimize stress, Olivia took a different approach to other animals in the sanctuary. Lolly and Billie, for example, were the sanctuary's two female zebras. They shared a large grassy paddock along the eastern side of the sanctuary. It is necessary to walk through their enclosure to get to other parts of the sanctuary. However, neither of the zebras seemed to want humans to get too close. They moved away from humans when they entered the enclosure and eyed them warily. Sometimes they even barked. The sounds, which resemble a loud cough, are intended as warnings, according to Olivia.

Billie the zebra arrived at the sanctuary with her mother, Molly, as the first two animals Olivia rescued. As described in chapter 1, Olivia first got the idea to start an animal sanctuary while recovering from a lightning strike. Her attempt to relocate two giraffes from an exotic animal park that was closing on the Hawaiian island of Molokai served as the catalyst for her animal-rescuing enterprise, but she was unsuccessful in saving the giraffes. As previously mentioned, she eventually agreed to send the giraffes to the Honolulu Zoo, but they died in transit. She did, however, manage to rescue Billie and her pregnant mother, Molly, from the same park.

Molly gave birth to Lolly shortly after their arrival. Molly would not allow Billie to come near the newborn zebra. She would chase her away, occasionally nipping or kicking at her. As the young zebra grew,

A rescued cockatoo. NEAVS.

though, Molly relented and allowed Billie to socialize with her young sister. Molly eventually died, but the sisters became inseparable. Despite the loss of the giraffes, bringing the zebras over from Molokai allowed Olivia to continue channeling her energy into rescuing animals, which she credits with helping her to recover from the cognitive impairments and psychological depression caused by the debilitating lightning strike. For this reason, Olivia says the zebras saved her life.

When entering the zebra enclosure, she always instructs volunteers "to think like a prey animal." "They don't know who you are or why you're in there," Olivia explained during my first tour of the sanctuary. "So for all they know you're coming to hurt them. The best thing to do is ignore them. Don't talk to them or look at them or give them any reason to think you're interested in them. Walk sideways to them so you're not facing them, keep talking to each other in low voices like you don't even know they're there. You can even grab some tall grass as you walk by and pretend to eat it, so they think you're just interested in grazing." Like many prey animals, zebras are actually quite capable of defending themselves from predators. "Unlike horses," Olivia said, "zebras will charge predators to defend themselves, kicking with their front legs and biting with those giant teeth."

One time, while feeding the zebras their morning mix of alfalfa pellets and hay, I had a chance to experience firsthand the usefulness of Olivia's technique for avoiding injury from the zebras. I heard some unintelligible human voices beyond the rock wall at the back of the sanctuary property. The zebras heard it, too, and moved away from their feeding area. Lolly continued to act particularly skittish as I fed the birds who live in a fenced-in pond that caregivers refer to as the "wetlands." When I turned on a spigot attached to a garden hose to replace some of the pond water lost to evaporation, she trotted past me, looking agitated. The zebras had not scared me at first, but after repeated admonitions that they can be dangerous and Olivia mentioning that Billie had bitten her shoulder once in what Olivia interpreted as an attempt by the zebra to groom her, I was more nervous around them. I followed Olivia's advice to try to think like them, to turn my shoulder to them, and to talk in a deep, reassuring voice. I pretended to bend down to eat grass, pulling clumps and holding them up to my mouth, while repeating, "It's OK, girls. I'm just grazing like you. Mmmm, yummy grass." Lolly let me pass without incident, but she seemed to eye me warily.

Later I found out that earlier that morning, volunteers had heard a feral pig on the other side of the rock wall dividing the zebra pasture from the adjacent property, and the zebras had seemed agitated by the noise. These observations seemed to provide evidence in support of Olivia's justification for the constant weeding and grounds keeping she insisted was necessary around the sanctuary. She said that preventing overgrowth of vegetation gave prey animals like the zebras a clearer line of sight and helped to reduce stress because it reassured them they were not being stalked by hidden predators. This is also the reason she rotates the alpacas, goats, and sheep who live at the sanctuary to different pastures around the property—so they can chew down the tall grass that would otherwise take over.

Olivia's approach to minimizing zebra stress is a form of engagement that anthropologist Matei Candea calls *interpatience*. On the basis of his ethnographic study of meerkat researchers, Candea developed this concept to understand meerkat ways of being with each other and their human researchers that occupy a middle ground between intersubjectivity and the absence of relation.[18] "Much of the time people spend with animals, and indeed with other people, is not so much interactive as 'inter-passive' or, better still, 'inter-patient,'" he explains.[19] Interpatience describes a seeming contradiction: relationships that are based on mutual detachment or disengagement. If patience is understood as "the active cultivation of inaction," then interpatience is "the mutual suspension of action, a cease-fire of sorts."[20] Candea witnessed interpatience when he saw researchers refrain from certain actions that might disturb the meerkats they were studying, to which the meerkats responded by refraining from running away as they typically do when humans are around.[21]

By engaging in interpatience, both zebras and humans create the narrow conditions under which each can be safe from the other while the caregivers feed the zebras or move through their space to care for the other animals at the sanctuary. Even while they seem to ignore each other, both sides are acutely aware of the other's presence. They engage with each other through inaction, allowing the zebras' preference to shape the conditions of that engagement. And, although the zebras lack the ability to leave the physical enclosure in which they live, within that space of confinement, they are able to influence the behavior of the caregivers in a way that at least mitigates the effects of their forced proximity to humans.

Practices of human–animal engagement that could be described as interpatience were not as common at other sanctuaries, but there were many other examples of caregiver concern for animals' emotional states creating opportunities for animals to have greater than usual influence over their own care. This was the case at Roosevelt Farm Sanctuary for a male turkey named Alphonse. Alphonse was brought to the sanctuary as a chick along with his brother Barry. Little is known about their previous living conditions. Barry was a very calm turkey who wandered around the sanctuary grounds, approaching people and standing quietly as they stroked his feathers. Alphonse was the opposite. He would charge people and peck at anybody who came near him, so he was put in his own enclosure where people could not get too close. Despite this general reaction to humans, a farm sanctuary caretaker in her mid-twenties named Maria developed a close attachment to Alphonse. Maria is an amateur bird expert. She raised her own parrots growing up in New York City and has an encyclopedic knowledge of different bird species and their individual peculiarities. One time, she told me about parrots in the Amazon rainforest that had started mimicking the sounds of the chainsaws that were being used to cut down trees around them for lumber. Maria described herself as a lifelong animal lover. She had already learned about the conditions of agricultural animals and had become a vegan when she was younger. She applied for a job as a caregiver at the sanctuary because she wanted to work with animals full-time.

Whenever anybody besides Maria entered Alphonse's enclosure, he would puff up his feathers so that he appeared to double in size and then charge at the intruder. Maria, however, learned to imitate turkey sounds and entered his enclosure with a hunched over posture intended to make herself seem smaller and less intimidating. Although neither Maria nor any of the other caregivers could identify precisely why Alphonse developed a tolerance, if not affection, for Maria, his behavior toward all other intruders to his enclosure suggested to his human caregivers that he had a clear preference that she be the only human to enter his enclosure.

Even though they did not know why the turkey felt the way he did about others in his space, Alphonse's actions stood as signs to his caregivers of his desires about who should and should not come into his vicinity. Through this assertion of his opposition to other humans entering his living space and its effect on the actions of his caregivers,

Alphonse exerted influence over who would clean his enclosure and give him food. Furthermore, through variations of degree in his refrainment from challenging Maria's presence, he also influenced her comportment while near him. In effect, Alphonse both chose which caregiver would care for him and trained her to behave in a certain way while doing so. But for his preferences to translate into altered human behavior in this case, the caregivers had to be both open to his capacity to express preferences through his engagement with them as a subject and willing to respond to those preferences accommodatingly. In the economy of compromises between sanctuary denizens, Alphonse's case is an example of caregivers yielding to his refusal to compromise over who could enter his personal space.

Summarizing her view of animal subjectivity, Maria told me, "What people don't understand is that animals have their own sensibilities. People think they know what animals want, but they don't realize that they have different sensibilities. It's something you have to learn over time by being here and being around them." Being open to the possibility of understanding these sensibilities creates a space in which caregivers like Maria can try to understand and respond to animal preferences. Writing about an experience he had in which a cat walked in on him while he was changing, Jacques Derrida wrote that in that moment, he saw the cat "as this irreplaceable living being that one day enters my space, enters this place where it can encounter me, see me, see me naked," and he wondered, what if she responded?[22] This question "comes down to knowing not whether the animal speaks but whether one can know what *respond* means. And how to distinguish a response from a reaction. . . . It would not be a matter of 'giving speech back' to animals but perhaps acceding to a thinking . . . that thinks the absence of the name as something other than a privation."[23] Acceding to such thinking, to the possibility that animal subjectivity could be something other than a privation, in turn opens the door to the possibility of a nonanthropomorphic yet still intersubjective relationship with animals that sanctuary caregivers like Maria strive to forge. Of course, it is important not to romanticize or exaggerate the transformative potential of these interactions. After Maria left the sanctuary to have a baby, other caregivers once again had to enter Alphonse's enclosure to clean it and feed him. Although they continued to try to respect his personal space by going as quickly as possible, they could no longer accommodate him like they did when

Maria was able to be his primary care provider. Unlike Maui, Alphonse ultimately lost much of his influence over the conditions of his care and was forced to surrender his ability to repel incursions by humans other than Maria into his personal space.

Responding to behavior that is perceived as aggressive by trying to leave animals alone is not always an option for caregivers. At Texas Companion Rescue, for example, it is imperative that dogs who exhibit behavior that appears aggressive—including growling, snarling, and nipping at people or other animals—quickly learn to curb that behavior or they will not be able to be adopted. At best, dogs who continue to exhibit such behavior may be forced to live at the shelter indefinitely since many adopters will fear that they are too dangerous to adopt. At worst, dogs that are deemed too aggressive to be rehabilitated may be killed. At the city shelter, killing was the standard response to animals that were deemed "unadoptable," at least until Texas Companion Rescue started pulling many of these animals from the shelter and placing them in their own adoption program. Only in extreme cases of repeatedly violent behavior would Texas Companion Rescue even consider killing an animal for behavioral reasons, but there are some dogs who have lived at the shelter for several months because their behavioral issues have scared off potential adopters.

Despite treating behavior that appears aggressive as a problem to be fixed, Texas Companion Rescue caregivers do not necessarily see such behavior as unjustified, as Pablo—the volunteer who led my orientation at Texas Companion Rescue—told me. As explained in chapter 1, Pablo is a self-taught dog trainer who likes to work with the "problem" dogs with whom other volunteers are afraid to work. He likes the challenge these dogs provide, and he loves the feeling of helping dogs get adopted. "Aggressivity is actually usually a reaction to the shelter environment," he explained. "Dogs exhibit tons of anxiety when first taken into a shelter. There's a difference between really aggressive and predictable reactive behavior." Recognizing the difference between dangerous aggression and predictable reactions to the stress of being enclosed in an unfamiliar place around unfamiliar dogs and humans is one way in which Pablo and other caregivers engaged with rescued dogs as individual subjects in the shelter environment. Pablo emphasized to me the need for shelter staff and volunteers to understand dog body language and pack behavior and the importance of trying to understand dogs on their own terms. "You don't train a dog to be semi-human. The point is to open yourself to the possibility of becoming a dog. To do this, the most important thing to learn is dog language. There is no such thing as the perfect animal for every situation; we need to recognize and understand dog behavior." Like Olivia's approach to engaging with the zebras, or Maria's efforts to understand and respond to Alphonse's sensibility, caregivers like Pablo try to see circumstances from the dog's perspective: reactive behavior is actually the appropriate response to the unfamiliar conditions of the shelter.

Unlike Olivia's approach to the zebras, this attempt to understand dog behavior is the first step in trying to alter it. By engaging in inter-patience, Olivia attempted to conform to zebra etiquette, whereas dogs are the ones expected to change their etiquette in the shelter setting. In a sense, dogs that exhibit reactive behavior must sacrifice an aspect of their dogness to become citizens of the shelter community— they must learn to respond to unfamiliar or scary circumstances in a way that conforms to human standards of appropriate dog etiquette rather than in the ways that make sense to them. In fact, dogs who excel at their obedience training even receive "Canine Good Citizen" certificates. On the other hand, dogs who do not learn to conform to human standards of dog etiquette are not able to more fully integrate into the shelter community and remain relatively isolated from dogs and other humans. This can become a self-perpetuating cycle, as continued isolation can contribute to further reactive behavior. A medium-sized, brindle-colored dog named Lamar happened to be one of these "problem" cases, exactly the kind of dog with whom Pablo liked to work.

I first met Lamar while shadowing Pablo. I later learned he was one of the only people at the shelter—including staff and volunteers— who felt comfortable taking Lamar out of his kennel. Pablo instructed me to stand back as he approached the cyclone-fencing door of the kennel where Lamar calmly sat. Lamar started to move toward the door, and Pablo stopped him with a quick "ehn" sound. Lamar sat back down, eagerly wagging his tail. Pablo fastened a lead harness around Lamar's head and guided him out of the kennel.

"Sit," he said, and Lamar sat. He then told me to approach Lamar with my hand out while pretending like I just ran into them on a walk. This was to replicate the conditions Lamar might experience while on a regular walk with his potential future adopter.

"Hi, how's it going? What a pretty dog you have. Can I pet him?" I said as I approached them.

One of Lamar's main issues was that he exhibited reactive behavior toward people and other dogs that approached him while he was on a leash, baring his teeth and growling quietly. When Lamar sniffed my hand and wagged his tail, Pablo immediately praised him and gave him a treat from a treat bag hanging off his belt. After this practice greeting, we took Lamar to a park trail with lots of dog-walker traffic and waited for other dogs to approach. As they came near, Pablo watched Lamar closely. If Lamar looked away from approaching dogs, Pablo would immediately reward him to reinforce the nonreactive behavior. If Lamar stared at the dog, though, Pablo would watch him intently and listen for any vocalization. At the slightest growl or tensing of muscles, Pablo would give a quick jerk to Lamar's leash and repeat a stern "ehn" sound. In these cases, Lamar would immediately relax and look up toward him.

Over the course of several training sessions with Pablo and Lamar, I saw that, except in rare situations with certain dogs that elicited a strong reaction from Lamar, the leash only seemed to be a safety precaution. Lamar could follow several different verbal commands and would stay, sit, or walk to a certain spot upon command from Pablo. After two sessions of working together, Lamar started responding to my verbal commands as well. Although many shelter volunteers expressed trepidation about interacting with Lamar, it was difficult for me to see why Lamar was so intimidating. Based on my observations of his training sessions with Pablo, he seemed to be incredibly intelligent, a quick learner, and very friendly to humans. Just as humans' personalities are complex and contradictory, however, none of these traits meant Lamar could not still be dangerous. After the conclusion of my fieldwork at the shelter, I heard that he bit a volunteer on the leg, seemingly unprovoked, and that the shelter was evaluating whether he was too dangerous to be adoptable. After letters of support from volunteers (including myself) and Pablo's dedicated advocacy on his behalf, Texas Companion Rescue ultimately decided that he had not yet proven himself untrainable. They decided to seek a foster home for him because they believed the shelter space was too stressful an environment for him to learn to fully overcome his reactive tendencies.

What stands out in Pablo's interactions with Lamar is his attentiveness to Lamar's subtle behavioral cues—the direction of his gaze or the tensing of his shoulder or neck muscles in a particular direction—in conjunction with a learned familiarity with the particular stimuli that provoke an aggressive reaction from Lamar. Like Maui's and Alphonse's human caregivers, Pablo does not know *why* Lamar expresses aggression in these contexts. He can guess that it means he does not want other dogs or humans to approach him in certain contexts, but why he does not want it and any more subtle nuances of that feeling are beyond Pablo's ability to interpret. That these cues point toward a more aggressive response in the immediate future, however, is enough information for Lamar's subtle bodily signs to cause recognition and a response from Pablo. Such efforts to recognize the specific intricacies of individual animal subjects help caregivers like Pablo attempt to alter behavior that in other circumstances may lead to the killing of animals.

In striving to understand, relate to, and respond to sanctuary animals as individual subjects with their own rich, nuanced personalities, feelings, emotions, interests, and desires, sanctuary caregivers participate in a praxis of empathic engagement.[24] They are endeavoring to practice what Lori Gruen describes as "entangled empathy."[25] Entangled empathy is a process through which people imagine themselves in the position of another animal and then make judgments "about how the conditions she finds herself in may contribute to her perception or state of mind and impact her interests."[26] Entangled empathy requires an awareness of the differences between the empathizer and the other animal as well as an understanding of the animal's species-typical behaviors and individual personality.[27] By employing this empathic praxis, caregivers can engage with animals like ethnographers attempting to understand other cultures.[28] As anthropologist Barbara Noske observes, good "participant observation is basically an exercise in *empathy* while at the same time one is aware of the impossibility of total knowledge and total understanding."[29] Due to that impossibility, the understandings caregivers gain through efforts to cultivate entangled empathy are always provisional; they remain open to change as caregivers continue to reassess the accuracy of their interpretations.[30]

As the story of Pablo and Lamar illustrates, efforts to understand the motivations of animal behavior also do not always lead to accommodation of the desires or feelings the animals may be conveying, like they did for Maui, the zebras, or Alphonse. Even while attempting to

A beagle who was rescued from a research lab. NEAVS.

understand dog language, Pablo felt he needed to reinforce a conventional human–dog power relation to modify Lamar's socially unacceptable reaction to other dogs and humans. To make him "adoptable," Pablo used his understanding of dog language to alter the way Lamar expressed it. He opened himself to the possibility of becoming a dog so he could help Lamar become more like how humans imagine the ideal dog should be. Because Texas Companion Rescue seeks to alter rather than accommodate animal efforts to resist human proximity, Lamar was not able to influence the conditions of his care in the same way that Maui, the zebras, or Alphonse did. However, in a more indirect way, Lamar was able to influence his care through the positive bonds he formed with me, Pablo, and a few other volunteers. Specifically, through these bonds, he indirectly influenced—to his benefit—the bureaucratic process of deliberating whether he would be allowed to live.

The main reason sanctuaries and shelters confine animals within a captive space—other than making it easier to administer the other forms of care described in this chapter—is to protect them from external dangers, including potential predators as well as humans who might be afraid of the animals or just not want them trespassing on their property. However, to minimize the impediment to animals' ability to be away from humans when they choose to, some sanctuaries weigh animal autonomy and safety concerns differently, choosing to allow animals as much freedom of movement as possible, even if it increases the potential risk from outside dangers. These sanctuaries do restrict animals' autonomy of movement to some extent, even if it is just a fence to protect animals from trespassing on the property of unfriendly neighbors,[31] but they try to avoid any unnecessary restrictions. VINE Sanctuary in Vermont, for example, is guided by this principle. Although VINE is not open to the public, I had two opportunities to tour the sanctuary and also worked as a volunteer for a day during one of them.[32]

VINE Sanctuary actually started as Eastern Shore Chicken Sanctuary in rural Maryland in 2000. Miriam Jones and pattrice jones, VINE's founders, were both experienced activists prior to starting their sanctuary, working on a wide range of social justice issues, including women's rights, LGBTQ rights, and disability rights. One day, they found a chicken who had fallen off the back of a truck. Where they lived in Maryland, they were surrounded by large-scale industrial chicken farms and slaughter facilities. The giant poultry processing company Purdue is based near there. The truck full of chickens had presumably been on its way to a slaughter facility. Trucks loaded with chickens as well as dead chickens along the side of the road were both common sights in that area. They did not have previous experience with animal rescue, but after finding the chicken, pattrice and Miriam decided to research chicken care and eventually to start Eastern Shore Chicken Sanctuary.

Their founding philosophy when they first started rescuing chickens was "birds will be birds." This meant that they would always try to make decisions based on what—to the best of their abilities—they thought birds, and specifically each individual bird, wanted for themselves, rather than what they as humans thought would be best for the birds. This meant, for example, that when birds wanted to nest in trees at night, if they showed that they could avoid predators (by jumping away from an outreached human hand), then they could stay there for the night. If they could not (and instead stayed on the original branch), they would bring them in for the night, since this meant they probably would not jump away from predators either. They have heard criticism of such practices from caregivers at other sanctuaries because they could be "exposing them to predators," but they have made the conscious decision to privilege animal autonomy over animal safety. "Sure, a predator could get them sometime, but they can generally look out for themselves, and so we give them the freedom to do so," pattrice explained.

In a chapter about sanctuary animals and captivity she contributed to an edited volume titled *The Ethics of Captivity*, Miriam discusses the qualified way in which caregivers at VINE understand autonomy as it applies to their animals. Humans at VINE use the term "as free as possible" to describe the conditions of the animals who live there, "as fences, enforced routines, involuntary medical procedures and regimes (including everything from forced sterilization to forced feeding), and other impositions certainly do not comprise a free state of being for those on the receiving end."[33] At VINE, she explains, choices regarding care in the sanctuary setting are made from the perspective that humans "live in a world that requires the rescue of members of certain species because other members of our own species will hurt and kill them if we don't" and that for many of those animals, "survival on their own is an impossible goal."[34] Thus, Miriam writes, "we do what we need to do, as ethically as possible, within the context of that reality."[35]

In 2009 they relocated from rural Maryland to a lush, wooded valley in rural Vermont. Initially, their plan was to continue just caring for chickens. But a private donor encouraged them to start caring for rescued cows as well. The donor provided the funding needed to purchase a hundred-acre parcel of land across the road from where they had relocated the chicken sanctuary. They also renamed the sanctuary VINE. Wild vines had climbed throughout the fencing and trees of the original sanctuary property in Maryland and grew throughout the new property as well. Vines serve as a poignant symbol for the sanctuary. As the sanctuary website explains, "vines both enact and represent the power of nature and the interconnectedness of all things. Vines pull down walls and snake through windows. They feed birds and serve as bridges between trees."[36] As an acronym, VINE also stands for "Veganism Is the Next Evolution." This refers to the idea, also explained on the sanctuary website, that in the "widest sense of the word, 'veganism' represents an essential next step for anybody who understands that the 'intersection of oppressions' of which social justice activists so often speak exists within and is supported by the matrix of beliefs and practices that promote and excuse the exploitation of animals and the despoliation of the environment."[37]

Now that they have expanded the mission of their sanctuary to care for cows and other animals, their guiding philosophy has also been extended to "cows will be cows," "sheep will be sheep," and even "emus will be emus," since a few rescued emus live at the sanctuary too. At Roosevelt Farm Sanctuary, and other farm sanctuaries, cows have plenty of space to roam, but they are generally limited in their movements to barns and fenced-in pastures. This is both for their own safety and the safety of humans and other animals at the sanctuary, as was the case at Roosevelt when Bob finally had to be separated from his companion Eloise. However, VINE's approach to structuring the living space of their cows and sheep is truly unique among the sanctuaries I have seen.

The hundred-acre parcel of land they purchased covers several forested hills. As you enter the property through a large gate at the bottom of a hill, a dirt road leads up from the gate to the top of the hill, where they have built a large metal-framed barn for the animals to use as shelter. The white structure is composed of metal arches with waterproof fabric stretched over them and shaped like a long half-cylinder lying on its side. The translucent fabric retains heat inside the structure when it is cold outside while also allowing some daylight to pass through the walls. The barn is open at both ends to allow animals to exit and enter whenever they want. The area around the barn and on the hill slope next to the dirt road leading up from the gate is grassy pastureland. Although they felt conflicted about cutting down any trees, they ultimately decided to clear some of the woods to make pastureland on which the cows and sheep could graze. Past the barn, though, the dirt road leads up into thick forestland, with a few more clearings that serve as additional pastureland for the animals. What's unique about this setup is that VINE allows the dozens of cattle that live there (thirty-nine at the time of my first visit) to roam freely over the hilly pasture and uncut forestland. The property itself is, of course, fenced in,[38] so the cows don't have complete freedom of movement. But on the sanctuary grounds themselves, the cows are free to wander wherever they want. This means that if cows wish to approach humans, they can. And if they wish to avoid humans, they never have to come near any (unless they need medical attention).

It is a surreal and enlightening experience to watch cows wander through the forest, scratching their sides against trees and munching on the small plants sprouting from the forest floor. I was several months into my fieldwork at Roosevelt Farm Sanctuary when a friend asked me if all farm animal sanctuaries look like farms. On the basis of my experience at Roosevelt and at the few other sanctuaries I visited, I had to say they did look like farms, at least the kinds of farms one might imagine as a child. They have big wooden barns, pastures, chicken coops, and pig wallows. And all the animals are housed in environments that look very much like how they would be drawn for a children's book about farm animals.[39] The word *rustic* comes to mind. Sanctuaries do not resemble modern, industrial farms at all, though. At most concentrated animal feeding operations (CAFOs), as contemporary factory farms are called, tens of thousands of animals are housed very close together in large, windowless buildings or packed into sprawling feedlots. VINE reminded me of this conversation because it looked like no farm I had ever seen or imagined.[40] I had never even considered that cows might want to spend large parts of their day grazing among trees rather than in an open pasture. It made me wonder what other unknown preferences domesticated animals might exhibit if given the opportunity.

During my first visit to VINE, pattrice gave our small group of visitors a short tour before we started our volunteer work cleaning up animal droppings from the barn and weeding thistles from the pasture. As we walked through the upper pasture near the tree line, we watched cows graze in the shade of tall trees. A shaggy, blond steer saw us approaching up the muddy dirt road. He turned from the large circular, metal hayrack where he'd been snacking and began to walk toward us. His name was Buddy. According to pattrice, Buddy was held in a small pen—"like solitary confinement"—where he lived before coming to the sanctuary. Buddy seemed much more interested in us than his food.

"He could have understandably come out psychotic or at least anti-social," she explained, "but instead he seems to privilege relationships above all else, even food." Buddy stretched out his large head, sniffing us and licking our hands. Like Flower the calf, Buddy reminded me of my dog. He was more calm and reserved than she is when she greets people, but no less determinedly interested in the greeting. "Buddy's a peacemaker," pattrice added. "He's attentive to all relationship dynamics around him, trying to calm other animals when they seem stressed by nuzzling them—cows as well as sheep, and even a squirrel one time." Although there are multiple possible motivations for Buddy's interest in interacting with others, what was clear was that his approach and expressed interest in us was facilitated by VINE's effort to let cows be cows. Unlike my encounter with Flower, nobody had any food to entice Buddy with, and in fact he had abandoned a pile of hay to approach us. Buddy was initiating a human encounter in that moment for his own reasons, whatever they may have been.

While VINE is certainly unique, it is not the only sanctuary that approaches animal care in this way. Writing about a similar sanctuary for pigs in the Pacific Northwest, feminist animal geographer Kathryn Gillespie explains,

> Sanctuaries are not monolithic, and some impose anthropocentric conventions of care and control more than others. Pig Peace aims to center the pigs and their experiences before education and advocacy, a priority not all sanctuaries share, and [Judy] Woods has engaged in what might be thought of as pig-led care

and knowledge production, letting the pigs instruct and lead her in formulating care practices that might allow them to flourish as individuals and as a species (this resonates with the approach that VINE Sanctuary in Vermont takes to sanctuary work and animal care).[41]

Through their approach to minimizing some of the negative effects of captivity, VINE and sanctuaries with a similar approach create spaces in which, at least in the kinds of interactions described here, animals and humans are able to engage with each other as fellow subjects and cohabitants in the sanctuary community without the power differential that shapes most human–animal relations, even if, as Miriam's comments about captivity make clear, the nonhuman animals still must contend with human controls and restrictions in other contexts.

## Improperty

One week in August 2017, my social media feeds were sprinkled with news stories shared by vegan and animal rights activists about a troubling story from the United Kingdom. One headline, from the *Guardian*, summed up the story succinctly: "Firefighters Eat Sausages Made of Piglets They Saved from Blaze."[42] The article described an incident in which a pig farmer had tried to thank some firefighters for saving two-week-old piglets from a fire that had broken out on her property by giving them sausages made from the same pigs six months later.[43] The farmer explained, "This is just what we do—we are not an animal sanctuary. We give the pigs the best opportunity and the best life they could have for six months."[44] This story jarringly highlights the contradiction between how sanctuaries treat formerly farmed animals and how the agriculture industry treats them. Even for many people who eat meat, this headline likely exposes and underlines the cognitive dissonance shaping the way many people think about animals used for food. One goal of sanctuaries, at least in their public role, is to further highlight and challenge this contradiction. Specifically, sanctuaries remove animals from animal-based consumption regimes in which they are legally, socially, and economically treated as living property, and they model for others ways of living with and relating to animals as subjects.[45] As referenced in the Introduction, anthropologist Katherine Verdery argues that property is a process of "making and unmaking certain kinds of relationships."[46]

Sanctuary care of rescued animals can thus be understood as a process of unmaking the property-based human–animal relationships in which these animals were previously entangled, moving them out of the zone of *bestia sacer*.

If there is one basic principle underlying sanctuary caregivers' ideas of proper human–animal relationships, it is that if animals are fortunate enough to make it to sanctuary, their lives there should be as free as possible from human control. Activists typically establish sanctuaries with the goal of creating spaces where "animals can live out their lives to be who they are without any obligations," in the words of a caregiver with whom I worked. Yet this ideal functions more as an aspiration than a fully attainable goal. As I showed in this chapter, the necessities of captivity—even in a sanctuary—require certain restrictions on animals' free exercise of agency. But in practice, this principle guides efforts to create lived spaces in which animals are treated as fellow subjects with at least some interests and needs equal to those of their human cohabiters, in contradistinction to the ways animals are often treated as property in more conventional contexts. The differences stand out clearly in sanctuaries focused on the care of formerly farmed animals or exotic animals like Roosevelt Farm Sanctuary or Rainbow Haven, where the daily lives of these animals are significantly different than they were prior to rescue. With rescued companion animals, such as cats and dogs, the differences are less obvious since these animals are often treated more like family than property outside the sanctuary context as well.[47]

Ultimately, though, even perfectly healthy companion animals can be legally killed by their owners, underscoring their legal status as property. Take, for example, an incident from early 2018 with parallels to the case described earlier about firefighters eating the flesh of the pigs they had previously rescued. In this case, a Vietnamese potbellied pig named Molly was slaughtered and eaten by the people who had adopted her from an SPCA in British Columbia. While shocking to many, the adopters' actions were not prohibited by the law. As one article explained,

> Although Molly's owner was vetted by the SPCA—and signed a contract specifically stating that the pet couldn't be killed or consumed—[SPCA caregiver Leon] Davis said it's not a criminal offence to breach that contract. Animal cruelty laws only apply when an animal suffers, he said, and investigators found

that Molly was killed humanely. . . . He's disappointed the law allows any owner to kill their pet—be it dog, fish or pig—at their discretion.[48]

Another case from 2014 involved a dog, Excalibur, in Spain. His owner, Teresa Romero Ramos, was a Spanish nurse who contracted Ebola after treating infected patients from Sierra Leone. While her husband and several health workers who came into contact with her were placed in quarantine, Excalibur was euthanized, even though there was no indication he had contracted the virus. Thousands of protesters took to the streets in Spain, and more than 390,000 people signed an international petition to spare his life, whereas, the *New York Times* noted, at that same time, about 150,000 people had signed a petition urging the Food and Drug Administration to fast-track research on a potential vaccine and treatment for Ebola.[49] As Lori Gruen argues in an op-ed in *Time* magazine, "Spanish authorities weren't thinking of Excalibur's life as valuable or of how devastating his death would be to his family [because] . . . animal lives are thought to be worth less than those of humans. If authorities can come and kill your family members because it is expedient, then we may be heading down a path that is more frightening than the virus itself."[50] This idea, that other animals are not just like family members but can literally be family members, is shared by many of the caregivers and activists I encountered throughout my research.

Ideas about the proper and improper way to treat animals are not, however, homogeneous across animal activist communities, and that is especially the case in the arena of cat and dog rescue, as evidenced by the No Kill–open admission schism in the companion animal shelter community. People for the Ethical Treatment of Animals (PETA), for example, sees euthanasia as the compassionate response—similar to what one might provide for a terminally ill human family member—to the suffering of animals that have been discarded as unwanted property. Although they are probably the most visible face of animal activism—challenging the propriety of the treatment of animals for food, clothing, laboratory testing, and entertainment—their tactics are often viewed as improper by activists and nonactivists alike. When it comes to euthanasia, though, PETA's rationale rests on the same rejection of the commodification of animal bodies that underlies the No Kill position. However, as Dinesh Wadiwel argues, where peaceable coexistence between humans and animals creates possibilities for friendship, such as with companion animals, this bond is placed in question by the modes of discipline, surveillance, containment and control that attend and are inherent to the practice of "pet ownership" and "domestication." The millions of pets "euthanized" in animal shelters annually highlight that even examples of seemingly happy cohabitation between humans and animals are framed within an "adopt, foster, euthanize" context of over-arching, and deadly violence. If we take this frame into account . . . then it becomes difficult to imagine what friendship might look like within this context.[51]

Indeed, the actualized killability, rather than the mere potential killability, of companion animals underscores their social status as disposable property. Starting from a similar position as PETA that animals should be treated as family rather than property, sanctuary activists reach the opposite conclusion precisely because the sanctuary is a space for fostering the kind of "improper" relationships that challenge an animal-property system.

Of course, the animal-property system is deeply entrenched in U.S. society. Even wild animals can easily be drawn into a property-based relationship with humans. Seeming to draw on a Lockean labor theory of property, courts in the United States have found that "wild animals reduced from the wild state in compliance with applicable law become property of an individual."[52] And wild animals that remain wild can still be categorized as property, as, for example, in the case of New York State, where "wild animals are state property even when they reside on one's private property."[53] There are some limits to property rights in animals, though. Legal theorist David Favre points out that as "living property," animals do in fact possess limited basic rights under anticruelty statutes, specifically the right to be free from pain and the right to have their basic sustenance needs met.[54] Nonetheless, as legal theorist Maneesha Deckha observes, law is an anthropocentric institution: "Statutes that purport to protect animals are limited in their effect since they are founded on and interpreted through anthropocentric assumptions about animal inferiority and reside in an overall legal framework that subordinates animals through their property classification."[55] Seeing animal oppression as fundamentally grounded in their social and legal status as property, legal scholar

Gary Francione explicitly calls for the abolition of animals' property status and the instantiation of animal rights in the law.[56]

Animals' legal classification is only one factor shaping their social and cultural status as property, though. As Kathryn Gillespie argues, "an animal does not have to be property in order to be the subject of violence and bodily appropriation, nor does a body have to be property in order to be commodified."[57] Although the "status of animals as property arguably makes it easier to objectify and commodify the cow and many other species for everyday use by humans and capital accumulation,"[58] the political–economic system in which humans relate to animals as commodities reinforces their *cultural and social* status as property as much as the legal system that reinforces it through property laws. In this political–economic context, humans relate to animals of all kinds—from farmed animals to wild animals—not just as living property but as "lively commodities,"[59] whose value emerges as a result of their status as living beings.[60] Ways in which animals can function as value generators may be readily apparent in the agricultural industry, entertainment industry, and pet industry, but as Maan Barua observes in her analysis of Indian lions and elephants as encounter-value-generating lively commodities in the tourist industry, virtually all animals can be subject to commodification, if they are not already entangled in circuits of lively commodities.[61] Caregivers in sanctuaries are thus rejecting not only a legal classification but also the mutually constitutive political–economic commodification of animals that, together with that legal classification, helps to shape the social and cultural status of animals as fungible, disposable, exploitable, killable living objects, or, in short, *bestia sacer*.

If they are rejecting the category of animal property and the conventional property-based relations between humans and animals that shape it, what, then, do the "improper" relationships of sanctuaries look like? Relating to dogs and cats as subjects, or even friends or family, is fairly easy for many of us to imagine, so to better illustrate how caregivers oppose conventional norms of relating to animals as living property, I will focus on the example of farmed birds.

Legislation like the Humane Methods of Slaughter Act ostensibly places small limits on property rights in livestock by requiring that livestock be rendered insensible prior to being slaughtered. But as Gillespie explains in her discussion of animal cruelty laws in general, even when a particular species is legally protected, animal cruelty cases require proof of intent for cruelty to the animal and this must be proven beyond a reasonable doubt, which rarely happens. . . . Indeed, those legal protections that do exist for nonhuman animals remain notoriously lax and insufficiently enforced. . . . In the context of agriculture, unsatisfactory welfare legislation also occurs because of legal exemptions at the state level called "common or customary farming exemptions" (CFEs). These allow animal farming enterprises to engage in practices that would otherwise be considered cruel (e.g. tail-docking, beak-trimming, and castration without anesthesia, etc.) because they are customary in the industry.[62]

Wadiwel notes that these kinds of limitations on animal cruelty based on the idea "that animals are not to *unnecessarily* suffer, also contains within it an implicit exception, that non human animal suffering deemed necessary is acceptable by law."[63] This means that restrictions like the Humane Methods of Slaughter Act and other anticruelty laws essentially reinforce animals' status as *bestia sacer* by further legitimizing the violence and deprivations to which they *can* be subjected. But even if being rendered insensible prior to being slaughtered provided some minimal relief of suffering to animals, not even this affordance is available to chickens, because the USDA has explicitly exempted poultry from even this minimum protection. This likely both contributes to and results from the fact that more farmed birds are raised and killed for food now than all other land animals put together. More than 7 billion chickens are slaughtered per year in the United States, and another 452 million are housed in factory farms for egg production. This intensity of production has also resulted in more farmed birds being rescued and cared for in sanctuaries than any other type of farmed animal. Farmed birds thus serve as a model case in the animal-property system, because their owners are legally free to treat them or dispose of them in whatever manner they choose. For this reason, birds living under the control of industrial agriculture are utterly subsumed within the category of *bestia sacer*.

In stark contrast to the commodification of farmed birds' bodies, however, activists like June, a volunteer I met at Roosevelt Farm Sanctuary, bring these birds into their homes and beds to live together as companions. June is in her fifties, a working-class, single woman with a job at a small commercial food company making vegan products. She makes enough money to get by, but she cannot afford health insurance, even after the Affordable Care Act was implemented. She lives near the sanctuary and spends much of her free time volunteering there or taking care of her own chickens. June *loves* chickens, deeply and wholeheartedly. She has four rescued chickens of her own. All former laying hens, they live with her inside her house and sleep with her in her bed. She calls them her girls, a beaming smile spreading across her face and pride radiating from her eyes every time she mentions them. At Christmastime, she took them to have their picture taken sitting on Santa's lap. She spreads sheets on the couch—chickens cannot really be house-trained—and watches TV with them while they perch in her lap or on her shoulders, nestling against her like cats.

At many farm sanctuaries, Thanksgiving, in particular, has become a focus for challenging the "proper" treatment of farmed birds through the inversion of the central role played by the bodies of turkeys on this holiday. Roosevelt, for example, hosts a turkey-centered festival every November. Intended as fund-raising and educational events, visitors participate in vegan Thanksgiving-style feasts and are then invited to help serve the turkeys at the sanctuary their own feasts of raw pumpkin pie, cranberries, and other fruits and vegetables.

Perhaps the most improper activist tactic of all is the act of simply taking animals from those with proper legal property claims, flouting the law to give animals the lives activists think they deserve. When they occur, such actions might entail raiding farmed animal facilities at night and taking as many animals as the activists can carry. What the owners would describe as theft of their living property these activists describe as liberation of living subjects. Taking animals in this way is a radical refusal of property-based human–animal relationships that challenges the ideological basis of such relationships by forcefully enacting their opposite: relationships based on a recognition of animals as subjects who cannot be owned by another being regardless of what the laws say.

Reminiscent of Engels's assertion that theft is "the most primitive form of protest,"[64] these activists practice a form of what anthropologist Eric Hobsbawm theorized as social banditry, a type of peasant protest and rebellion.[65] Unlike Robin Hood–style social bandits, however, these bandits are stealing property, not to give it away to those who lack wealth, but to give the property over to itself, to liberate it from its property-ness. In a sense, they give animals property rights in themselves. Although bandits and caregivers cannot extend legal rights to animals or force the courts to recognize animals as legal persons,[66] by treating them as subjects entitled to rights, they essentially imbue the animals with de facto rights, at least in the context of their relationships with them. But there is a paradoxical irony in this act, because, while saved from being a particular form of property—a source of food, for example—the animals do not fully shed the property status that made their theft possible in the first place. As Hobsbawm observes, "the crucial fact about the bandit's position is its ambiguity. . . . The more successful he is as a bandit, the more he is both a representative and champion of the poor and a part of the system of the rich."[67] Similarly, the more successful these bandits are at liberating animals, the more those animals are reintegrated into a system of property. This is because the lives of animals in sanctuaries are made possible by the fact that legally, they remain property, only now they are property of the sanctuary. Despite the forging of relationships based on the caregivers' recognition of their other-than-human subjectivity, legally speaking, animals remain property without the rights of legal

A gravely sick piglet is carried to rescue. Animal Liberation Victoria.

persons. Even in the case of compassionate euthanasia, the animals are so easily killable precisely because they are not legal persons. As of this writing, assisted suicide for humans is legal in only eight states and the District of Columbia (and it is authorized by a state supreme court ruling in Montana), but animals can be euthanized anywhere in the United States.

This ouroboros-shaped pattern of depropertization through propertization is similar to what we see in the model of the Creative Commons license, in which people can surrender their copyright interests in intellectual property by granting certain usages of that property. But the reason why the Creative Commons licenses that grant certain uses retain legal weight is that they are supported by the underlying copyright that the holder could reassert whenever a work is not used in accordance with the license. They subvert the system of copyright but are also only possible within it.

In the space of the sanctuary and in their homes and private relationships with animals, caregivers can model improper ways of relating to animals as subjects rather than property, but as long as rescued animals' social and political lives can only exist within the sanctuary—as long as sanctuaries are some of the only zones of exception from a world of bare life[68]—then those lives will generate ethically problematic questions, such as what it means to be free when your whole world is enclosed by a fence. And despite caregiver aspirations, sanctuary animals are also not totally free from harm or control within those fences. As I have shown in this chapter and will explore further in chapter 4, practices of care are necessarily entangled with forms of violence or harm. While spaying and neutering, for example, serve sanctuaries' larger rescue mission by ensuring as much space as possible for more rescues, they also inflict violence on the bodies of animals. In working through the contradictions and dilemmas created by the social and material conditions sanctuaries face, caregivers are creating emergent forms of animal ethics that are adapted to the realities of trying to live differently with animals. But the internal contradictions of captive freedom reveal that these animals are neither fully autonomous subjects nor property. They are instead improperty, living beings within a shifting spectrum between property and subjecthood, possessing limited rights within the sanctuary context even though they are not legal persons.

In her research on a wildlife rehabilitation center in Guatemala, geographer Rosemary-Claire Collard discovered a parallel but significantly different process of unmaking and making human–animal relationships.[69] This facility takes in wild-caught animals rescued from the exotic pet trade so they can be dehabituated to humans and released back to the wild. Collard argues that this work of rehabilitation entails taking apart animals' lives as commodities and putting back together their lives as wild animals.[70] While the sanctuaries I visited also seek to unmake the lives of animals as property, they cannot replace those lives with new ones free from human interference. As long as the larger political–economic and legal contexts that make it impossible for animals to be full rights-bearing subjects outside of sanctuaries remain intact, humans will always be a part of their lives. So instead of trying to sever animals entirely from their dependency on humans, like Collard's rehabilitation center, they endeavor to unmake property-based relationships with animals by forging alternative relationships with them. However, the same political–economic and sociolegal factors that would render animals *bestia sacer* outside sanctuaries also place constraints on these alternative relationships within sanctuaries. In other words, property-based relationships transform into improperty-based relationships as sanctuary workers try to enact their visions for human–animal sociality while navigating the dilemmas and contradictions of sanctuary work. Understanding this transformation reveals some of the limitations that confront sanctuaries in their efforts to move society closer to realizing sanctuary visions for human–animal relations.

Through the different dimensions of care described here, sanctuary caregivers strive to forge relationships with animals as fellow subjects, unmaking the property-based relations in which many rescued animals were previously entangled. As a result, some animals can at least partially invert conventional species power hierarchy and assert some influence over the conditions of their own care, but they also must face limitations on their freedom. Many of the limitations related to the dimensions of care described here require animals to lose freedom of movement and association in exchange for the benefits of care they receive. To put it bluntly, at this historical moment, animals must accept confinement in the bigger cages of sanctuaries to partake in the benefits of life, health, and potentially even happiness that sanctuary care can afford.

Rescued chickens roosting together in a coop. We Animals.

## Chapter 3
# Creating and Operating Sanctuaries

### The "Don't Start a Sanctuary" Conference

Every fall, Farm Sanctuary hosts the Farm Animal Care Conference at its 175-acre facility in upstate New York. As described in chapter 1, Farm Sanctuary was established in 1986 as the first sanctuary for formerly farmed animals, creating a model and inspiration for the hundreds of other farm sanctuaries that have followed. Its New York facility is located on wooded, rolling hills in the Finger Lakes region. Red, barnlike buildings and fenced pastures with grazing cows evoke the bucolic family farms of the early twentieth century, farms that have since been almost entirely replaced by large, industrialized agricultural operations in the United States. After a half-hour drive from the closest rental accommodations I could find, I arrived around 8:30 in the morning, just as the conference was about to start. A few dozen attendees were already gathered in a small room in the administrative building, waiting for the first presentation to begin. The audience consisted of a mix of caregivers from sanctuaries that were already in operation who had come for further training, people who rescued and housed a few animals and were now hoping to transition to actual sanctuaries, and aspiring sanctuary founders who wanted to learn more about what sanctuary life entailed before trying to build their own. Most of the attendees were from the United States and Canada, but at least one contingent of caregivers was from as far away as a sanctuary in Australia.

The Care Conference was created to provide aspiring sanctuary operators with all the information necessary to start and maintain a successful sanctuary. When I attended, it cost $175 per person and spanned two days, consisting of nine hours of panels each day covering every conceivable issue sanctuary operators would need to consider. The topics included sanctuary fund-raising, sanctuary administration, animal care operations and programs, visitor and volunteer programs, shelter, farm equipment and barn cleaning, and individual sessions specifically addressing the care needs of chickens, pigs, turkeys, rabbits, cattle, sheep and goats, and ducks and geese. All the attendees received a binder with printed copies of the presentations and other resources covering everything from legal requirements to insurance and media relations. Each day also included a vegan breakfast and lunch. The presentations related to fund-raising, administrative organization, and educational programs took place in the meeting room where the conference started. The various sanctuary employees who oversaw these elements of Farm Sanctuary's operations led the presentations related to their areas of expertise.

The animal care sessions took place in the second half of each day during walking tours of the sanctuary as we visited the living areas for each species being discussed. Susie Coston, Farm Sanctuary's national shelter director at that time, led all these sessions. Referred to as the "farm animal whisperer" by many involved in sanctuary work, Susie had been working at Farm Sanctuary for fifteen years and oversaw all of the New York facility's animal care staff. Susie has never taken any courses in animal care. Long before coming to Farm Sanctuary, she earned a degree in fashion and was planning to go into advertising, but she quickly realized she hated it. After her brief foray in fashion, she followed in the footsteps of her teacher parents and earned a special education master's degree to work with disabled children. This job was also not a great fit, so she started working with animals during her summer breaks. Finally, she had found a job she loved. She gained six years of animal care experience from working for a veterinarian and another sanctuary in West Virginia before starting at Farm Sanctuary. As she explained to the attendees, at that point, she had been working with animals for more than twenty years and could not be happier.

Susie is as well known in sanctuary circles for her generosity of time as she is for her expertise in the unique intricacies of farm animal care. Virtually every caregiver I encountered through my field-work at Roosevelt and visits to other farm animal sanctuaries not only knew who Susie was but had called her at some point for advice or guidance in treating various animal health issues. Her encyclopedic knowledge of the unique needs and health issues of every species—and virtually every individual animal—made each hour-long session feel like an entire semester of vet school on whichever animal she was discussing.

Susie and the other presenters shared invaluable information for anybody who wanted to run a successful sanctuary, and its accuracy and effectiveness had been tested in the crucible of Farm Sanctuary's three decades of pioneering work in farm animal rescue and care. But by the afternoon of the second day, as we walked through the sanctuary and listened to Susie explain all the requirements for maintaining the health of cows, goats, and sheep, I occasionally heard some conference attendees from other sanctuaries scoff under their breath at pieces of information—like the best materials and structure for cattle fencing or best practices for preventing parasites—that they seemed to think were unrealistically expensive or too difficult to carry out with their limited staff. Any tiny sprouts of interest in someday opening my own sanctuary were withering under the overwhelming amount of information packed into the conference's two days. As I heard the quiet bits of critical response from these attendees, though, I realized there might be a good reason for this. I remembered something a friend who used to work at Farm Sanctuary years ago told me: some of the sanctuary workers jokingly referred to this event as the "Don't Start a Sanctuary" conference.

Perhaps a more accurate title than the "Don't Start a Sanctuary" conference would be the "Know What You're Getting Into" conference. As intimidating as the conference's presentation of the many difficulties of running a sanctuary was for some attendees, the overarching message was not one of discouragement so much as it emphasized the serious responsibilities running a sanctuary entails. Susie set the tone at the beginning of the first day. "Last year in the United States fifteen sanctuaries closed," she told the audience. "Thousands of animals were left homeless. This is not a glamorous job. It's dirty, dangerous, hard work. You *have* to gain experience before starting a sanctuary. This conference serves as a reality check—just the tip of the iceberg this weekend. It's *so* much work, it's life consuming. I would not start a sanctuary. Seriously, that's why I let somebody else do it and just walked in."

One attendee raised her hand. "I just started a sanctuary, and I'm now having second thoughts."

"You'll have so many more," Susie replied. Later, while stressing the importance of adequate staffing, she added, "Everyone goes in with a big heart, but it can become overwhelming so fast, and you'll close. You always have to do everything the same every day for the animals, no matter what. So if you're short staffed, you'll be beyond exhaustion, running on nervous energy."

Many aspects of sanctuary operations and maintenance shape the possibilities and limits of caring for rescued animals in captivity. From funding to administration, land needs and infrastructure, personnel management, and overall mission formulation, as well as the unique considerations and preparation that go into founding new sanctuaries, sanctuary workers must continuously balance a multitude of concerns. While different kinds of sanctuaries focus their efforts on different social categories of animals—such as companion animals, exotic animals, and food animals—they are united by the common goals of animal rescue and care. Owing to the practical necessities of meeting these shared goals, sanctuaries also share a common range of organizational and economic challenges.

In this chapter, I examine these challenges through the framework of the Care Conference to illustrate the range of different responses to these challenges across different sanctuaries and how these responses configure animal subjects. All animal sanctuaries are structured around particular ideas of the animal as a subject of care that both shape the resource management, governance, and policies of the sanctuary and are shaped by the larger political–economic context in which they are situated. I will therefore examine how political–economic constraints can conflict with sanctuary goals and how caregivers try to navigate these conflicts, especially the contradictions that arise from enlisting animals in the fund-raising process while simultaneously trying to shelter them from circuits of animal commodification. Finally, I describe how the political–economic challenges to sanctuary operation often also require sacrifices of caregivers for the benefit of the sanctuary community.

## Funding

The Care Conference is part of the larger political–economic network that links myriad types of animal rescue operations throughout the United States, and the major issues it addresses also reflect significant features of that political economy with which every sanctuary must contend. It is not surprising, then, that the first session of the conference focused on the single most important element of sanctuary operation outside of actual animal care: fund-raising. Samantha Pachirat, Farm Sanctuary's national director of education and strategic initiatives, led the session via a Skype video call projected on a screen at the front of the meeting room. Originally from St. Louis, where she worked at the St. Louis Zoo for two years, Samantha started working at Farm Sanctuary in 2000 after witnessing the terrible living conditions of cows at an allegedly "humane" dairy farm. Her previous experience at Farm Sanctuary includes stints in both the Education Department and the Development Department, on which she drew for her presentation that day.

"Fund-raising is a thing that people tend to shy away from, but it's a crucial foundation to a sanctuary," she told the audience. "You need to find start-up capital, build a membership base, manage donor relations, run successful fund-raising events, fund capital projects, secure grant funding, and solicit in-kind donations." Initial start-up funding for sanctuaries often comes from the personal savings of a founder, or potentially a benefactor. This was the case for Rainbow Haven, the exotic sanctuary introduced in chapter 1. Olivia and her husband, Sam, built their sanctuary slowly, drawing on their private savings to build the physical infrastructure that housed their first animals. Rita and Ted, the founders of Roosevelt Farm Sanctuary, also drew on their own savings to buy the land for their sanctuary and start building their care facilities. Unlike these two organizations, however, Texas Companion Rescue grew out of a local social movement rather than the vision of a few individual founders. Texas Companion Rescue coalesced from the local No Kill movement and, as a result, drew its initial funding from an already established funding network of donors and supporters. By the time it leased its first facility for housing rescued cats and dogs, this initial network of financial support was already in place. Rainbow Haven and Roosevelt are more typical examples of sanctuary origin stories. Like Farm Sanctuary as well, sanctuaries often start with an individual or couple with a strong personal ambition to start rescuing animals. This means that they often start by drawing from their own personal financial resources. Since owning multiple pieces of property is not feasible for most people, this also means that they often build the sanctuary on their own private property, where they also live.

This start-up model was the plan many of the aspiring sanctuary operators to whom I spoke had in mind when they came to the conference, but it was not the one advocated by Farm Sanctuary. Echoing the conference's emphasis on robust preparedness, the guide in the binder provided to attendees cautioned, "For sanctuaries, the saying 'if you build it, they will come' refers to animals, not funding. It takes enormous amounts of time and expertise to raise the resources necessary for the operation of a sanctuary."[1] One important component of successful fund-raising is a donor database. "Before you have a barn or an animal, you need a database in place," Samantha explained. "A database is essential to fund-raising."

There are many tactics for building donor databases. Sanctuaries send representatives to table at events related to animal advocacy or veganism and vegetarianism, where they gather people's contact information on sign-up sheets. They also collect contact information from sanctuary volunteers and visitors who come for tours or "open house" events hosted at the sanctuaries. While it's an invaluable component in fund-raising, database management can also be expensive. Some organizations use basic software like Microsoft Access to manage their databases, but there are also specific—more expensive—database programs designed for fund-raising that enable organizations to track donor retention and engagement levels and provide tools and guidance in designing and measuring the effectiveness of funding solicitation materials. Samantha recommended a program called Boomerang, which ranges in price from $99 to $499 per month, depending on the number of records in the database. She also suggested that sanctuaries have a dedicated employee-managing database in addition to the requisite software. "It's easy to prioritize animal needs over a database, but ultimately that database is part of animal needs too," Samantha explained.

This statement about animal needs reiterated another component of the conference's preparedness message: the idea that a desire to help animals—and even actually tending to the physical needs of animals—is not enough to run a sanctuary. Every aspect of running a functional nonprofit animal care organization becomes an "animal need." However, because these organizations are suspended in a larger political economy in which the needs of nonprofits are commoditized by for-profit corporations, "animal needs" can in turn become commoditized, even when the goal of sanctuaries is to remove animals from economies in which they already function as commodities. Though they may be able to remove the animals in their care from certain forms of economic exploitation, the need for funding and the resources it buys—such as agricultural animal feed and veterinary pharmaceuticals—ties sanctuaries and their animals to multiple circulations of capital within the larger economy, which still relies on animal commodities as a significant source of profit.

A database is useful only if it is used in conjunction with fundraising efforts like direct mail solicitations. Depending on its size, individual donations will make up most to all of an organization's annual budget. This is why Samantha emphasized the importance of a robust donor database. For most nonprofit organizations, direct mail is still one of the best ways to build and maintain a donor base, although many are seeing increasing success with social media. There are two categories of direct mail solicitations: acquisitions, which are directed at potential new people, and in-house appeals, which are directed at people who have already made previous donations. Acquisition is important to compensate for the natural attrition rate that occurs in any donor base. The goal is to be constantly maintaining—or, even better, always growing—the number of active donors.

Conducting acquisition mailings is another way in which sanctuaries interface with the larger nonprofit political economy. Nonprofit organizations, including animal rights and animal welfare organizations like PETA and the Humane Society of the United States, rent and trade their donor lists to list-brokering companies, such as the California-based Names in the News. Organizations provide a sample of their mailing materials and a list of at least five thousand donors if they want to trade, and the broker matches them with other organizations that may be willing to rent or trade their lists. For example, if an organization was not interested in a trade, then it may instead decide to rent its list for a fee, along with specific contractual terms for onetime use in a mailing. It might also reserve the right to approve letters or whole mail packages. Because the return rate is very low—often between 1 and 3 percent—organizations frequently send out acquisition mailings to hundreds of thousands of people at once. Acquisition mailings can lose money at first, especially with the cost of list rentals, but ultimately, they can recoup costs as new donors stay on and continue to donate.

List trading and renting are the reasons why donating to a particular cause often leads to a deluge of solicitations from organizations focused on similar or related causes. Years ago, I donated thirty dollars to Farm Sanctuary to sponsor a turkey. I was surprised to suddenly start receiving solicitations from a range of animal rescue–oriented organizations from which I had not previously received mail. Since I couldn't afford to donate very much on the meager income of a graduate student, it seemed to me to be a bad idea to share my information with other organizations that might channel my limited donation budget elsewhere. Careful evaluation of list performance, however, enables organizations to strategically employ list rental and trade to achieve a net increase in acquisitions. Evaluating list performance requires using a number of different organizations' lists and tracking the results of *every* fund-raising effort to see which lists perform best. Lists that perform well for Farm Sanctuary include lists from organizations with vegan education and anti–factory farming advocacy missions. By focusing particular donor appeals on legal advocacy work in which they've engaged, they have also found some success using the list from the Animal Legal Defense Fund, a nonprofit legal advocacy organization focused on animal protection causes. Lists from other kinds of sanctuaries, such as horse sanctuaries, work best, though. They have found that their mission is most relatable to people who already support sanctuaries so that their appeal crosses species better than it does other animal issues.

In-house mailings, targeted at proven donors, reliably bring in much more funding than acquisition mailings. The guide in the conference binder suggests sending out three or four in-house mailings each year and focusing each one on a different project or campaign donors can contribute to. Examples include requests for donations to support the building or renovation of new animal facilities or to fund expensive veterinary care for an injured animal. In-house mailings are also tested for effectiveness in message and design. To test a particular mailing package, an organization uses a control package and a test package to see which one works better. The test package may include a more graphic image of an injured animal, for example. If the test package elicits more responses, then its features can be incorporated into future mailings. These tests require extra expenditures at first but can more than compensate for the initial costs when they lead to more effective mailings.

Premiums, which are small gifts, such as address labels or stickers, are sometimes included in these mailings to catch people's attention and encourage donations. Farm Sanctuary has found through its testing that including premiums actually depresses responses, although they apparently work for other organizations, such as the Humane Society of the United States, because they continue to include premiums in their mailings. The exception to this for Farm Sanctuary is giving adoption certificates to people who sponsor animals through their adopt-an-animal program. On the basis of my own experience sponsoring a turkey, adoption certificate premiums may work as an incentive because they are appealing to people who want to sponsor animals in other people's names. I sponsored a turkey as a birthday present for an animal-loving family member, and the certificate provided the ideal medium to share the news. In general, though, Farm Sanctuary has found that when a premium appeared to serve as motivation for a donation, it was less likely to keep that donor than donors it got through a commitment to the organization's mission.

Another tool used in mailings is the gift string—a formula for requesting donations from previous donors based on the amount they last gave. There are different formulas for designing gift string requests, but Farm Sanctuary has found the best formula to be 1.5 times the previous donation. So, if a donor gave $50 last time, then the mailing would suggest a few options starting with $75 and going up incrementally from there. This tool does not work well for many organizations, but for Farm Sanctuary, it has been very effective. The fact that it has discovered a successful formula underscores the value of a database and good database software. Only through keeping track of previous donations from every donor and testing the results of various requests was it able to find such a productive formula.

Every detail of the mailing package can impact donor response, even postage. For Farm Sanctuary, donors who give $100 or more respond better when they get first class postage, and those who donate less than $100 respond better to bulk mail postage. The number of inserts in a particular mailing can also impact responses. Farm

Sanctuary's testing has shown that less is more. Too many inserts can depress responses because too much information can be overwhelming. Sticking to one goal per mailing is thus also more effective than trying to save on postage by sending multiple pieces of information in one mailing, such as a request for a donation along with an event invitation.

Perhaps the most important component of any effective mailing is the writing style. The text in a mailing is crafted to catch and keep a reader's attention long enough to get her to read through to the "ask"—whatever the mailing is requesting to be given. For this reason, mailings often employ bold font, underlining, bullet points, and large pull quotes. The language itself is often punchy and dramatic. People are unlikely to read the whole thing, so creating a sense of urgency helps to retain attention longer.

The ask itself is most effective if it can grab people with a specific request that also relates more broadly to what it means to support the organization. Specific cruelty cases often work best for sanctuaries in this regard. For example, talking about the general conditions to which dairy cows are subjected in large factory farms may be too abstract for many donors, but referring to a specific cruelty case of a cow that was rescued from a dairy farm with graphic details about her mistreatment can elicit more responses. While the larger institutional conditions that negatively impact animals may seem too big to change with a donation, personalizing these conditions with the biographical details of individual animals makes these subjects of rescue more relatable to donors, and thus more helpable as well. Images of the animals and the effects of their mistreatment can also elicit sympathy and further strengthen an animal's relatability, but they lose their effectiveness if they are too graphic. They work best when they are just graphic enough to convey a sense of cruelty without causing the potential donor to be overwhelmed and turn away. For Farm Sanctuary, urgency in the timing of the ask—like requesting funding for an animal that was just rescued with severe injuries that need immediate veterinary treatment—creates the biggest bumps in responses, though precisely because they are urgent, they are often difficult to time with a direct mailing, which takes time to prepare. These sorts of urgent asks therefore usually work better in online appeals.

This strategy of employing descriptions of animal suffering to solicit funding for animal care highlights a significant tension in sanctuary work, a tension that arose repeatedly throughout the conference. While their personal stories can help to make animals more relatable as individual subjects worthy of rescue and care, monetizing their experiences through fund-raising appeals also simultaneously reinscribes them as mechanisms for producing value.[2] Interpolating donors into the experience of rescue itself aggravates this tension further. Acknowledging that thinking about fund-raising opportunities in the middle of a rescue could be difficult, Samantha nonetheless stressed to the conference attendees that when you can involve donors in a rescue even before it occurs, "it's a rare moment to seize if you can." Farm Sanctuary has seen "extremely good results from people who really support rescue." Practically, sharing animals' stories of mistreatment and rescue is an essential fund-raising tool for sanctuaries. However, at the same time as it enables sanctuaries to care for these individual subjects of rescue, it refigures them as objects of value, though notably a different kind of value than they may have generated in their previous lives as lively commodities[3] or animal property. The problem this poses is that it potentially conflicts with or undermines the sanctuary mission of "transforming cultural perspectives that see animals as a valid source of economic value in any context."[4]

The process of fund-raising impacts the subjectivity of donors as well as animals. It sells donors the opportunity to become animal rescuers, at least by proxy, if not directly. This does not mean donors' support is motivated by selfishness or self-interest. Most sanctuary supporters I've met through my research care deeply about the well-being of the rescued animals they've encountered and sincerely support the missions of the sanctuaries they fund. At the same time, though, their financial support for the sanctuaries enables them to inhabit the subject position of animal benefactors, and the value of this experience to donors is something sanctuaries actively recognize. Effective donor relations are therefore crucial to sanctuaries. Many have an employee specifically dedicated to donor stewardship. Expressing appreciation for support is an essential component of that stewardship. Farm Sanctuary sends thank-you letters within a few days to anyone who donates more than five dollars. Thank-you calls or permanent on-site recognition—even if just a laminated sign—can also be useful tools in solidifying donor relationships, especially with bigger donors. Major donors also appreciate being able to visit sanctuaries for special tours with more exclusive, behind-the-scenes access to animals and other facets of the sanctuary. Staying in touch in general is important to many donors, which is why many sanctuaries also send out newsletters or e-newsletters with personal updates and photos of animals. It tells them, "You're a part of the sanctuary," Samantha explained. Donor databases also play an important role in donor relations, as they allow sanctuaries to keep notes about personal interactions with donors as well as their donations. The ultimate goal of these donor relations tactics is to deepen the sanctuary's relationship with donors. As Samantha told the conference attendees, "It's less expensive to retain donors than acquire them." Enabling them to see themselves and feel appreciated as coparticipants in sanctuaries' rescue missions—to make them a part of the sanctuary—is one of the most effective ways to ensure retention.

One of the guiding principles of fund-raising is to "give everyone a chance to give," as Samantha advised the conference attendees. Online fund-raising is thus becoming an increasingly vital part of an effective fund-raising strategy. As mentioned, e-appeals are useful in urgent situations when it would take too long to use direct mail. Farm Sanctuary's testing has shown that these are most effective when they are very succinct, because people are willing to give even less attention to email than to paper mail. Websites, of course, also provide an easy way to donate. All of my field sites have prominent donation buttons on the home pages of their websites to make donating as easy as possible for anyone who visits the sites. In fact, Roosevelt and Texas Companion Rescue have donate buttons on both the top and bottom of their pages.

Offering an annual membership to donors is another common way to make them feel like they belong to the sanctuary community, while also offering benefits that function as premiums. Because sanctuaries' annual expenses remain the same—or even increase—annual memberships also provide a means of building a permanent funding base to meet ongoing needs and lock in a long-term commitment from donors. Prices for memberships vary across organizations. PETA, for example, uses eighteen dollars because it has found through testing that that is a particularly effective price. Roosevelt's memberships are thirty dollars for an individual and fifty dollars for a family. According to their website, benefits of membership include free admission to the sanctuary during visiting hours; discounts at sanctuary events and on branded merchandise in their online store; discounts at several vegan and vegetarian restaurants, a vegan tattoo parlor, and a vegan clothing and shoe store; and a "warm feeling knowing that you are helping out the most abused animals in the world—farm animals."

Finally, fund-raising events provide opportunities to make donors feel like part of the sanctuary by bringing them into direct contact with animals, caregivers, and other sanctuary staff and volunteers. Farm Sanctuary, for example, holds an annual gala where it honors celebrity guests for their commitment to farm animals. The 2015 guests of honor were the musician Morrissey—a vocal vegan and animal rights advocate—and Tracey Stewart and her husband, Jon (former host of *The Daily Show*), who later established their own Farm Sanctuary–affiliated sanctuary in New Jersey. General admission tickets for the gala were $500 per person or $5,000 for a table. Having a table option allows existing donors to introduce family and friends to the organization's mission. The relatively expensive cost means many donors cannot afford to attend, but these events still sell out. These high-priced kinds of events create a space for wealthier donors to experience philanthropic sociality, participating in the sanctuary's rescue mission while mingling with other wealthy donors and celebrities.

As explained in chapter 2, many farm sanctuaries hold an annual fund-raising event timed to coincide with Thanksgiving. Donors purchase tickets to the event—$150 dollars at Roosevelt—where they are served a catered, multicourse, vegan, Thanksgiving-style meal. There is also a silent auction for items and gift certificates donated by artists, restaurants, spas, and other vegan-oriented businesses. After the humans eat and bid on auction items, they step outside to see the guests of honor: the sanctuary's turkeys. Inverting the traditional Thanksgiving meaning of "serving turkey," caregivers lead the turkeys into a courtyard constructed of hay bales, where they serve them a cornucopia of raw vegetables, cranberries, and pumpkin pie. The event not only brings in tens of thousands of dollars in funding every year but also helps to reinforce animals' status as subjects of care as well as donors' roles as active participants in the community of care that serves them. Roosevelt also makes this experience available to less-wealthy donors who wouldn't be able to afford a celebrity gala–style event by providing the option to volunteer at the event, which entails doing setup, prepping and serving food, or cleaning.

Texas Companion Rescue hosts a range of smaller fund-raising events throughout the year, often partnering with local businesses. Four local pubs, for example, host the Pubs for Pups Pub Crawl. Participants pay a thirty dollar fee and receive an event-themed T-shirt, a pint glass, and four beer tickets. Because Texas Companion Rescue focuses its rescue efforts on companion animals, the event relies on a different type of inclusiveness than other sanctuary events. Texas Companion Rescue supporters often become members of its rescue community through adoption of their own cat or dog first. In fact, while the organization conducts a range of fund-raising, its primary ask is for the in-kind donation (donations of goods and services rather than money) of providing a permanent home, or at the very least a foster home, to rescued animals. As actual rescuers of their own animals, many supporters then expand their commitment to animal rescue through activities that support the shelters' rescue and care of other animals. Since Texas's warm climate allows most bars and restaurants to have outdoor seating areas, events like the Pub Crawl enable participants to socialize at fund-raising events along with their dogs. As the crowd moves from bar to bar, all wearing identical, brightly col-

Rescued turkeys enjoy a pumpkin pie. We Animals.

ored T-shirts emblazoned with the organization's logo, it also enables them to fold other bar patrons into the fund-raising event, educating them about Texas Companion Rescue's mission and potentially eliciting more donations.

The Care Conference session on fund-raising ended with a question-and-answer period, during which attendees expressed some of the concerns they had about sanctuary funding efforts. One attendee asked, "How do you handle pressure from major donors who want to steer your mission?"

"The vast majority are not like that," Samantha explained, "but it's a fine line. You're looking for people who support you, but there's a partnership. It's OK to adjust goals a little bit to fit donor interests, but you have to ask yourself does it still fit our mission and have honest conversations with them. Maybe they'll be persuaded, but give donors a chance to be collaborators and have some agency. There's no justification for contradicting your mission."

Although organizations generally keep their relationships with large donors private, some major celebrity animal advocates have received a fair amount of media attention for their philanthropy. Former game show host Bob Barker and cocreator of *The Simpsons* Sam Simon have had ships named after them by the antiwhaling direct action organization Sea Shepherds in recognition of their generous financial support. There is no reason to believe that wealthy donors such as Simon or Barker have interfered with the missions of the organizations they support, but colleagues who have worked at organizations involved in animal rescue initiatives have told me that donors of this magnitude can and do influence individual rescue cases by requesting organizations take on cases they may not have otherwise deemed a good use of resources. In general, these donors choose to give their financial support to organizations whose mission they already support, so they may have little motivation to try to influence the mission to serve their own agenda; they are supporting the organizations precisely because they share a common agenda. However, the concern underlying the question also reflects an element of the political economy of animal rescue. It may not negatively impact organizations or their missions, but large donors are capable of buying enough clout to influence specific rescue cases that affect individual animals. If these cases end up in successful rescues, then this can be for the best for those animals, but it also raises concerns related to a tension—highlighted by the next few questions—between an organization's rescue mission and its advocacy mission.

"What about considering vegan versus nonvegan sources in fundraising?" asked another attendee. "Where our sanctuary is based there are like two million people and only six vegans. Are donations from nonvegans like 'blood money'?"

"Half of Farm Sanctuary donors are not vegetarian," Samantha replied. "Veganism is mentioned in our materials, but *not* in our acquisition materials. The vast majority of people oppose factory farming cruelty, so we can find a common ground in anticruelty messaging. We use a 'big-tent pole' kind of focus in acquisition. Donors may accept or even appreciate veganism as an aspiration and support organizations that promote veganism while not being vegan because they support the anticruelty mission."

"Our organization has multiple mandates," said the next questioner. "One is humane education, and the other is rescuing animals; should we include both in our donation solicitations?"

"Direct mail is about emotion, urgency, catching attention," Samantha replied. "It's about sending the message that helping animals is a people problem, so that's what we're doing. Education is an important strategy, too, but it's hard to get education funding through direct mail. 'Animal people' are more motivated by directly saving animals from cruelty."

These two questions and responses point to a tension that arose multiple times throughout the conference: education and advocacy for better treatment of animals in general versus rescuing individual animals from cruel treatment. Rescuing and caring for individual animals requires financial resources that would be impossible to get if organizations were to sever all ties to the larger economy that still treats animals as commodities and natural resources. Given that many people who support animal rescue and oppose animal cruelty still consume animals and their by-products in various forms, it would be especially detrimental to refuse donations from people who have not fully embraced a vegan lifestyle, as the second questioner implied. In addition to participating in a larger economy largely driven by animal-based industries, sanctuaries also have to make decisions about how to balance their dual missions of rescue and education. This is where large donors have the greatest potential to influence decisions.

Some rescue cases provide perfect media opportunities to further an organization's education mission as well. In 2014, for example, Sam Simon—who died from colorectal cancer at the age of fifty-nine on March 8, 2015—worked with PETA to buy a Southern California chinchilla farm. The 425 chinchillas they rescued were put up for adoption, while the media coverage provided an opportunity for PETA to further spread its antifur message. That year, Simon also funded the rescue of an Indian elephant that had been mistreated at a temple in India and some bears in the United States. "I have a desire to help animals," he told reporters at the chinchilla farm. "The question of whether it makes financial sense, it's my money and I get to do what I want with it. It's an expensive hobby I picked up at the end of my life."[5] From Simon's personal perspective, the question of whether it makes financial sense may not matter, especially because he already knew he was terminally ill. In the larger context of animal rescue strategy, though, it still resonates. Considering the number of animals rescued and the media opportunity it provided, the chinchilla rescue may have made good strategic sense, but rescuing one elephant in India could potentially be construed as a waste of resources compared to the larger number of animals or better media coverage in which funding a different rescue may have resulted. Choosing how best to allocate resources often involves difficult choices like this for rescue organizations—choices in which saving some animals means not saving others. Organizations must decide how to balance the goals of their dual and potentially conflicting missions in making these choices, and the influence of the financial patrons they necessarily must invite to join their missions can at times be a significant factor shaping those decisions.

## Administration

Following a short coffee break after the presentation on fund-raising, the conference attendees once again took their seats in the small meeting room for the next presentation on sanctuary administration. Leila Moody, who was at the time Farm Sanctuary's chief operating officer and chief financial officer, led this session. Leila earned an MBA from Northwestern's Kellogg School of Management and gained several years of experience working as a director of finance and administration for a financial services company and as an independent consultant for a range of for-profit and not-for-profit companies.

She also volunteered at a cat rescue and rehabilitation organization in Chicago. She came to Farm Sanctuary in 2012 as the CFO and expanded to the COO position as well in 2014.

Leila started her presentation by focusing on how to establish a sanctuary as an institutional entity. The first decision sanctuary founders must make is whether to be a private or a public institution, which is primarily determined by funding sources. Those with access to reliable, long-term sources of income can afford to remain private, but they won't legally be able to make public solicitations in the future. Sanctuaries that plan to depend on the public for financial support will have to incorporate as not-for-profit corporations. There are several steps in establishing a nonprofit. First, the sanctuary will need to incorporate in the state where it will be located. Incorporation regulations vary from state to state, but states usually provide instruction guides for establishing nonprofits.

One of the most important steps prior to registering with the state is formulating a mission statement. The conference binder cautions attendees to think "carefully about your purposes and goals, so you can establish the capacities you may need for future programs (such as the ability to have registered humane officers on staff, tax exemptions, etc.)."[6] Carefully planning how to define a sanctuary's mission in advance is important because nonprofit tax status only covers the organization while it's operating within its stated mission. It is thus easier to state the mission broadly enough to cover the range of things an organization will want to do rather than revising the mission statement later. For example, Rainbow Haven's mission statement reads,

> Our mission is to positively impact the environment while educating Hawai'i's children about their place in the natural world. Our goal is to assist in the development of an environmentally responsible generation of youth. We are licensed to rehabilitate and possess endangered species, allowing us to teach about the fragile ecosystem we impact on a daily basis, while giving visitors a rare chance to see the animals up close. Native animals brought to us with injuries are cared for and released when able. Our resident animals will live out their natural lives at the facility.

It broadly articulates a youth educational mission to foster environmental responsibility combined with a rescue mission to rehabilitate, care for, and house animals. The breadth of the statement enables

Rainbow Haven to perform a wide range of educational or animal care–related activities with donor funds without falling outside the purview of its nonprofit designation.

Processing a state nonprofit application generally takes about six to eight weeks, and once it is established, states charge the nonprofit corporation annual registration and filing fees. After establishing a state nonprofit corporation, an organization can then apply for federal 501(c)3 nonprofit status with the Internal Revenue Service. This allows donor contributions to be tax-deductible, gives the organization some tax exemptions, and makes it eligible for bulk mailing rates with the U.S. Postal Service. Importantly, obtaining 501(c)3 status also gives an organization legitimacy in the eyes of the public, especially donors. Following state incorporation and obtaining 501(c)3 status, an organization needs to then register with each separate state where it wishes to solicit charitable contributions. Larger sanctuaries, like Farm Sanctuary, that solicit donations at a national level must register in every state.

Nonprofit corporations must also follow specific accounting procedures to maintain their nonprofit status. This is yet another reason why donor databases are useful—they record much of the financial information organizations need to report. If an organization fails to file IRS tax form 990 three years in a row, its nonprofit status is automatically suspended. Making this information readily available to the public can also lend organizations further legitimacy. Texas Companion Rescue posts 990s directly on its website, and both Roosevelt and Rainbow Haven provide links on their websites to where people can find their tax information on GuideStar.com, an online database of information about U.S. nonprofits.

To incorporate, states require organizations to establish a board of directors, an election process for board members, and a set of bylaws. Leila advised the attendees that it is helpful to find people to join the board who can bring resources with them, especially professional skills. Many inchoate sanctuaries will have to start with a board consisting of the people already involved in building the sanctuary, but the guide in the conference binder cautions that this can inhibit a sanctuary's growth and development in the long run and suggests that the ultimate goal should be "an independent board of directors whose primary responsibilities are to assess the overall effectiveness of the organization and to bring in financial resources." An independent board of directors can also provide a "checks and balances" mechanism to prevent a sanctuary director from making decisions that could be detrimental to the sanctuary, such as taking on animals that the sanctuary does not have space for or cannot afford. Olivia, the director of Rainbow Haven, told me that she intentionally gave her board of directors approval over any new rescues because she recognized that if the decision were left up to her, she would take in every animal that came along.

Leila concluded her presentation on sanctuary administration by addressing budgeting, an essential tool in making responsible use of funding and resources. "Organizations with small infrastructures," she said, "can do a lot of good work with a relatively small budget." But costs climb rapidly as organizations scale up. Farm Sanctuary, for example, had a $9.5 million annual budget in 2014, up from approximately $6 million in 2009. It saw a large increase when it acquired a second California location.

She acknowledged that an accurate budget can be difficult to estimate, but—echoing the earlier presentations' emphasis on preparedness—she told the attendees, "It is critical to create a plan for spending and earning. Start slowly and watch your costs as they build. There are always unanticipated expenses, so if you budget your known expenses to break even with no wiggle room, you'll run into problems. Things break on farms like you will not believe. Distinguish between ongoing and onetime costs, plan fund-raising so you're receiving it before you need it. You should have income in advance of when expenses hit. For example, if you budget a barn, also consider the increased utility costs, labor for those additional animals, and so on. Budget for the lifetime care of animals. Some species are a lot more expensive than others, so you need to consider the life span of an animal and the ongoing expenses she will require, like bedding, feed, veterinary care, including the proximity of vets and how much transport might cost. Also consider housing, including heating, cooling, water, and sewage for barns and facilities. Be realistic about what you can take on."

This last sentence about realism made it clear that she was not only suggesting that the attendees make sure to have sufficient funding secured in advance of taking on the responsibility of a new animal but that they also recognize the limits on how much responsibility they can afford to take on at any given time. It was the closest anyone at the conference had come so far to addressing the idea that sanctuaries should not take in animals they cannot care for. In the section on budgeting, the conference binder adds, "Many well-intentioned sanctuaries have closed because of their failure to budget well. It is difficult to say no, but always saying yes can lead to financial crises." The possibility of turning down a rescue complicates the figure of the animal as subject of care and rescue. When discussing donor appeals, Samantha encouraged attendees to share animals' biographical details—particularly any cruel treatment inflicted on them—to elicit sympathy for individual animals and their plights. In this context, donors ideally identify with animals as unique individuals in need of care. The imperative to be realistic about what a sanctuary can take on, on the other hand, encourages people who are already inclined to see animals as individuals in need of rescue and care to recognize instead that they are also members of a massive collective of other individuals in need of care and rescue, most of whom cannot realistically be helped given the incredibly limited resources of sanctuaries. In other words, responsible sanctuary management can at times require rescuers to resist the sympathetic impetus to help that they simultaneously seek to foster in donors.

Another element of sanctuary operation that has a serious impact on budgeting is staffing. Many sanctuaries initially rely on volunteers. Depending on how large they grow, some even find it possible to run on volunteer work exclusively. Rainbow Haven, for example, relies entirely on volunteer labor. Nobody who works there, including Olivia, receives a salary. Olivia is also the only full-time volunteer, though she does run a residential internship program that brings vet students to the sanctuary for several weeks at a time. In general, volunteers' availability and commitment can fluctuate, and the need for a reliable labor force leads many sanctuaries to hire at least a few staff members. This means they must budget for staff wages as well as payroll expenses. Sanctuaries with employees also need to account for labor laws related to minimum wage, overtime, break requirements, unemployment, and worker's compensation and be aware of how workers' status as employees or independent contractors will affect compensation. Likewise, they must conform to Occupational Safety and Health Administration requirements by maintaining records of injuries and illnesses.

Again counseling attendees to be realistic about budgeting, Leila told them, "Don't overhire for your budget." Sanctuaries that rely on paid labor must worry about more than just budgeting costs, though. The quality of labor is as much an issue as the number of laborers, and a failure to adequately compensate employees can lead to an unending cycle of training and rehiring.[7] Providing benefits is one way of strengthening employee retention, though this can also place a larger strain on the budget. "One of the primary dilemmas sanctuaries face with employees is that they need skilled labor—people with a robust understanding of the care requirements of a range of species—but they don't always have the budget to adequately compensate that level of skill." One caregiver with whom I worked closely at Roosevelt Farm Sanctuary became an expert in farm animal care through years of experience but was seriously considering a career change because she only made fourteen dollars per hour. As this example illustrates, relatively low wages work against building and retaining the kind of skilled, experienced caregivers sanctuaries most need. Increasing the employee budget would be one solution, but this would require shifting money away from other expenditures, such as animal care, and that would require making more tough decisions about which animals can be rescued.

### Sanctuary Property and Infrastructure

Susie spent the first half of the second day of the conference reinforcing points from the first day and addressing all of the other major issues with which aspiring sanctuary operators would need to contend, starting with choosing the physical property where a sanctuary is based. Ideally, she explained, this property should be owned by the organization rather than the founders. This helps create a protective barrier between founders' personal finances and those of the sanctuary, so that if the founders encounter personal financial problems, these will not also impact the sanctuary and the animals.

A related concern to who owns the property is whether anybody will live there. Because some founders do start sanctuaries on their own property, that is often the same property where their house is. "If you don't have anybody else," Susie explained, "you can never leave. Continuously living on the property leads to burnout. It's hard to let go." Both the founders of Roosevelt Farm Sanctuary and Rainbow Haven live in houses on the same property as the sanctuary and have different ways of coping with the risk of burnout. At Roosevelt, Rita and her husband, Ted, mostly focus on administrative work in offices based in their house and allow hired caregivers to oversee the animal care operation. Because they have a paid staff, they are also able to travel occasionally without leaving the animals uncared for. At Rainbow Haven, Olivia does oversee all the animal care herself. However, she and her husband, Sam, plan vacations every year. Olivia uses her internship program to make sure there are several trained vet students in residence at the sanctuary to run the animal care operation for the few weeks they are gone.

If the sanctuary is not going to be based on property the founders already own, then there are several factors to consider in choosing a location. Both urban and rural spaces come with benefits and drawbacks. Urban areas increase opportunities for education and outreach, but more expensive property and stricter zoning restrictions can limit the size of the sanctuary. Rural sites near farming areas afford access to much cheaper feed and bedding supplies and vets who are more experienced with farm animals, but they are more removed from potential visitors. Roosevelt has managed to find a good compromise between these two options by locating its sanctuary in a rural area that's a little over two hours from New York City. They receive a steady flow of visitors and volunteers while also enjoying the perks of a rural location.

Building effective and safe infrastructure also requires careful advanced planning, because species needs and capabilities vary widely. "I would love to wipe out buildings and start over now that I know what I know," Susie told the attendees. "If you have the ability to start from scratch, have a strategy. Now that we're not using haylofts, I wish we didn't have them. If you have a downed cow, the only way to help her up is with a tractor, but you can't lift a cow with a tractor in a barn with a hay loft."

Appropriate fencing also varies by species and requires an informed understanding of different species' capabilities to plan effectively. Fencing for chickens, for example, would be useless if used for cattle. In fact, "beef cattle can tear through anything," Susie explained. "One time we introduced new cattle to the sanctuary. We had a camera crew down there to film how wonderful it would be for them to enter their pasture for the first time, and these one-ton animals tore right through the electric fences. I was like, 'Run!' Fencing is one of the biggest expenses a sanctuary has." Sometimes individual animals need to be taken into account as well. "We had a pack of goats that would jump the fence all the time in California," said Susie. "But then one day an old one got caught by his back legs, so we had to raze the fence. Lame animals will never stop trying to be with the herd, so you have to accommodate them."

In addition to knowing which fencing works best with each species, it is necessary to know what predators are indigenous to the area where a sanctuary is located and what fencing works best to keep them out. "You also have to make sure you have predator-proof fencing for all animals, which is easier said than done," Susie told the attendees. "There is no such thing as absolutely perfect fencing, but knowing what you are up against is critical. They have big coyote kills in California because farmers don't have barns. The mister fans in barns would have to run twenty-four/seven in California. So they need fencing that can keep out coyotes." As this California example illustrates, the environmental conditions where a sanctuary is based also affect decisions about animal care and sanctuary infrastructure.

## Caregiver Management

The theme of preparedness that ran through the first day of the conference was even more prominent on the second day. "Know how to care for the species you take in," Susie told the audience. "Before even getting a chicken—know everything. One of my biggest frustrations is when sanctuaries that have been in business ten years call about the most simple thing that my one-year interns could do with their eyes closed. Right now we have 130 animals on medication at Farm Sanctuary. There's not one animal on this property my caregivers can't restrain. If they can't, they're not a caregiver yet. To train a full caregiver here, it takes at least two years. Before taking on any animal of any species, you *must be* trained in the very basic care required to keep that animal safe and healthy. A lot of sanctuaries are not doing individual medical care, which they *should be doing*. At Farm Sanctuary, we do everything but major surgeries at this point."

The sites where I worked evidenced a similar commitment to care capacity. Texas Companion Rescue employs vets and vet techs to treat injured or sick animals, while Roosevelt Farm Sanctuary had between three and five experienced caregivers on staff while I was there who knew how to treat most minor injuries and administer a range of veterinary pharmaceuticals. It also has a local vet who comes to the sanctuary to treat large animals, and—like Farm Sanctuary—it has a close relationship with the Cornell Veterinary School in Ithaca, where it takes seriously sick animals it cannot treat in its own medical facilities. At Rainbow Haven, Olivia has an extensive amount of self-taught veterinary knowledge, but she also runs her internship program for vet students to both provide them with opportunities to gain clinical experience and have skilled assistants with prior experience in veterinary medicine. In addition, she has a close relationship with a local veterinary office, where the interns can work shifts for experience, as well as a condo near the beach that she offers to licensed vets who want to trade veterinary care for a free vacation spot.

Returning to the topic of budgeting from the first day, Susie advised the attendees to "plan ahead and create a budget for your first year, and then make a five-year plan before you start taking in any animals. And have a contingency plan. If funds dried up, we'd start placing our animals—that's part of our contingency plan. The number of sanctuaries that closed because of a failure to plan well is scary. One that recently closed was a one-woman show with 250 animals. It's not an easy choice if you're in love with a pig and have to decide between $5,000 surgery and putting the pig down. You also need a plan in place if you die. A sanctuary run by only one or two people often has to shut down just due to injury or illness. Animals shouldn't have to rely on you surviving—that's not fair. If you take them all in, and they'll have to be put down if you die, then you're a bad person." At Rainbow Haven, Olivia has set up a trust to take over the sanctuary if something happens to her. "I left the sanctuary to the animals," she likes to say.

Next, Susie turned to issues related to staffing. "This job can be very repetitive," she said. "I love what I do, but I'm really tired a lot. You have to take care of people to try to avoid burnout. Burnout and exhaustion is a big cause of injury." To illustrate her point, she described an incident in which she was tired and failed to move out of the way quickly enough as a large cow slammed her against a wall. The cow slammed into her repeatedly, leaving her with broken ribs and an injured spleen. "Cows can kill people. They have killed farmers." This story also illustrates another issue that Susie emphasized throughout her presentation: the need to have a thorough understanding of the personalities, temperaments, and physical needs of individual animals. After this incident, the caregivers altered the fencing setup for this cow to keep her from having physical contact with people. "She eventually died of cancer, but she got to spend the rest of her life living happily with her favorite cow friend."

The constant reminders of animal mortality in sanctuaries make emotional burnout as much a concern as physical burnout. "You never get over them dying," Susie explained, "and you shouldn't. I don't want my staff not to cry. But burnout is the number one loss of staff, and you're going to die inside every day." To counter the effects of burnout, Susie emphasized the importance of compassion and open communication. "Staff won't necessarily tell you when they're not comfortable doing tasks, so talk to them. Don't have them do stuff you're not willing to do. Compensate them fairly for their work, and allow them to take days off and vacations even if you don't feel there is time. Don't be martyrs or expect them to be. If you cannot provide all of this, reduce animals or increase staff! It's important to keep your staff happy—they're as much individuals as animals are."

This last comment highlights a tension that I witnessed throughout my fieldwork as well as through past experiences in animal rights activism. Staff at animal advocacy organizations sometimes feel that they are expected to sacrifice themselves for the benefit of the animals, working long hours without adequate compensation because there is always more to do. Caregivers with whom I have worked, for example, leave work late because they are the only ones on duty and they have to finish feeding all the animals. One caregiver was chastised for letting the animals down when she ended up on a jury after reporting for jury duty. A lawyer acquaintance who worked at an animal advocacy organization was even reprimanded for taking time off work to take her dog to the vet after he was attacked and injured by another dog. Susie's statement that humans are as much individuals as the animals foregrounds this paradoxical trend in animal rescue movements through which the figure of the individual animal subject can eclipse or partially erase the individual human subjects involved in producing those animal subjects. Without the attention to human individuality that Susie advocates, the humans in animal rescue can have a tendency to blur at times, at least from the vantage point of management and their expectations, into mere mechanisms in the process of producing animal subjects.

For sanctuary founders, however, there can be an opposite effect. "Founders syndrome," Susie warned the attendees, "is the number one thing that's going to destroy this movement." She was referring to the situation—found throughout the nonprofit world—in which founders exert excessive control over their organizations and refuse to listen to others' advice. "I've never seen a pattern of founder's syndrome like I have in the animal rights movement—it's a massive problem." It seems to happen most often when the organization is strongly identified with a particular person, she explained.

"The founders this happens with are the ones who are no longer directly working with their staff, especially ones who started out working with the animals. There are a lot of resources online for founder syndrome, but unless the board can intervene, there's very little you can do to address it. The major symptom is that the founder makes *all* decisions without any formal process or input. This happens when key staff and board members are selected by the founder, and they are all friends and family—'yes men.' Anybody who challenges the founder is gone. And then they'll call other sanctuaries to trash the people they're firing. The founder sees everything to be about them and not about the mission, the animals, the cause. Don't stay and destroy your staff if this starts happening. You need to surround yourself with people who will tell you when you're wrong or when you're being a jerk. You're always learning. The day you think you know everything, you should quit. It's a small movement with five million celebrities, but none of us are actually celebrities. Do not lose sight of the cause— the mission. This is not about you; it's about them! I love those animals with all my being, and I hope when I die other people do too."

Taken in conjunction with her admonitions about treating both staff and animals as individuals, this impassioned denouncement of founder's syndrome presents a complex critique of the interrelated constellation of subjectivities within a sanctuary. In asking potential founders to approach their rescue mission with humility, she is emphasizing the centrality of the animal subject to the sanctuary mission. At the same time, she is decentering the position of the founders. In the dynamic Susie presents, animals are both individual rescue subjects and members of an endangered collective, while human caregivers—founders as well as staff—are also simultaneously individual subjects and part of a caregiving collective in service to the animals. Furthermore, by relating to animals as rights-bearing subjects (regardless of their actual legal status), human caregivers transform the sanctuary space into an interspecies community in which both animals and humans operate as citizens. The caregiving relationship creates a hierarchy in the sense that the caregivers both serve and in some ways control the animals, but on each level of that hierarchy, the individuals that compose each collective are equal—no one is more important than the others, and both levels are equally important to the equilibrium of the multispecies community. Together, these two interconnected collectives arguably form a posthuman citizenry. In their book *Zoopolis: A Political Theory of Animal Rights*, philosophers Sue Donaldson and Will Kymlicka conceptualize a robust framework for a societal arrangement in which humans and domesticated animals could live together as co-citizens.[8] Owing to the many dilemmas of captive care and the ways in which caregivers address them, most sanctuaries do not afford animals all the rights of membership that would come with animal citizenship in Donaldson and Kymlicka's model,[9] but most do to some extent conform to the three core elements of citizenship they lay out: "residency" (a recognition that the sanctuary is the animals' home and they belong there), "inclusion in the sovereign people" (the animals' interests "count in determining the public good" within the sanctuary space), and agency (animals should "be able to shape the rules of cooperation" within the sanctuary community).[10] The first two elements are in fact the core elements of a sanctuary ethos, because sanctuaries exist to provide a residence to rescued animals, and serving their interests is the goal of sanctuary care. Although the degree to which different sanctuaries intentionally incorporate the third element into their daily operations varies, animals within all sanctuaries shape the rules of cooperation and thus the conditions of their own care, as I have shown in previous chapters through the examples of Bob and Eloise, Lamar, Flower, Lolly and Billie, Maui, Magma, and Buddy.

Susie's ideal vision for the structure of a sanctuary serves as an aspirational goal for many caregivers with whom I have spoken, but in practice, it remains elusive. During the course of my research, I encountered staff at one sanctuary who were so frustrated with what they explicitly identified as "founder's syndrome" that they were contemplating quitting en masse. Fortunately for the sanctuary, the staff and caregivers managed to reach a détente. Though not always this extreme, staff and management tension remains an issue throughout the animal rescue movement. As Susie suggested, relying on more collective decision making is one way to ameliorate these tensions. One of the caregivers involved in the narrowly averted mass resignation hopes to someday start her own sanctuary based on a consensus model in which all the caregivers will make collective decisions about animal care and sanctuary procedures, though she also worries about whether all sanctuary responsibilities can be best accomplished under this model. Emergency medical decisions, for example, may not allow time for a consensus process. Nonetheless, she cannot imagine it being worse than working for someone who is suffering from founder's syndrome.

Continuing to emphasize the importance of preparedness, Susie next turned to other issues that founders will have to address. "Some of the other pitfalls you have to worry about," Susie explained, "are taking in more animals than you can handle, taking animals you don't know how to care for, an inability to raise funds, and attempting to do all the work alone. There are sanctuaries popping up all over the place run by one person with a full-time job—they will close in a year. If you have more than a few animals, you need a staff. You can't rely on volunteers alone. And it's hard to find ones that can handle challenging tasks. You also can't do it if you're going to need a full-time job. Ten billion animals die a year; you can't save them all.[11] You have to be able to say no. Farm Sanctuary says no to eight hundred animals a year. If you can't sleep at night saying no to an animal, don't start. Taking too many animals too quickly is the number one mistake sanctuaries make. You need to build up slowly. There are sanctuaries I wouldn't place with because of their inability to raise funds."

While staff are necessary for any large sanctuary, Susie also went on to stress the value of volunteer and intern programs. Most volunteers at sanctuaries are at least partly motivated by a desire to interact with the animals. "They want to feed, pet, and brush them," Susie explained, "but volunteer work often involves cleaning duties and physical work, so be very clear about what kind of work volunteers will be doing. Have projects ready for the volunteers before they arrive, and make sure you have all material resources you'll need for volunteer work." Farm Sanctuary used to allow volunteers to come whenever they wanted, but the lack of reliable consistency didn't work well. So it implemented a system through which it asked volunteers to make a weekly commitment.

The sanctuaries where I worked all handled volunteer management differently. Roosevelt Farm Sanctuary had the least formalized volunteer process. It requested that people sign up in advance through its website and had a calendar where people could see which days did not yet have volunteers scheduled, but it did not require any kind of formal commitment. Volunteers could choose to help caregivers—which usually entails cleaning animal areas—or to work with administrative staff on other tasks. It also relied on volunteer support at its fundraising events.

Rainbow Haven had no formal sign-up process, but most of the volunteers had regular days on which they came in the morning or afternoon to help Olivia and the interns with animal feedings. Olivia also requested some of the more experienced volunteers to be on-call while she was on vacation in case interns needed help with anything. While I was working there, weather forecasts predicted a tropical storm might hit the island while Olivia would be away. She asked me to be on-call to help the interns out with moving all the animals to secure facilities if it looked like the storm was going to be serious. In the end, the storm fizzled out, and they didn't need any help.

Unlike the other two, Texas Companion Rescue has a highly organized volunteer system. As described in chapter 1, potential volunteers must first submit an online volunteer application and attend a volunteer orientation, which is held once a month. The orientation has a twenty dollar registration fee, with a ten dollar discount for students, minors, and seniors. The orientation provides an overview of all the different areas where people can volunteer and ends with break-out sessions for people who want to work with either dogs or cats. Volunteers must commit to six hours of volunteer work per month, and most jobs require additional training after the orientation. Volunteers also log in to a computer system to record their hours and can take on more responsibilities as they gain experience. This level of organization provides a large corps of skilled and reliable volunteers that enables Texas Companion Rescue to operate with a relatively small paid staff.

Intern programs are another way sanctuaries can supplement their labor needs. At Farm Sanctuary, interns work forty hours a week for stints that last from one to three months. Intern programs provide reliable labor while allowing for more training than regular volunteers could receive. "This gets more done for the sanctuary and gives the interns a more rewarding experience," Susie told the attendees. "It also serves as a staff recruitment tool and helps to develop better activists." Conversely, intern programs can serve as a filter. "People often say I'd do anything to work for Farm Sanctuary, but that's not always true. An intern program gives them a chance to see how they fit with the work, the organizational culture, and living in a rural place." The application process for Farm Sanctuary is the most rigorous among the organizations I visited. It starts with a written application, followed by a phone interview. It may also include letters of recommendation, as I recently learned when a student in one of my courses asked me to write her a letter for her intern application. If the application is successful, then the applicant has to sign a contract committing to the internship and pay a $150 deposit to hold her spot, which she gets back after she completes the internship. The deposit is to make sure the applicants are serious. "Not every animal lover is a good fit. People do back out or come and leave after a week." Because the internships are unpaid, Susie stressed the importance of expressing appreciation. "Remember they're not getting paid; this is a special time in their lives, so appreciate and connect with them on a daily basis."

Intern programs do come with potential costs as well as benefits, though. They take time from experienced staff to train and supervise interns, and occasionally interns bring their own problems to the sanctuary. Farm Sanctuary has had issues with interns using drugs, having personal conflicts with each other, and more serious problems like suicidal depression and anorexia. At Rainbow Haven, one intern got caught using ecstasy. After that, the board of directors created a more stringent screening process. Olivia now does background checks on interns that entail investigations of their social media presence, similar to the ones conducted by universities of their student applicants and employers of their job applicants. If prospective interns proudly display their partying prowess on their Facebook profile, then they have little likelihood of landing an internship there.

### Advocacy Mission

Finally, Susie focused on the topic of a sanctuary's role as an advocate for animals. "By investing time in basic visitor program elements, you will greatly increase the impact your sanctuary has. The more we educate the public, the quicker we can make the world better for farm animals." Farm Sanctuary sees between four thousand and five thousand people come through on guided tours each year. "That's four to five thousand chances to get people to change the way they eat and live their lives, to go vegan or vegetarian or at least cut down on meat and save more animals. When someone pets Antoinette the turkey and says 'I'll never eat turkey again,' we've not only saved Antoinette's life, but all the lives of the turkeys that person would've eaten in their life."[12]

Farm Sanctuary offers tours Wednesday through Sunday, every hour on the hour. The tours have a standard fact-checked script with breaks where guides can share individual animals' stories based on which animals the tour happens to encounter. "They come in almost dead and then you tell their stories: who they are, where they come from, and how happy they are there now." The best stories, according to Susie, are anything that shows animals have preferences and feelings, "like the pig who broke out of her dog crate to nurse her piglets in back of the transport truck. This shows that pigs have maternal feelings too. Really, animals do most of the work of connecting with people." At this point in the presentation, Susie showed the audience a slide of a smiling man nuzzling his face against a goat's neck.

Both Roosevelt Farm Sanctuary and Rainbow Haven conduct regular tours in which visitors meet and learn the biographies of individual animals. At Roosevelt, tour guides also include details about animal agricultural industries, while tours at Rainbow Haven focus on issues related to the exotic pet trade and threats to wildlife. Texas Companion Rescue does not conduct formal tours, but its facilities are open to the public so visitors can interact with all the animals who are available for adoption.

As Susie's explanation of tours suggests, many sanctuaries see their rescued animals as ambassadors who can educate the public about what they see as the abuse or mistreatment of animals.[13] Tours at Roosevelt occur on the weekends during the spring and summer. The tour winds through the sanctuary, stopping at each of the housing areas for the different kinds of animals at the sanctuary—chickens, ducks, goats and sheep, cows, and pigs—while a tour guide describes the typical living conditions and treatment of each of these types of animals in the industrial food system. Tour guides also encourage visitors to consider reducing their consumption of animal products or adopting a vegan lifestyle, emphasizing what they see as a direct connection between consumption choices and the impact of those choices on the lives of farmed animals like the ones visitors meet on the tour. As explained in chapter 2, some sanctuaries do not allow public tours of their facilities to minimize the potential stress to animals having to engage with lots of human visitors. They limit their public outreach to social media because they see the sanctuary space as existing solely for the animals in residence. They seek to resist what they see as a sort of instrumentalization of animals that results from situating them as educational ambassadors to the public. Even for these sanctuaries, though, animals still function as ambassadors for the sanctuary in a fund-raising capacity, as they use stories and images of individual animals on their websites and fund-raising materials to compel people to make financial donations.

Tours do present some risks. All visitors to Farm Sanctuary sign liability waivers, which is true of Roosevelt Farm Sanctuary and Rainbow Haven as well. People are not allowed near sick animals, and guides are trained to read behavioral cues in animals that could signify dangerous situations, such as cows stretching their necks and bugging their eyes, which can indicate agitation. Animals with patterns of aggression are also not on tours. For example, as Susie explained, "adolescent cows go through a jerk phase around two. They also can just play too rough, especially bottle-fed calves that weren't disciplined by their mothers." This is likewise true for bottle-fed puppies at Texas Companion Rescue that weren't socialized by their mothers. Puppies raised by their mothers generally know not to bite too hard, whereas the bottle-fed puppies need extra training to make sure they don't hurt people unintentionally.

Despite the safety precautions, visitors can have a distorted sense of their safety because the animals are cute and friendly, and many of them belong to species that are not considered dangerous. Susie described one incident in which a cow used her horns to throw an empty baby carriage up into the air. After that, no carriages were allowed on tours. "Another time, for some reason, a lady dumped popcorn on her child's stroller so turkeys would eat off her baby. A male turkey jumped on the stroller, lost his balance, and started flapping the baby with his wings." Farm Sanctuary now limits tours to children who are twelve and older. "Groups of kids can change animals' energy. Goats and steer will head-butt kids even when they're nice to adults. It's important to educate kids and to introduce them to animals, but you have to do it safely."

The decision to allow visitors access to animals is part of a calculus of safety and animal autonomy that sanctuaries balance differently. Giving tours during which visitors interact with animals affects both where animals are allowed to go in the sanctuary and how much choice they have in avoiding human contact. Take goats with a penchant for butting small children with their horns, for example. Since the goal of the tours is to educate people about the treatment of farmed animals, it would curtail the impact of their educational outreach to prevent children (and, by extension, adults who would not come without their children) from visiting the sanctuary. To prevent goats from injuring children, it is thus necessary to have fences to keep the goats and children separated. Although fences at sanctuaries serve multiple purposes, including separating different species of animals that might injure each other or eat each other's food, the architectural design and spatial segregation of animals in many sanctuaries are partially shaped by the decision to allow groups of human visitors near animals. The issue of visitor safety is only heightened at exotic animal sanctuaries like Rainbow Haven, where potentially more dangerous animals, such as monkeys, zebras, and ostriches, could seriously injure a visitor. Finally, in addition to influencing the spatial organization of animals' daily lives within sanctuaries, allowing public access in the form of tours can impact animals' autonomy by limiting their ability to regulate their proximity to humans. Sanctuaries that provide access to the public in service to their educational goals "necessarily must impose further limits on animals' already limited autonomy in exchange."[14]

Aside from visitor safety and limitations on animal autonomy, the advocacy mission raises another risk for sanctuaries, as noted by ecofeminist philosopher Karen S. Emmerman. Emmerman argues that sanctuaries can never provide complete restitution for the original acts of confinement and exploitation inflicted against rescued animals, but they risk giving that impression to many sanctuary supporters: "Once an animal is in sanctuary and people get to meet her, know her, hear her story of exploitation and trauma, a caring response ensues. The animal is romanticized, thought about, and held in awe in much the same way the animals in zoos are. We feel relief at seeing an end to her suffering and have a sense that things have gone well in the world."[15] She thus emphasizes that it is important not to lose sight of the fact that sanctuaries are "one step in the work of moral repair rather than the final destination."[16] As sites of "new beginnings wrapped in an inescapable past and captive present"—and for many animals who continue to bear the physical and psychological effects of their previous captivity, "also of continued trauma"—Emmerman argues that sanctuaries are "places where we get a glimpse of humans doing the very best kind of moral work," but "even the very best kind of moral work is tainted in some sense" when "lifelong captivity is the best we can offer animals."[17] Similarly, Lori Gruen observes,

> Even when captive animals have their futures secured, are provided with access to the outdoors, have space to develop stable social relationships if they are social species, have ample opportunities to express species-typical behaviors, are not removed from their groups except when it is directly in the interest of that individual and the particular group to which he or she belongs, are provided with healthy and plentiful food in a way that is enriching, and are provided with opportunities to exercise and develop species-typical cognitive and behavioral skills, they remain captives. . . . Animals in captivity often suffer physically and psychologically, have their liberty interests frustrated, and have their Wild dignity violated. Releasing them to the wild may restore their liberty and dignity, but it will undoubtedly lead to tremendous suffering and probable death. Keeping them captive is wrong and releasing them from captivity is wrong. . . . There may be no ethical way to rectify the wrong we have done.[18]

Emmerman and Gruen highlight the fact that as long as sanctuaries need to exist, their missions are incomplete. The challenge this creates for the advocacy mission of sanctuaries is communicating to people that while sanctuaries may be a response to the conditions that render animals *bestia sacer*, and they may provide a partial reprieve from those conditions for a very limited number of animals, they are not by themselves a remedy to those conditions.

### "Don't Start a Sanctuary" Reprise: A Case Study

An experience from the beginning of my fieldwork illustrates many of the problems that can arise when a sanctuary is unable to contend with all the concerns related to funding, administration, infrastructure, and management presented at the conference. Before conducting research at the other sanctuaries featured in this book, I briefly volunteered at a sanctuary in Florida that struggled with many of the potential problems Susie and the other presenters cautioned against. On the first day I came to Quiet Glen Animal Sanctuary, about twenty miles outside of Ocala, Florida, I almost drove right past the entrance to the driveway, but I spotted the tattered flag and the carved wooden sign with the sanctuary's name just in time. Inside the sanctuary, ramshackle fences formed lopsided corrals for ponies on one side of the dirt driveway and a large-horned cow on the other. As I drove to the parking lot, I passed enclosures for dogs, birds, and coyotes. Although the coyote enclosures were new and solid looking, the other structures were made of tilting wooden frames supporting sagging chicken wire. Across from the large waterfowl enclosures with small concrete ponds full of murky water, the home of Lynn, the sanctuary founder, sat among a labyrinth of dog kennels, a deer paddock, and a fenced-off area for garbage. Next to Lynn's house were some storage sheds and a short flat-bed trailer. This is where two sanctuary volunteers, Donald and his wife, Kim, lived. Next to their trailer was an outhouse, which functioned as both their private toilet and the sanctuary's only public restroom. Donald and Kim moved to Florida from New Jersey in the late 1990s. After Donald was laid off from his job, they were unable to pay their rent and became homeless. Lynn met them when they were living out of a tent in the nearby Ocala National Forest. Lynn, who I later learned was known for helping humans in need as well as animals, offered for them to move into the trailer in exchange for helping with caring for the animals at the sanctuary. They had been there for about a year when I arrived.

Among the animals housed at the sanctuary were coyotes, ducks, geese, peacocks, pigeons, chickens, deer, cranes, pigs, a goat, an emu, horses, a cow, various reptiles, and a fox. In stark contrast to the other sanctuaries I visited, most of these animals lived in enclosures that did not look like they were cleaned very often. The fox's enclosure stood out as particularly unsuited for him. Somebody had found him with an injured foot, possibly from a trap, and brought him to the sanctuary seven years ago. Lynn nursed him back to health, but he didn't seem happy at the sanctuary. Every time I peeked into his tiny fenced-in enclosure between the deer paddock and the garbage bins, he was running in circles and looking around anxiously. He was always visible to anybody who walked by because he had nothing in his

A well-cared-for rescued fox. NEAVS.

enclosure to hide under or behind. The fox's repetitive circular pacing was most likely a manifestation of stereotypic behavior, abnormal repetitive movements with no apparent goal or function that are sometimes observed in captive animals.[19] Stereotypic behaviors frequently occur in animals kept in especially confined or stressful environments, such as laboratory animals or animals in factory farms.

On one side of Lynn's house were several dogs living in kennels who would bark incessantly throughout the day. The sanctuary did dog adoptions, Donald told me, but these were infrequent because it did not have an active adoption outreach program like Texas Companion Rescue. "But the sanctuary isn't even supposed to have dogs," he added. "Lynn built it to take care of other animals, like exotics, but people keep bringing dogs here because they know they won't be killed like they would at the local animal shelter, and Lynn can't turn them away."

My first task as a volunteer was to assist a man named Tim in moving three male coyotes to the large new cages he had built for them. The other volunteers called him Dr. Tim because he provided veterinary care to animals that were sick or injured. He had a biology degree from college but no official veterinary training other than what he'd taught himself from books and the internet. Tim lived about thirty miles from the sanctuary in The Villages, one of Florida's many gated retirement communities. He was bored with retired life, so he started volunteering at the sanctuary. Nine and a half years ago, Tim introduced himself to Lynn after seeing several of her solicitations for donations in the local paper. She asked him if he knew anything about reptiles. He told her he knew a bit about reptiles, and she said he was just the man she was looking for. Tim's first task at the sanctuary was to look after a ball python, a skink, and some gopher turtles, and the responsibilities blossomed from there. Since then, Tim has also become an amateur primatologist, spending hours observing and recording data on the wild colonies of rhesus macaques that settled on the nearby Silver River decades ago when they escaped from a tourist attraction.[20]

As we tried to move the first coyote, cherry-Kool-Aid-red blood trickled between his teeth. Tim warned me and the other volunteers to expect this. It was from the coyote biting down on the restraint poles, the kind with wire loops on the end that dogcatchers use to slip over the heads of stray dogs. "It makes their gums bleed," he said. I hoped that the next two would not do the same thing, but they did. More unsettling than the blood—or their wide-open mouths as they writhed with the plastic-coated wire cords around their necks—was their silence. I expected coyotes to yip and howl when they were agitated or excited, but these coyotes made almost no sound at all, even as their eyes rolled wildly and they jerked against their restraints.

Tim had devised a plan to avoid dragging the "boys," as he called them, across the sanctuary from their old cyclone fence enclosure, where each sat cramped in a small kennel space, to their new individual cyclone fence enclosures with slightly more space than that afforded by the minimum dimensions for a coyote cage mandated by the state: eight feet wide by twenty feet long by six feet high were the dimensions necessary to avoid a fine. Tim had single-handedly designed and built three connected cages that were eight feet high out of pieces of fencing from scrap piles near the parking lot. The cages were so well crafted that I did not even notice the wheel welded to what was formerly part of a sliding gate until Tim explained where the materials had come from. To move the coyotes, he built a litter out of pieces of plywood. The plan was for Tim and I to slip the loops of our restraint poles over their heads and then maneuver them onto the litter so two other volunteers could carry them to their new homes. Coyboy, the first and fiercest, rolled off the litter almost immediately, so Tim carried him under one arm while we each held our restraint poles with the loops pulled taught around his neck. Scrapper and Myboy were either more cooperative or more petrified since they stayed on the litter while the four of us carried them to their new homes, with another volunteer opening and closing the many gates that made up the triple level of security Tim designed for the new coyote paddock. All three of the coyotes along with a young female were left near the sanctuary gate as puppies, and the sanctuary had been caring for them ever since. No one knew where they had come from or why they were left there, but a lot of the volunteers thought they might have been orphaned by a hunter and left there by somebody who felt sorry for them.

After we finished moving the coyotes, Tim told me that he had taken on the coyotes as a special project. "I try to provide a comfortable and psychologically stimulating environment for them." He showed me a bunch of old blankets and towels in a big heap under a wooden frame covered in tarps. Tim explained that he gave these to the coyotes to play with and told me that when I came to the sanctuary to volunteer, I should swap out new, clean ones for the old ones, which the coyotes often left scattered around their cages in shredded pieces. Tim also had a special stash of stuffed toys and new tennis balls in a garbage bag that he saved for the coyotes. He hid it by the blankets so other volunteers did not give them to the several dogs who live at the sanctuary.

After the move, the coyote housing consisted of the brand-new triple-cage structure for the boys, a similar adjacent single-unit structure for Minnie, a young female coyote, and a third individual unit attached to the back of Lynn's house for Winnie, an older female. I asked Tim why the coyotes were all separated, and he explained that Lynn thought the boys were displaying aggression toward each other. Tim believed they could work it out on their own, but Lynn did not want to take the risk. The girls, though, had been living together previously. "They were separated because Minnie is more wild than Winnie," he explained, "and Lynn thought she was making Winnie less dog-like." Lynn did not like this because she enjoyed being able to walk out her back door and play with Winnie. She was also left as a puppy outside the sanctuary several years ago, but unlike the other coyotes, Lynn had spent a lot of time playing with her as she grew into an adult, and she now acted more like a pet dog than a wild coyote around Lynn.

Lynn's influence over the sanctuary ran deep and extended beyond desired effects such as taming Winnie.[21] When I first started volunteering there, Lynn was staying in a rehab facility for an unspecified illness. Tim was hesitant to discuss her financial situation because he wanted to respect her privacy, but he intimated that her situation was somewhat tenuous because her insurance company was planning to quit paying for her care. "She's kind of in the same situation as these animals," he said, waving his arm to indicate he was referring to the animals at the sanctuary. When I asked him what he meant, he said, "Well, if she were to die, the sanctuary would have to shut down immediately. I don't think she has much to leave behind to keep it running. And if she dies, I'm afraid all the animals would have to be put down."

Conditions definitely could have been better at Quiet Glen, especially compared to the other sanctuaries I visited, and Lynn was aware that the sanctuary did not make a very good impression on outsiders. I was forbidden from taking photographs while there. Lynn made this rule clear to all visitors because she was worried that, in her words, "They'll come after me." Donald told me that while cruising the web, she once found pictures a visitor had taken at the sanctuary and was upset they had been posted without permission. Others reflected this concern over judgment of the quality of care Quiet Glen provides to its animals. Though I said nothing critical about the conditions of the sanctuary, Tim seemed to guess what my first impressions were while he was showing me around after we were done with the coyotes. "It's not pristine, but all the physical and mental needs of the animals are being met," he said.

Quiet Glen could have served as a model at the Care Conference to illustrate all the problems the presenters wanted future sanctuary operators to be prepared to address before founding their own sanctuaries. Aside from the general lack of cleanliness and dilapidated infrastructure, for example, the captive conditions of animals like the fox and the coyotes showed that the caregivers were not actually able to attend to the psychological well-being of all their animals. Despite their new enclosures, the coyotes displayed stereotypic behavior similar to that of the fox, darting back and forth in a straight line from one end of their cage to the other. Even though there was more space in the newer enclosures, they were located in the center of the sanctuary and were made of cyclone fencing that left the coyotes, like the fox, visible to anybody who walked by. The limitations on freedom of movement and the ability to avoid human proximity imposed on these animals were noticeably steeper at Quiet Glen than they were for most of the animals at the other sanctuaries I visited. Given how long the fox had been living like this, it seemed probable that these conditions would continue to be the status quo in these animals' future, at least as long as the sanctuary continued to exist. Resting as it did on Lynn's continuing survival, the existence of the sanctuary itself was also precarious. As Tim had pointed out, there was no contingency plan in place to guarantee the continued operation of the sanctuary if Lynn died. Unlike Rainbow Haven, for example, where Olivia had set up a trust to enable the sanctuary to continue to operate in perpetuity, the lives of all the animals at Quiet Glen were tied directly to Lynn's—a situation that, as Susie suggested, is poised for disaster, particularly for the animals. Sadly, a year after my time volunteering at Quiet Glen, I learned that Lynn had died. Fortunately, state animal welfare officials and other sanctuaries in the area worked together to find new homes for all the animals. This, of course, would not be an option for facilities located in areas without the same safety net of other rescue organizations to lend assistance.

## Sacrifice and Solidarity

Toward the beginning of her discussion of a sanctuary's advocacy mission, Susie told the audience, "In practice, the first priority of a sanctuary is the animals' comfort and safety." However, she later confronted the attendees with a potentially controversial statement that seemed to contradict this earlier idea: "We've saved about five hundred animals. Out of 9 billion killed every year, that's basically zero percent. We're doing what we're doing to educate people to get them to stop eating meat," she said. "There's so many little sanctuaries popping up, but if you're not doing education and outreach, it's not a sanctuary— then the animals are just your pets. Don't try to become a sanctuary if you're not going to do advocacy. Sanctuaries play a very special role in this movement—we're here to get people to stop eating animals, that's our job, that's our only job."

Many of the people in the audience nodded in agreement, and nobody challenged this statement. Indeed, the idea that sanctuaries are a tool for educating people about better treatment of animals is common throughout all the sites where I worked. It also, however, highlights the deepest tension in the conflicting facets of the figure of the animal subject of care and rescue. The idea that getting people to stop eating (or otherwise mistreating) animals is the only (or even primary) goal of the sanctuary movement reflects a vision of its mission in which individual animal subjects are enlisted to a cause that they did not sign up for, even if it ultimately might benefit them and their fellow animals still consigned to the realm of *bestia sacer*. It is a tension that the sanctuary movement may not be able to resolve but only reproduce. As the act of rescue transforms animal objects into animal subjects, the sanctuary's advocacy mission simultaneously reinscribes them as a different kind of object in service to an alternative value system. When Susie said that sanctuary animals' well-being was their number one priority and that their only goal was to get people to stop eating animals, she was not contradicting herself so much as reflecting the contradiction at the heart of the movement—the multifaceted figure of the animal that is simultaneously a subject of rescue and care in a co-constitutive relationship with human rescuing subjects as well as a sympathy-eliciting object suspended in financial and ethical systems of value.

Focusing specifically on farm sanctuaries, but offering a critique relevant to other kinds of sanctuaries as well, Sue Donaldson and Will Kymlicka describe this dynamic as the "refuge + advocacy" model and propose that sanctuaries endeavor to implement an alternative "intentional community" model in which sanctuary animals are co-citizens with humans in the sanctuary space.[22] As they explain, the models they present are analytical constructs—"a framework for analyzing sanctuary practices"—rather than descriptions of actual sanctuaries,[23] but they draw the features of the "refuge + advocacy" model from practices at actual sanctuaries. They identify four domains in which they argue many farm animal sanctuaries "have often adopted unduly paternalistic policies that may diminish the wellbeing of their animal residents, and violate their right to exercise meaningful control over their lives."[24] Specifically, these entail limitations on animals' ability to associate or interact with other animals,[25] on animals' ability to engage in sexual reproduction and offspring rearing, on animals' ability to move freely throughout and fully experience the sanctuary environment, and on animals' ability to engage in what may feel to them like meaningful or fulfilling forms of labor.[26] As this chapter and the preceding ones have shown, the first three domains have shaped human–animal interactions at my main field sites, as a result of both human efforts to place limitations on animals (for their well-being or the well-being of others) and animals exercising agency within these domains in ways that shape and influence the conditions of their care. The fourth domain, which Donaldson and Kymlicka summarize as "work," relates to the idea that animals may find significance or personal satisfaction by engaging in activities that caregivers might try to avoid because they consider them exploitative.[27] Some of the activities that they identify as potentially qualifying as meaningful work to animals, such as chickens laying eggs that are used to feed other members of the community or older animals caring for younger animals or socializing new arrivals at the sanctuary, are activities I also frequently noticed across my field sites.[28] However, it is also true that caregivers refrained from what they would have perceived as exploitative activities, such as selling eggs or wool for profit or otherwise relating to animals as lively commodities.

The crux of Donaldson and Kymlicka's critique of sanctuaries with features of the "refuge + advocacy" model is that, in general "they have focused intensively on keeping animals safe and on meeting their basic needs" and "have focused much less attention on imagining different possible lives for animals, and on enabling animals to tell us how they want to live and to contest our ideas of what they need."[29] Essentially, they argue that this approach to sanctuary care treats animals more like wards than citizens.[30] As they note, "increased freedom and choice for animals brings increased risks—of predation, of injury, of fear or confusion. But as Jonathan Balcombe has said, the best life is not the safest life."[31] What they see as missing in the emphasis on safety through "protection from harm, neglect, exploitation, commodification, or instrumentalization, and through provision of basic needs" is "a commitment to creating communities that are more spacious, complex, varied, open, unpredictable, and free, in which animals are actively enabled to have a say in how they will live."[32]

To achieve this goal, they argue, it is necessary to "move away from ideas of sanctuary as refuge to sanctuary as a new kind of intentional community whose future directions can be shaped by all of its members."[33] This "intentional community" model, "in which the perimeter/ fences aren't markers of captivity, but rather boundaries that can actually support agency and flourishing," would require

> setting up the conditions under which the animal residents, as individuals and groups, can indicate to us how they want to live, rather than us imposing preconceived ideas of what they need or want based on alleged species norms, or on our ideas of what constitutes acceptable risks, desirable freedoms, and possible kinds of flourishing. It means starting from the basic assumption that, under the right conditions, animals may often be in a better position than we are to figure out how they want to live, and in ways that we may be unable even to imagine. . . . The first and most fundamental step is to recognize animal residents as full and equal members of the community, with a right to help shape the community. This is impossible if paternalistic decisions regarding safety, resources, or human convenience continuously limit animals' freedom and agency—their ability to explore ways of living, and communicate to us what they want.[34]

It is true that few sanctuaries, if any, provide animals with the ideal conditions of Donaldson and Kymlicka's "intentional community" model, although many might come closer than their binary analytical constructs would suggest. As the first three chapters of this book have, I hope, demonstrated, animals are already shaping the conditions of their care despite and in response to caregiver choices that may qualify as "paternalistic." This is not to say their agency is not constrained and limited, but caregivers are listening to animals, and sometimes animals are making themselves heard even when the caregivers fail to listen. And to be clear, Donaldson and Kymlicka do acknowledge that sanctuaries they visited "fall along a continuum, displaying features of both models, to varying degrees."[35]

Despite their failure to meet the ideal conditions of intentional communities and to always provide the full range of citizenship rights to animals, I would argue that many sanctuaries still function as multispecies communities of co-citizens working through the challenges of balancing animals' physical and emotional well-being under conditions of captivity. But even if all the goals of the "intentional community" were attainable (and it is not clear that the dilemmas of captivity can all be resolved sufficiently to make that possible), it may be difficult, if not impossible, for caregivers to fully move away from the idea of sanctuaries as places of refuge given the massive scale and pervasive impacts of the many kinds of violence perpetrated by humans against animals that are a "constant specter hanging over and motivating sanctuary work."[36] Donaldson and Kymlicka are correct that treating animals "as agents, as members, and as co-creators of ongoing, shared communities leads to very different outcomes than viewing them as refugees in need of humanitarian care," but in practice, many sanctuaries are doing both at the same time, while finding it challenging to entirely forgo the latter.

The treatment of animal subjects is also not the only impediment to a fully intentional community as Donaldson and Kymlicka conceive it. Just as there is the figure of the animal that is simultaneously a subject of rescue and care and an ambassador for education and fundraising, there is also a second contradictory figure at the heart of the sanctuary movement mirroring this first one, but obscured by the sanctuary mission focus on animals: the human rescuing subject who is often expected to sacrifice time and even physical and emotional well-being for the benefit of the animals. If sanctuary caregivers are

co-citizens in the multispecies sanctuary community, then they may
be what political theorist Wendy Brown calls "sacrificial citizens,"
a concept she uses to describe the ethos of citizenship under neo-
liberalized democracy that expects citizens to act as "responsibilized
human capital" willing to make sacrifices to serve the requirements
of the economy.[37] In her explanation of sacrificial citizenship, Brown
articulates specific examples that reflect the same general acquies-
cence to austerity measures that may be asked of the caregivers Susie
described who are expected to dedicate themselves fully to sanctuary
work:

> While, in transition from liberal to neoliberal democracy, citizen
> virtue is reworked as responsibilized entrepreneurialism and
> self-investment, it is also reworked in the austerity era as the
> "shared sacrifice" routinely solicited by heads of state and heads
> of businesses. Such sacrifice may entail sudden job losses, fur-
> loughs, or cuts in pay, benefits, and pensions, or it may involve
> suffering the more sustained effects of stagflation, currency
> deflation, credit crunches, liquidity crises, foreclosure crises,
> and more. "Shared sacrifice" may refer to the effects of curtailed
> state investment in education, infrastructure, public transporta-
> tion, public parks, or public services, or it may simply be a way
> of introducing job "sharing," that is, reduced hours and pay.
> Regardless, as active citizenship is slimmed to tending oneself
> as responsibilized human capital, sacrificial citizenship expands
> to include anything related to the requirements and imperatives
> of the economy.[38]

The labor demands that can be made on sanctuary workers create expectations similar to those directed at Brown's responsibilized human
capital. If the caregiving relationship forged between humans and animals creates a posthuman citizenry within the space of the sanctuary,
then arguably, caregivers who are expected to behave as responsibilized human capital (albeit for the benefit of the animals and the fur-
therance of the sanctuary's mission rather than the imperatives of the
larger economy) are in effect sacrificial citizens.

Running a successful sanctuary requires a lot more than a passion
for animals and a willingness to take them in. As described in this
chapter, financial concerns, in particular, place a range of limitations

on sanctuaries, especially on the goal of removing animals from capitalist regimes of animal commodification. This is why many sanctuaries find it necessary to enlist animals into the fund-raising process to garner enough donor interest and support to continue operating, and financial constraints and inadequate staffing and management can also place limits on sanctuaries' abilities to fulfill their missions. As my experience in Florida illustrates, no amount of goodwill can compensate for the deteriorating conditions of an overburdened sanctuary, and the animals are not the only ones affected in such circumstances. Caregiver sacrifice may become a necessity for sanctuaries struggling with too little staff and resources or too many animals, which are really two ways of describing the same dilemma. If this makes caregivers into sacrificial citizens, then their participation as such in the sanctuary community plays an essential role in making the kinds of intersubjective relationships that transform animals from *bestia sacer* into sanctuary citizens of their own, even while their use as sympathy-eliciting mechanisms for generating funding also helps to keep them suspended as improperty within the spectrum between property and subjecthood.

Brown's concept of sacrificial citizenship is useful here because caregivers must make sacrifices for the requirements of the larger interspecies community at times, but it only tells part of the story. Sanctuary humans care for other animals because they care *about* other animals. They choose to do sanctuary work because they support the mission of sanctuaries, and we must not forget that many of them are volunteers who do the work for free. But even the full-time, paid workers choose the work out of a commitment to the sanctuary mission. For this reason, they can be understood to be participating in and building what anthropologist and labor studies scholar Kendra Coulter calls "interspecies solidarity."[39] Susie's emphasis on the importance of treating sanctuary employees well certainly reflects caregiver concerns about their labor and how it affects them physically, mentally, and financially, as I have seen firsthand during my fieldwork. But it is also true that caregivers willingly and often happily accept some of the sacrifices they make to help the animals they care about and for, and this choice also reflects their commitment to transforming the social status of animals more broadly—the socially transformative goal of the sanctuary mission that Susie emphasized. In accepting the human costs of their sanctuary work, caregivers actively forge solidarity with the non-human sanctuary co-citizens. As Coulter argues,

> akin to care ethics, interspecies solidarity can be understood as both an activity and a political value. . . . Individual acts of solidarity matter, and they can disrupt dominant perceptions and power relations. They can also set a domino effect in motion which propels a broader set of processes. Moreover, solidarity can prompt and inform larger, collective forms of political work. Caring can be and can become political. . . . [Interspecies solidarity] is an invitation to broaden how labor as both a daily process and a political relationship is understood and approached. Accordingly, interspecies solidarity is both a path and the outline of a destination that encourages new ways of thinking and acting, individually and collectively, that are informed by empathy, support, dignity, and respect.[40]

Indeed, as acts of interspecies solidarity, caregiver sacrifices can actually be an important part of the depropertizing subject-making relationships formed through sanctuary care. It is not that they *should have to* make sacrifices to forge solidarity, but in the current political–economic structure, it is unavoidable. Humans and other animals are both subject to the exploitative processes of capital in different ways, but sanctuary caregivers are willing to accept the personal costs that system imposes on sanctuary work to challenge systems of animal exploitation. To the extent that this makes them into sacrificial citizens, however, it is important to note that it is a departure from Brown's conceptualization of this category in that they are sacrificing for a political goal other than the ongoing upward accumulation of capital. For this reason, caregivers' roles as sacrificial citizens in the sanctuary community need not be an impediment to the realization of an intentional community of fully equal co-citizens. It is a hard fact that sanctuary resources are limited. But as long as the sacrifices caregivers make are made with knowledge and consent as reasonable concessions to the actual resource limitations of sanctuaries rather than the result of mismanagement, and fair dignified treatment of caregivers is a guiding value of the sanctuary mission, those choices can contribute to building a broader interspecies solidarity and make sanctuaries an important part of what Coulter describes as "a new kind of intersectional, interspecies politics that sees diverse people and animals seeking justice and fairness side by side."[41]

There is one more impediment to the realization of the intentional community ideal for many sanctuaries, and it involves a very different kind of sacrifice in sanctuary work that I have not yet addressed. The next chapter explores this final paradox of sanctuary care: the fact that saving animals' lives sometimes requires sacrificing animal lives.

A curious rescued sheep. We Animals.

## Chapter 4
# Animal Death

"It's weird, but sanctuaries are actually full of death. A lot of things have to get killed at sanctuaries," said Seth, one of the Rainbow Haven interns. Responding to a question from me about what had surprised him most about sanctuary work, Seth immediately articulated one of the central paradoxes of animal care. Sanctuaries, by definition, are spaces designed explicitly to foster life, but death is as woven into the fabric of sanctuaries as the practices of care that keep animals alive. As examined in the previous chapters, care routines at sanctuaries are generally guided by the goal of giving animals better lives than they previously had.

Drawing on Agamben, I have argued that animal sanctuaries provide animals with zones of exception where animals can be protected to some extent from the deprivations of the realm of *bestia sacer* that exists outside of sanctuaries. Although sanctuaries may shield their chosen animals from the conditions of bare life, this does not mean that sanctuary animals are also shielded from the effects of biopower. Foucault describes biopower as the "power to foster life or disallow it to the point of death."[1] As I have shown in previous chapters, in the course of employing a range of biopolitical practices, sanctuaries face many dilemmas that require them to make difficult decisions about how best to foster life. This chapter focuses on one of the most difficult dilemmas for caregivers to navigate: fostering the life of certain animals sometimes requires sacrificing the lives of others. These dilemmas arise in situations in which caregivers must kill animals to feed others, kill animals to protect others, and kill animals to "save" them from their own pain and suffering. Caregivers respond to these dilemmas with a specific mode of care I call necro-care.

## Necro-care

The fact that sanctuaries are, in Seth's words, "full of death" is counterintuitive since sanctuary caregivers oppose a range of modern practices that they see as relying on animals' killability. Approximately 55 billion animals (9 billion terrestrial animals and 46 billion marine animals) are killed for food annually in the United States,[2] and approximately 3 million unadopted animals are killed each year in U.S. shelters.[3] The death toll is so large that many animal activists see it as a form of genocide, invoking comparisons to the Holocaust or the institution of slavery in the Americas.[4] Expanding on these analogies, an anonymous quote often attributed to the direct-action activist group the Animal Liberation Front situates "animal liberators" in an activist lineage with those who opposed slavery and the Holocaust: "If we are trespassing, so were the soldiers who broke down the gates of Hitler's death camps; If we are thieves, so were the members of the Underground Railroad who freed the slaves of the South; And if we are vandals, so were those who destroyed forever the gas chambers of Buchenwald and Auschwitz."[5] One controversial example of activist efforts to highlight similarities between the Holocaust and animal agriculture was a 2003 photo exhibit called *Holocaust on Your Plate* produced by Matt Prescott with the support of PETA. The exhibit was composed of sixty square panels with photos of animals in factory farms and slaughterhouses next to photos of prisoners in Nazi concentration camps. Prescott explains that the "methods of the Holocaust exist today in the form of factory farming where billions of innocent, feeling beings are taken from their families, trucked hundreds of miles through all weather extremes, confined in cramped, filthy conditions and herded to their deaths."[6]

It is worth noting that there are legitimate historical linkages underlying these analogies. Cary Wolfe argues that such examinations of the parallels between the technological manipulation of life in factory farms and Nazi concentration camps highlight how "practices of modern biopolitics have forged themselves in the common subjection and management of both human and animal bodies."[7] In fact, he elaborates, the organizational structure of the processes Nazis used to kill the victims of the Holocaust were "derived from production models developed by Henry Ford (a notorious anti-Semite), who in turn reveals in his autobiography that the inspiration for his assembly-line method came from a visit to a Chicago slaughterhouse and witnessing its mechanized disassembly line for making meat out of animal carcasses."[8]

However, there are a number of problems with such analogies. As a rhetorical argument intended to shift perspectives about animal treatment, their persuasive power is undermined by the fact that they offend people who see the comparison as trivializing these historical events at best, or even worse, dehumanizing the human victims of these atrocities by suggesting their suffering and deaths are no more significant than those of nonhuman animals. For example, in response to PETA's *Holocaust on Your Plate* exhibit, Abraham Foxman, the national director of the Anti-Defamation League and himself a Holocaust survivor, said,

> [The exhibit is] outrageous, offensive and takes chutzpah to new heights. . . . The effort by PETA to compare the deliberate systematic murder of millions of Jews to the issue of animal rights is abhorrent. Rather than deepen our revulsion against what the Nazis did to the Jews, the project will undermine the struggle to understand the Holocaust and to find a way to make sure such catastrophes never happen again.[9]

Furthermore, these comparisons also elide significant differences between modern treatment of animals and historical events like the Holocaust. Roberta Kalechofsky, a member of Jews for Animal Rights, makes this point in her response to the *Holocaust on Your Plate* exhibit:

> While I sympathize with PETA's aim—and am a member of PETA—I objected to this use of the Holocaust. . . . The agony of animals arises from different causes from those of the Holocaust. Human beings do not hate animals. They do not eat them because they hate them. They do not experiment on them because they hate them, they do not hunt them because they hate them. These were the motives for the Holocaust. Human beings have no ideological or theological conflict with animals.[10]

Despite the historical links between industrial animal slaughter and the Holocaust noted by Wolfe, as well as the structural parallels in both the magnitude of individuals killed and the techno-organization of the processes of killing, modern animal agriculture enterprises are unique from events like the Holocaust in that they use death as a means of resource extraction.

Noting that there is in fact a poverty of language in how we discuss practices like industrialized animal agriculture, Dinesh Wadiwel argues,

> While we might point to resemblances between examples of human violence toward other humans—such as concentration camps—and draw parallels to human violence towards animals in industrialised slaughter and experimentation, there are of course limitations. Indeed a focus on these comparisons not only reveals a poverty of language in describing the horrors that are imposed upon animals, but misses the fact that our use of animals contains specific modalities of violence that cannot be compared, in any way, to contemporary instances of violence towards humans. In the most direct sense, we breed animals on an industrial scale to be killed and eaten, something that cannot be compared to any contemporary forms of human violence towards other humans . . . [because what] we do to animals exceeds and goes beyond human violence towards other humans.[11]

Agricultural animals are killed as part of the process of value production, not to exterminate their species from the face of the earth. And while these animals, much like enslaved humans, are treated as living property, the surplus value they generate—derived from the flesh and secretions of their bodies and the bodies of their progeny—comes not from productive animal labor as much as the reproductive animal labor invested in producing animal bodies. Animal agriculture is an extractive industry that treats animal bodies as self-replicating living resources. Their deaths are a means to the end of extracting value from their bodies,[12] but—unlike the Holocaust—death of the population targeted with killing is not an end in itself.[13]

Because they currently do rely on the production of both life and death, contemporary animal economies draw equally from both poles of biopolitics. On one hand, as Wolfe argues, "the practices maximizing control over life and death, of 'making live,' in Foucault's words, through eugenics, artificial insemination, and selective breeding, pharmaceutical enhancement, inoculation, and the like are on display in the modern factory farm as perhaps nowhere else in biopolitical history."[14] On the other hand, such practices also typify what political philosopher Achille Mbembe calls necropolitics, "the contemporary forms of the subjugation of life to the power of death," or necropower.[15] Feeling that the notion of biopower is insufficient to account for these forms of subjugation, Mbembe employs this notion to account for the contemporary creation of *"death-worlds,* new and unique forms of social existence in which vast populations are subjected to conditions of life conferring upon them the status of *living dead.*"[16] Mbembe's model of death-worlds is "late-modern colonial occupation," such as the contemporary occupation of Palestine,[17] with its concatenation of multiple forms of power: "disciplinary, biopolitical, and necropolitical."[18] Although focusing their power on radically different populations of living beings, animal economies also combine these multiple forms of power in the creation of death-worlds in which animals are also made to live until and *so that* they can be killed in order to extract surplus value from their bodies, conferring on them a similar status of living dead.[19]

It is this status that sanctuaries seek to negate through their rescue of and care for animals. Yet even within sanctuaries, death is inescapable. Sanctuaries in many ways function as life-worlds juxtaposed against the death-worlds of modern animal economies, but they, too, employ forms of necropower against certain animals in order to foster the lives of others. In his study of breeding programs for the endangered whooping crane, Thom van Dooren writes that the care necessary for fostering the reproduction of future generations of cranes is often "intimately and inextricably entangled with various forms of violence," sometimes even necessitating the sacrifice of other species for the benefit of the cranes.[20] Care for certain animals often coincides with the "domination, coercion, and abandonment of" other animals, giving rise to what he calls "regimes of violent care."[21] Expanding on Van Dooren's conceptualization of this interconnection between practices of care and practices of violence, I have identified a more specific form of violent care that actively employs death in the service of fostering life: necro-care.

## Sacrificial Others

One significant component of violent care that Van Dooren identifies is the practice of sacrifice, although sacrifice in this context does not necessarily lead to death. To successfully breed whooping cranes, conservationists have found it necessary to require captive birds to live in "diminished environments and be exposed to ongoing stresses, including artificial insemination," a potentially violent experience for birds, especially if they actively resist.[22] These captive breeding cranes live a "sacrificial life" in the sense that it is a "life given, and not by one's own choice, for the good of others."[23] Although they are not killed—indeed, they are intentionally kept alive through regimes of biopolitical care—their lives are nonetheless sacrificed as part of an effort to care for their species. "Sacrificial surrogates" from other species are also enlisted into the breeding project. At one location, a quail colony was established to act as "royal tasters" to test new batches of feed for the whooping cranes "to ensure their desirability and safety . . . after an incident in which a new batch of food was contaminated by microtoxins" that sickened the cranes.[24] The use of individual animals in this way is the result of "species-thinking,"[25] a specific kind of "sacrificial logic" that "positions individual organisms of both the endangered species in question and numerous other species . . . as 'killable' in the name of the greater good of conservation."[26] This logic guides the choice to use "individuals from a range of other species of 'least-concern.'" While "least-concern" is a conservation category designated by the International Union of Conservation of Nature to assert that "a species is not presently at risk of extinction," it also functions as an "ethical taxonomic category" that marks "individuals of these species as available and expendable forms of life in the service of other, more needy, beings."[27]

Although not based on official designations, some sanctuaries also create categories of sacrificial others when caregivers weigh the interests of rescued animals against those of other animals of less concern to the sanctuary mission. Meeting the specific dietary needs of different animal species, for example, introduces a unique dilemma for sanctuaries that care for carnivores.[28] Sanctuaries with carnivores must contend with the fact that some animals need to die so that others may eat. In these situations, the sacrifice of some animals to foster the lives of others constitutes necro-care, a unique mode of care in which the death of certain individuals is an integral part of care for others.

At Texas Companion Rescue, feeding animals does not require that caregivers kill animals themselves, though they do need to provide their animals with meat-based food. Cats are obligate carnivores, meaning they must consume meat to survive. Dogs are omnivorous, but their nutritional needs are most easily and affordably met with a meat-based diet as well. There are actually debates in vegan circles over the practicality and ethics of putting cats and dogs on vegan diets. Although more expensive than regular food, commercial vegetarian and vegan dog food products exist that can provide a nutritionally balanced diet for most dogs with no health complications. Whether a dog is content on such a diet is a more open question. Cats, on the other hand, generally do not do as well on plant-based diets. Some vegans claim to have successfully gotten their cats to adopt diets of specially formulated vegan food that meets all of their nutritional needs, but I have personally known vegans who had a difficult time getting their cats even to try vegan food. Vegan diets can also lead to serious health complications for many cats. The author of a book on raising vegan cats confided in me that he had to put his cats back on a carnivorous diet after they developed health problems. Similarly, for many years, I had a feline companion named Panza who had a chronic urinary tract condition that required specially formulated cat food, making a vegan diet impossible, even if I had been willing to impose it on him. Most cats and dogs at Texas Companion Rescue are therefore fed regular commercial pet food. Dogs and cats with special medical requirements eat prescription pet food, but these are also meat based.

Roosevelt Farm Sanctuary, on the other hand, is like most farm sanctuaries in that it has no carnivorous animals, aside from a few barn cats. Some animals, like chickens, ducks, and turkeys, hunt for insects and will eat meat if it is provided, but their health can be easily maintained with an all-plant-based diet. Pigs are also omnivorous, though Roosevelt's pigs thrive on a diet of commercial grain pellets, produce donated by a nearby grocery store or traded for sanctuary-produced compost with a nearby farm, and leftover prepared food from a local Buddhist temple. Only the three barn cats at Roosevelt are provided with animal-based food since the relatively small number of rodents they catch and eat are not enough to meet their nutritional needs.

However, Rainbow Haven, like other exotic and wildlife rescue sanctuaries, has several omnivorous and carnivorous animals. Like the barn cats at Roosevelt, these animals sometimes find their own sources of meat. For example, Conan is an extremely friendly capuchin monkey who came to Rainbow Haven after being taken by humane law enforcement officers from somebody who was keeping him as a pet on the other side of the island. Conan was malnourished and living in a small, dirty cage when they found him. They contacted Olivia, the sanctuary director, and she agreed to take him in. He now lives in a spacious, multiroomed cage complex with slides, swings, grass-covered ground, and his own small cement pool of water. There is a small area immediately inside the cage that is separated from the living area by a locked gate. When feeding Conan and the two female macaques, Coco and Rita (also rescued together from a situation very similar to Conan's), who live in the contiguous cage, caregivers enter this area through a locked gate and then lock the gate behind them to make sure there are always two locked gates between the monkeys and the outside, a double precaution against escape. This is for their safety as well as the safety of others. Monkeys would be extremely difficult to catch in the verdant rain forest vegetation around the sanctuary. Aside from being both dangerous to and at risk of injury from humans and dogs, they would pose a potential danger to native animal species.

Each monkey gets a small metal dog bowl of various chopped pieces of fruits and vegetables, such as carrots, grapes, lettuce, bananas, avocados, and apples. Like Roosevelt Farm Sanctuary, Rainbow Haven receives daily donations of old produce from a local grocery store.

A rescued capuchin.
NEAVS.

The monkeys' meals vary by what's in the donation boxes each day. Sometimes, the donations include expired Oscar Meyer Lunchables boxes, which usually contain some combination of crackers, cheese, and lunchmeat. When this happens, the monkeys may also get a few small pieces of ham or cheese, though their diets as provided by caregivers are otherwise usually herbivorous.

The multiple levels of physical barriers to the monkey cages protect the monkeys from the outside world, but they do not necessarily protect the outside world from them. The sanctuary has a few dozen chickens who now live in their own fenced-in chicken yard, but they used to be allowed to roam free on the property. One day, Olivia told me, she was walking by the monkey cage with her mother, who was visiting from the mainland, when they noticed a curious chicken staring at the low stone wall that borders the cage. Conan had placed bits of food along the top of the wall outside the wire fencing of the cage and was patiently watching the chicken. As the chicken walked up close enough to the wall to peck at the food, Conan reached through the bars of his cage, grabbed the chicken's head, and pulled it off. Olivia and her horrified mother watched in surprise as Conan ate his prize.

The decapitated chicken was not the only bird to suffer an attack from Conan. Other times, when he was not quite quick enough, he only succeeded in scalping other chickens. Olivia bandaged their heads, using a honey poultice to hold the flap of skin against their skulls until they could heal. One of these chickens had to be fed separately from the other chickens because she was no longer fast enough to compete with the other ones for food. In addition to the chickens, who are no longer allowed near the monkeys, Conan uses his food bait trick to lure wild birds close enough to grab. Occasionally caregivers find feathers inside his enclosure, the only signs left from a successful ambush.

As Conan's bird hunting illustrates, the monkeys will eat meat, even though their diets are mostly plant based. One snack they particularly enjoy is spiders. Small, spiky crab spiders spin webbing throughout the sanctuary's many birdcages. Every few weeks, the webs must be cleared out. During these cleanings, caregivers collect the spiders in plastic containers and carry them over to the monkey cage. The monkeys know what is coming and gather by the wall of the cage in anticipation. They reach through the fencing, grabbing little handfuls of spiders and tossing them in their mouths like popcorn.

Rainbow Haven also has resident carnivores who cannot so easily catch their own prey and thus must have prey provided for them.

The sanctuary has a few birds of prey, who, like cats, are obligate carnivores. Siren is an 'io, or Hawaiian hawk. She lost a wing after getting hit by a car. The veterinarian who tried to treat her decided it was better to amputate rather than try to set her broken wing. After that, she was given to the sanctuary, where she has lived ever since. Hoot, a barn owl, and Pug, a pueo (a rare Hawaiian owl), also came to the sanctuary after being injured in accidents.

Pug, Siren, and Hoot all subsist on baby chickens and mice. Ideally, the birds would be able to hunt their prey before eating them. At least, this would provide them with the opportunity to engage in species-typical behavior that could potentially provide them with some psychological enrichment. However, to enable them to practice this species-typical behavior, it would be necessary to provide them with other live animals whose own subjective interests would conflict with those of the carnivores. In any situation in which animals are being fed to other animals, caregivers must make decisions about whose interests to prioritize. Olivia tries to strike a balance between the interests of the birds and the interests of the mice and baby chicks she uses to feed them, even while ultimately prioritizing the birds of prey. Caregivers first kill the chicks and mice as quickly as possible and then feed them to the birds. Although the interests of the mice and chicks are of less concern than the interests of the birds within the sanctuary's hierarchy of value, they are not entirely insignificant. They are a sacrificial population, but their interest in not suffering still influences caregivers' actions. On the other hand, while the mice and chicks likely die less painfully or traumatically than they would in the talons of a bird of prey, they still lose their lives. And while the birds are able to eat animals they might hunt in the wild, they are not able to experience the species-typical behavior of hunting prey. In this way, caregivers strike a compromise of sorts. Necro-care in this context requires the sacrifice of food animals, but it also allows for some consideration of their interests.

Pug and Siren are fairly shy around humans and are fed their mice and chicks in a tray, but Hoot, who does not seem to mind the presence of humans, gets to at least approximate the experience of hunting. Whoever is feeding her sticks the first body through the mesh of her cage, and she swoops over to grab the food with her talons. She then flies back to a branch in her cage to tear off pieces of meat. The person feeding her then opens the door to her cage and closes it on the neck of the second body, leaving the head sticking out of the cage. When she's ready, Hoot swoops back over and grabs the second body, pulling it loose from the head, which falls to the ground outside the cage. The next day, whoever comes by in the morning to feed other nearby animals tosses the decapitated heads into a small turtle pond at the bottom of Hoot's cage, where one of two eager turtles who live there immediately gobbles them down.

In addition to the turtles, Hoot shares her cage with two pheasants. Kristin, one of the veterinary interns, told me that Olivia also tried housing some quail with Siren, but one of the quail landed on a branch next to her, and she promptly ate it. While feeding the pheasants under Hoot one day, I was distracted by Seth talking to me from outside the cage. Standing in the enclosed space between Hoot's cage and a second pheasant cage, I turned to face Seth with my fingers still holding on to the door to Hoot's cage. Suddenly I felt something hit my fingers. Hoot had flown over and grabbed the wire around my fingers in her talons.

"What the hell?" I was startled but uninjured.

Seth chuckled. "Oh, she's just hungry. We didn't feed her yesterday. Birds of prey don't need to eat every day."

Several weeks later, I made the same mistake again. While Kristin was feeding Hoot a mouse, I leaned against the outside of the cage with my hand and suddenly felt a sharp pain in one finger. I pulled it away and turned to see Hoot clinging to the cage on the other side of where my hand had been. Although seemingly drowsy during the day, she gets quite alert when it's time to feed. There was a small bloody spot on one finger where I assumed she pricked me with the sharp tip of one talon. Although I at first thought this was an accident, I later saw Olivia demonstrate how she trained Hoot to land on an outstretched arm before receiving her food. She could land directly on bare forearms without breaking the skin. This led me to suspect that perhaps Hoot had intentionally pierced a finger that she had perceived as food. It was a good reminder that humans, too, can be food, even if the owl posed no real threat.[29]

The killing of mice and chicks so the hawk and owls can live reflects a difference in how these animals are valued. There are multiple dimensions to how this valuing unfolds. Siren and Pug both belong to endangered species, which from a conservation perspective could make them more valuable than the mice and chicks. All three birds of prey are also beautiful, majestic animals. They may not be quite big enough to qualify as charismatic megafauna—widely popular large animal species, like the giant panda, that are the zoological equivalent of celebrities—but the three birds do have an undeniable aesthetic appeal. On a more personal scale, Olivia helped save each bird from a medical condition that would have led to death in the wild. She named them and developed a personal connection to each bird as an individual subject. Olivia definitely derives value from their interactions, and the same may be true for the birds as well. All of these factors no doubt contribute to the birds' value vis-à-vis the mice and chicks. However, the biopolitical organization of the sanctuary also plays a significant role in shaping its hierarchies of value. The sacrificial element of necro-care employed in the feeding of carnivores creates two categories of animals: the sacrificed and the saved. As targets of the sanctuary's life-fostering biopolitical practices, the birds, as saved animals, are imbued with a kind of care value that cements them as animals of "most-concern." The mice and chicks, on the other hand, are too useful to the project of saving these animals to be saved themselves.

As suggested by the weighing of prey interests against the interests of the birds, being members of a sacrificial group of lesser concern does not mean that the mice and chicks are of no concern at all. Killing animals is not easy, no matter what category of care they belong to, as I further illustrate later in this chapter. Olivia has the baby chicks flown in from another island. She wraps a plastic bag around their shipping container and puts them in the large deep freezer in the barn. "They're killed with carbon dioxide and cold to make it painless and quick," she explained. Olivia breeds the mice herself. The fact that the mice are bred and cared for at the sanctuary until they are killed for food illustrates how flexible these categories of care can be. Mice cross over from a target of biopolitical care to an instrument of necro-care when their sacrifice becomes necessary for the care of the birds. To make their deaths as quick and painless as possible, Olivia or one of her interns kills mice by using their fingers to snap the mice's necks at the base of their skulls. They then put the mouse and chick bodies in Ziploc baggies and store them in the freezer portion of a refrigerator in Olivia's garage. They alternate feeding the birds mice and chicks, laying the baggy on the hood of a car to defrost in the sun before feeding them to the birds. The mice and chicks are members of a sacrificial population of food for other animals, but they are also subject to the life-fostering effects of biopower until their bodies are needed.

As mentioned, employing necro-care while navigating the dilemma posed by the conflicting interests between the saved and the sacrificed is not necessarily easy for caregivers. One time, I was in the barn, and Kristin called me over to help her in the room where the mice lived. She was "graduating" mice, which entailed choosing which mice were ready to be killed and putting them in a separate terrarium to await their deaths. She needed me to take the mice she was choosing and put them in the terrarium. While we worked, I asked Kristin if she had ever killed anything before coming to the sanctuary. "Yes," she said. "The lab where I worked does animal testing. I used to have to kill mice there when they needed to be euthanized." It was actually this work that had sparked Kristin's interest in veterinary care. She sees many forms of medical animal experiments as necessary and valuable research, but she was hoping to become a lab vet so she could work in labs to try to ensure animals suffered as little as possible.

Kristin's mouse selection process was partly guided by age—mice rarely die of old age at the sanctuary—and partly by which mice had cancer. As I helped her with the mice, she saw one that had a small tumor on his leg and handed him to me so I could place him in the terrarium. Tumors were very common, and Kristin kept an eye out for them, reasoning that it was good to try to weed cancer genes out of the breeding population and that these mice were going to die sooner anyway. She had killed several mice with tumors, and their bodies were laid out in a line. She pointed out some of the bulging little tumors to me. She encouraged me to touch one. It was harder than the surrounding tissue, but still furry and soft on the surface. The use of eugenics in the selection process is another aspect of necro-care at Rainbow Haven. On one level, the mice are being killed to foster the lives of other species, the various birds of prey who rely on them for sustenance. On another level, though, some of the same mice—the ones with cancer—are also being killed to improve the health of the overall population of other mice. The same act of killing, or sacrifice, simultaneously contributes to the biopolitical care of multiple groups.

In one sense, the eugenic rationale may also help further justify the act of killing, creating yet another ethical category to guide necro-care: the unhealthy genetic contagion in addition to the source of food for others. But this category produces its own dilemmas. One mouse Kristin killed had two large tumors on her sides, but Kristin realized right after killing her that she might have been the mother of a new batch of "pinkies," as the hairless, pink, altricial newborn mice are called. She showed me the dead mouse, a drop of blood trickling from her nose. She had one visible lump on her side, and Kristin pointed out that her nipples appeared to have been recently nursed. I could not see any milk, though, and did not have a frame of reference to which to compare them. Kristin was concerned about the pinkies that she may have just orphaned, worried that they would have no mother to care for them now. However, the ethical category created by the logic of eugenics also provided a way of coping with the dilemma it produced: "On the other hand," Kristin said, "I guess we don't want cancerous mice to be passing on their genes anyway. We'll have to wait and see what happens with the pinkies. If she was the mom, then we'll probably find them dead soon."

Kristin is also conflicted about using the mice for food. She likes them and genuinely feels bad for them when she finds tumors. Shortly before Olivia left to go on vacation with her husband for a few weeks, Kristin even put aside two older mice that were being bitten by the others in a small retirement cage. Olivia, smiling and mildly apologetic, told her they were still going to be food when she got back. Despite—or perhaps because of—this compassion, Kristin also has seemingly no hesitation in killing them with a quick neck snap as soon as she spots a tumor. Nobody named the mice (their sheer numbers would have made this impossible even if anyone wanted to), but Kristin's ambivalence about killing them at times created moments of inchoate individuality. The retirement home for the two old mice, the concern over the potentially orphaned pinkies—in these moments, particular mice became subjects of concern beyond their status as living food. These moments are temporary ruptures in the parallel mechanisms of sanctuary biopower. The care for rescued individuals that is at the core of the sanctuary's mission bled over into the necro-care directed at the population of bird fodder, blurring the boundaries between the two.

Such ruptures occurred at other moments as well. One time I was helping clean the other rodent cages near the mice, which contained several chinchillas, a few guinea pigs, and a rat, all of whom are permanent residents, not potential food. I was replacing the uneaten hay in their food trays and the sawdust in their toilet trays—the sanctuary composts all the rodent droppings and urine-soaked wood shavings. While I was working, Kristin was cleaning the mouse terrariums—six in total—and at one point a mouse escaped. I helped her catch him, but I knew he was going to be killed eventually anyway. At that moment, I personally felt the friction between the two modes of care. In capturing the mouse rather than letting him get away, I was preserving him to be sacrificed as a subject of necro-care. I helped clean the mice terrariums the next day, this time with Seth. I found a one-eyed mouse—normally the kind of injury that would be grounds for "graduation"—but rather than calling Seth's attention to him, I slipped him back in with the others before anybody could kill him. I was only deferring an inevitable death rather than the more permanent escape I could have allowed the escaped mouse, but in this case it felt like the equivalent of the choice I resisted the previous time. I told Seth afterward, and he later shared the story with Kristin. She teased me about it, but she was also quite serious about wanting to find the mouse so she could kill him. She felt that it would be putting him out of his misery. Following the one-eyed mouse incident, Kristin would not let me help with the mice again. She did not discuss it further with me, but I realized that by breaking the rules that one time, I was destabilizing the logic of sacrifice that enabled these practices of necro-care. By making such an exception for one mouse, I implicitly challenged the process that helped to remove personal responsibility from the decision-making process about when to kill a particular mouse. Whether or not it was her intention, removing me from the process guaranteed that I would not similarly disrupt the process again.[30]

Ethical choices about how to apply necro-care are also influenced by understandings of animal behavior derived from ethological knowledge about how animals act and hunt in "the wild." After Kristin had finished her internship, I learned that when the caregivers cleaning the terrariums find dead pinkies, they often feed them to Dot, the rat. A few days after I learned this fact about Dot and the pinkies, I brought it up with Olivia.

Amy, a new intern, suggested Olivia could show me, and Olivia reached into a mouse terrarium. Amy had replaced the three veterinary interns after their internship ended. She was a short, energetic woman in her late teens from Queens. Amy had finished high school and was now in the middle of a volunteer-traveling expedition before starting college. She found Rainbow Haven doing internet research on places in cool locations where she could volunteer. Unlike the previous interns, she was not interested in becoming a vet. She still wanted to work with animals someday, though, and was considering getting a license to do animal-assisted therapy with humans.

"Oh, no, is it a live baby?" I asked.

Olivia turned around quickly and was raising her hand up toward the rat cage as she came around. "Not anymore," she said. "I dispatched it." She handed the dead pinky to Dot, who snatched the body and went inside an empty toilet paper tube to eat it in privacy. I must have looked shocked, because Olivia became more serious and said, "In the wild, a rat would naturally eat them. If a rat finds a mouse nest, she clears it out. They're competition for food." In this case, ideas about what is "natural" for rat–mouse interactions helped to justify this sacrificial act of necro-care. Unlike the birds of prey, Dot did not need mouse protein to survive, but ideas about rat predation practices on mice further expanded the category of animals to whom the mice could be legitimately sacrificed. Dot got to eat the mouse both because she is a member of the category of saved animals to whom others could be sacrificed *and* because her eating mice is justified by scientific understandings of rat behavior privileged by caregivers, even though she did not actually need the mouse for nutrients.

## Euthanasia

Euthanasia—the killing of animals that are incurably sick or untreatably injured to spare them further suffering—is the most direct form of necro-care in that it directly affects the individual it is supposed to help; it literally transforms death into a form of care for that individual. Derived from the Greek words *eu* for "good" and *thanatos* for "death," it means "good death." For a being who can no longer live any semblance of a good life, a good death may be the best kind of care one can provide.[31] Euthanasia, however, can also function as a form of sacrificial necro-care for the benefit of others.

Kristin's reaction to my giving a temporary reprieve to the one-eyed mouse provides one example of how euthanasia contributes to the larger system of sacrifice in sanctuaries. As I explained, by breaking the rules for determining which mice would be killed, I implicitly challenged the process that helps to remove personal responsibility from deciding which animals are to be killed. This process protects individual caregivers from having to bear too much emotional weight for the necessary work of killing. In this context, the mouse needed to be sacrificed so as not to disrupt this responsibility-diffusing mechanism—he may have been euthanized in a literal sense because he was old and infirm (although it is debatable if his quality of life was so impaired that it justified a mercy killing on its own), but he was also euthanized as a sacrifice to the maintenance of the system that determines when euthanasia is applied.[32]

Euthanasia can also function as a form of sacrificial necro-care in relation to the material well-being of the larger sanctuary community. Roosevelt Farm Sanctuary intentionally tries to avoid this dilemma by aspiring to always privilege the veterinary needs of their animals over concerns about resource limitations. As illustrated by the story of Flower, the calf with leg braces described in chapter 2, Roosevelt commits to spending whatever resources are necessary to give the best life possible to each animal in its care. It does eventually decide to euthanize animals with untreatable medical conditions that severely impair their quality of life, but I did not hear of financial considerations ever influencing a decision to euthanize an animal while I was there. I was never present during a euthanasia procedure, but some of the animals I met while there were euthanized over the period of time I volunteered. For example, one day after arriving at the sanctuary, I learned that Rude Boy had been euthanized. Rude Boy was an elderly pig who had been brought to the sanctuary several years before by some anonymous rescuers who did not disclose where they found him. At first, I assumed he was euthanized because of his arthritis, which often forced him to crawl on his knees and required daily medication. The discomfort may have been a contributing factor to his general surly disposition—Rude Boy seemed to prefer to be left alone and would sometimes nip at volunteers who got too close. From occasional exchanges with different caregivers about his condition, I gathered that the staff was generally concerned about his quality of life, but they all seemed to agree that his joint pain was not so severe that euthanasia should be seriously considered yet. I assumed that his condition had worsened, but Theresa (the caregiver who introduced me to Flower) explained that they had taken him to the vet because he'd lost his appetite, and the vet discovered that his abdomen was full of inoperable tumors. This is when they finally decided to euthanize him, not because it would have been too expensive to treat his condition, but because they thought it would have been impossible to alleviate the severe pain and discomfort caused by the cancer.[33] Nonetheless, Rude Boy's death did free up space and resources at the sanctuary for other animals to be rescued in the future. Even when the death of an animal is not a result of sacrificial logic, the economies of resources that structure sanctuaries infuse all deaths with benefits for others.

Finally, euthanasia can function as a form of sacrificial necro-care when caregivers see keeping an animal in captivity as doing more harm than good. In chapter 2, I described how I participated in a letter-writing campaign on behalf of the dog Lamar, who had bitten a volunteer at Texas Companion Rescue. Although the organization eventually decided not to euthanize him, I later learned that another dog named Broxton who came into the shelter after I finished my fieldwork there was killed following a similar incident in which he bit another volunteer. A volunteer named Alba, a retiree who immigrated to the United States from Italy in the 1980s, tried to rally members of a private Facebook page for volunteers to lobby on his behalf, but this time, the lobbying was unsuccessful. Killing an animal for aggressive behavior is very rare at Texas Companion Rescue. The organization is explicitly guided by a No Kill philosophy, which means they never kill animals due to resource or space limitations like open admission shelters do. However, they also endeavor to minimize the amount of time animals have to be in the shelter before they can be adopted to a permanent home.

If an animal has been deemed too aggressive to be adoptable, then this necessarily means the animal will spend her whole life in the shelter, and, moreover, the animal will likely have less mobility and social stimulation than other animals in the shelter because only staff trained to deal with dangerous animals will be able to interact with her. In these circumstances, the animal's quality of life is a significant factor in the decision-making process. Dogs, in particular, do not do well living in a shelter environment for long periods of time. Some become noticeably despondent, while others that were previously amicable start to develop more aggressive reactions to humans and other animals. But once it has been decided that a dog is too dangerous to adopt, the shelter's economy of resources suddenly becomes a factor in the decision-making process as well. Permanently housing an unadoptable dog not only takes space and resources from adoptable dogs—essentially sacrificing those dogs instead if they cannot be pulled from the city shelter before they are killed—but it also takes human resources away from other animals in the shelter by requiring caregivers to spend time caring for the dog that could instead be used to care for other animals.

While I was not present for the deliberation over Broxton's fate—in fact, no animals were euthanized while I was volunteering there—based on conversations with staff and administrators about the euthanasia policy, it is most likely that the decision was primarily an ethical one shaped by the idea that a permanent shelter life could not be a good life and that, in fact, killing a dog in that situation would truly be an act of euthanasia. However, like the death of Rude Boy the pig, Broxton's death functioned as a sacrifice, albeit unintended, for the well-being of other animals in the shelter as well as future animals who had not yet been rescued. Indeed, the economies of resources in shelters and sanctuaries together with the vast populations of as-yet-unrescued animals outside of sanctuaries create a second economy, an economy of sacrifice in which every death in the sanctuary functions as a sacrifice for another animal that has yet to be rescued, while every life in the sanctuary functions as an ongoing sacrifice of all the animals that will not survive to take its place. The very limited finitude of sanctuaries' capacities to rescue and care for animals makes sacrifice unavoidable. Put simply, as Susie stated at the Care Conference in chapter 3, sanctuaries cannot save everyone, which means acts of euthanasia will always distribute care beyond the individual being euthanized. In this sense, the death could be understood as good for others as well as for the one who is dying.

## External Threats

Necro-care also plays a role in regulating how sanctuaries deal with animals outside their sphere of care, particularly uninvited guests who pose a threat to the safety of their rescued animals. For captive-bred animals repatriated to the wild from conservation programs, other animals are sacrificed through "habitat modifications," such as the killing of predators as well as competitors "to give released animals a better chance of survival."[34] "Predator control" plays an important role in the care practices of sanctuaries as well. The first line of defense is sanctuary architecture, which shapes animal spaces both to segregate animals that could harm each other within the sanctuary and to segregate all the animals within a sanctuary from potentially harmful external threats. When architecture is not sufficient to protect sanctuary animals, though, "predator control" may also require the sacrifice of certain animals.

The monkey cages at Rainbow Haven illustrate how the physical architecture of the sanctuary restricts the movement of animals to prevent them from endangering the welfare of others. Material infrastructures are equally important in preserving the safety of the animals they contain by keeping other animals out, though. Take, for example, the Norwegian brown rat *(Rattus norvegicus)*, a member of the muroid family of rodents. One of the most widely dispersed mammals on the planet, the brown rat can now be found virtually everywhere where humans have settled. The name is a misnomer derived from mistaken assumptions about its origins in the late eighteenth century—the brown rat most likely originated from central Asia. Brown rats are omnivores and thrive in close proximity to human habitations. Rats and their fellow muroids, mice, are perhaps the most common uninvited guests in sanctuaries. For these expert scavengers, the constant supply of grains, hay, and seed mixes needed to feed most herbivorous sanctuary animals is the ultimate jackpot. Rainbow Haven has a strict policy requiring that the door to the food storage closet remain closed whenever somebody is not in there filling food dishes. As Olivia warns, "it only takes a second for a mouse to run in when you're not looking. And then, when we find mouse poop, we have to clean out the whole closet and check every bag to be sure she hasn't had babies anywhere."

Unlike small mice, rats' appetites extend beyond the pillaging of animal feed. They will also kill for meat. Caregivers at Roosevelt Farm Sanctuary occasionally see rats, but they've had nothing like the rat problem that plagued Farm Sanctuary, where the Care Conference described in chapter 3 was held. As Susie explained to the attendees of the Care Conference, caregivers discovered that rats were gnawing their way into the chicken coops and dining on chickens at night. With the ability to exert approximately twenty-four thousand pounds of pressure per square inch, rat teeth are capable of chewing through solid materials such as wood, brick, cinder blocks, concrete, and aluminum. Rats are also capable of slipping through openings half an inch wide. To protect its chickens, the sanctuary had to construct chicken coops with a layer of steel mesh in between the outer and inner wooden walls and floor, and even then the coops were not impenetrable. Caregivers exercise constant vigilance, checking the coops for holes morning and night to ensure that no invaders came in while the chickens were sleeping and that they aren't trapping the chickens with a predator when shutting them in for the night. Roosevelt Farm Sanctuary also has had some issues with predators like bears, who have wandered onto the sanctuary property and broken into chicken coops in the past, but all the chicken shelters on the property are now bear-proofed with fences and solid doors.

Rainbow Haven has its own unique predator threat to deal with: mongooses. In one of the many examples of humans trying to alleviate an invasive species problem by fighting fire with fire, only to ignite a second equally destructive fire, humans introduced mongooses to Hawai'i in the mid-1800s. They hoped the mongooses would hunt rats, multiple species of which had come to the islands centuries before by boat with Polynesian settlers and later with European explorers. However, rats are nocturnal, while mongooses are diurnal. "Rather than forming a predator-prey dynamic that could rid the islands of rats and save native bird species from their predation, rats and mongooses together made bird hunting a 24-hour affair, with rats on the night shift and mongooses on the day shift."[35]

Mongooses are common in the area where Rainbow Haven is located, and one had killed a duck a few days before I began volunteering. As a facility that does endangered species rehab, which includes the three nenes (a species of goose native to the Hawaiian islands) at Rainbow Haven, the state requires the sanctuary to have a "predator control plan" in place to protect endangered species like the nenes. Olivia's control plan for the mongooses entailed catching them in cage traps and quickly killing them with a bb gun. Because mongooses are a nonnative species with no legal protection, addressing the problem of predator control with practices of necro-care is not only a viable solution but also a legally sanctioned one. Because the Hawaiian islands are, geologically speaking, relatively new volcanic formations, a large percentage of the animals on the islands are nonnative, which is defined in Hawai'i as "any species that were introduced to the islands with human assistance."[36] Merely being nonnative does not necessarily provide a sufficient legal basis for killing animals, however. Laws related to nonnative species often make a distinction between "nonnative" and "invasive," with the latter applying to species that pose a risk of ecological or financial harm. As other social scientists have observed, the concept of "invasive species" has been used to reinforce xenophobic spatial ideologies about who or what belongs within national boundaries, contributing to hierarchies of value that render certain species killable while protecting others.[37] While "invasive species" is not an official regulatory category in Hawai'i like it is under federal law, the state uses a synonymous category of "injurious wildlife" as a regulatory designation applied to any species "which is known to be harmful to agriculture, aquaculture, indigenous wildlife or plants, or constitute a nuisance or health hazard."[38] Designated as "injurious wildlife," mongooses in Hawai'i have historically been subjected to population management efforts that include trapping and killing or the use of a poison called diphacinone. Furthermore, because they are "injurious wildlife," such killing is allowed under the state's animal cruelty laws.[39] Hawai'i's animal cruelty statute prohibits mutilating, poisoning, or killing any animal "other than insects, vermin, or other pests; provided that the handling or extermination of any insect, vermin, or other pest is conducted in accordance with standard and acceptable pest control practices and all applicable laws and regulations."[40]

These conservation-oriented legal designations establish a framework for the taxonomic ethical categories that the sanctuary employs in targeting mongooses as objects of necro-care. "Species-thinking," legal requirements, legal exemptions, and the privileging of saved animals in the sanctuary hierarchy of value all work together to make the logic of sacrifice easier to implement in the application of necro-care: killing predators preserves the safety and well-being of rescued animals. The sanctuary's regime of care and violence and its differential impact on various animals emerges "out of the intersection of legal and ecological frameworks of value that render animals like mongooses killable and animals like nenes in need of saving."[41]

Aside from the significant threat to the actual safety of sanctuary denizens posed by animals like rats and mongooses, the other big issue related to uninvited guests at sanctuaries is the stealing of food. All of my field sites have ongoing rodent problems. Unlike Rainbow Haven, however, none of the other sites take overt action to kill invaders. Instead, they outsource pest control to their cats. Roosevelt has a few barn cats who spend most of their time hanging out in the visitor center and purring on people's laps, but they occasionally catch rodents or birds. Aside from cats, Roosevelt Farm Sanctuary's only other method of pest control is the use of live traps to catch (and release away from sanctuary property) an occasional rodent. This is because the vegan principles that shape the sanctuary's mission conflict with the intentional killing of other animals, even animals considered to be pests. Cats, however, provide a sort of ethical loophole since they cannot be stopped from hunting unless they are locked inside. Texas Companion Rescue also has a few free-roaming cats who catch the mice that live around the kennels, while the cats inside the cat adoption area probably rarely see a mouse brave enough to wander inside.[42]

In addition to its other methods of necro-care, Rainbow Haven has a mouser. Olivia told me the story of how the cat came to the sanctuary. She was assisting with a feral cat–neutering program to which she donates time and resources on the island, and they were neutering a very young kitten. Per the technicians' request, she took him home to make sure he came out of the anesthesia with no complications. When he woke up, he went completely wild and clung to her side with his claws. So she hung out with him in their bathroom until he finally mellowed out. She had not been planning to keep him after he recovered, but he endeared himself to her so much that she decided to adopt him. While relating this story, Olivia also mentioned that she got into an argument with representatives of the Hawaiian Division of Forestry and Wildlife (DOFAW) over their feral cat control methods. They told her that as a wildlife rescuer, she could not be in favor of saving feral cats.

"Yes, I can!" she said. "You just have to do it responsibly with public education about feeding and a good trap-neuter-return program." People are going to feed them anyway, she reasoned, and DOFAW's alternative was to kill them with trays of antifreeze, a solution she found completely unconscionable. It was easy to see why—antifreeze contains ethylene glycol, a sweet-tasting chemical that can cause kidney and brain damage, blindness, and ultimately death when ingested.

The use of certain sanctuary animals as agents rather than targets of necro-care blurs the sacrificial categories of food and pest. Aside from the cat, whom Olivia rescued and incorporated into the sanctuary regime of life-fostering care, Rainbow Haven has other animals who benefit from their own participation in rodent control. One day, while feeding the birds in the cages on the lawn, I noticed holes in the ground inside some of the cages. Mice were darting out of the holes and grabbing bits of birdseed that had fallen to the ground. I saw two mice inside the cage of Sadie and Squawker, a pair of eclectus parrots like Magma, who was introduced in chapter 2. Squawker has a green head but is otherwise featherless, a result of self-inflicted feather pulling like Magma's. Sadie is red and blue but still has all her feathers. Sadie has a southern accent she picked up from her previous human companions, and Squawker makes lion sounds he learned to imitate when he was kept near the lions at the Honolulu Zoo. One time I touched Sadie's back while I was in their cage refilling their food and water dishes, and Squawker showed me how he got his name by blasting a deafeningly loud shriek directly in my ear.

When I told Seth about the mice, he said, "We're going to have to kill them. I'm not happy about it, but Olivia said that's what we have to do." Kristin and I cleaned out the old food and feathers in the bottom of the cages to minimize mouse attractants, but that alone was not enough to address the problem. To get rid of the mice in the bird cages, the interns flooded the mice holes with a hose. When the mice ran out, Betsie, Olivia's Rottweiler, caught them and killed them with her teeth. Olivia trained her to bite them but not eat them. During this process, Betsie looked like she was chasing a ball, wagging her tail and making a game of chasing the mice. Turning the killing into a game and enlisting the participation of other animals can add more purpose to the act of killing—necro-care in this context not only prevents the spread of "vermin" in the sanctuary but also provides enrichment for Betsie. However, as Seth's ambivalence shows, it can also enhance discomfort with the act of killing by not affording it what some may consider the appropriate tone, such as somber necessity. In other words, for some participants, it risks making too light of an unsavory task even while for others it makes the task more palatable.

Sometimes sanctuary architecture and techniques of necro-care are still not enough to prevent external threats to sanctuary animals. After I left the sanctuary, I heard that Squawker had died from an unknown illness. The theory around the sanctuary was that one of the wild birds that occasionally rest on top of the cages on the lawn had defecated into Squawker and Sadie's water. Squawker may have contracted a zoonotic infection from bacterial or viral contamination in his water. If so, he died from an unwelcome invader that is too small to trap, by means of a vector that cannot be blocked by cage wire. Unlike the safety precautions in place around the monkey cages, it is extremely difficult to prevent wild birds from getting close enough to sanctuary birds to pass on contagious diseases.

Some uninvited guests, on the other hand, pose almost no problem at all and are allowed to coexist with the sanctuary animals. Despite their thievery, this is the case for the pigeons at Roosevelt Farm Sanctuary that roost in the barns and steal food when they get the chance. One day, I spotted a nest in the rafters outside the pig barn, and I told Jean, a caregiver from France. He worked on vegan outreach campaigns in France before immigrating to the United States, where he taught French at the elementary and middle school levels before moving to Roosevelt to work at the sanctuary. He looked in the nest to see if it was empty, in which case he might have moved it. But there was already an egg in it, so he left it alone. In the case of Roosevelt, ethicopolitical principles directly conflict with techniques of necro-care that could be used to keep out external threats. Choosing not to kill does not necessarily mean that death is avoided, though. Pigeons pose no threat to farm sanctuary animals, but as mentioned, rats do. Allowing a rat to live could lead to the death of chickens. In this context, choosing not to exercise necro-care would nonetheless lead to a fatal result.

At Rainbow Haven, one intruder causes minor annoyance but is still mostly ignored: the bufo toads, also known as cane toads. Another nonnative species, bufo toads are large, nocturnal, brown toads that can grow up to nine inches or more. They have paratoid glands running down their backs that secrete a toxin that can cause convulsions, paralysis, and death in other animals if left untreated. Dogs, in particular, are at risk of bufo poisoning because the toads are the perfect size to fit in a curious dog's mouth. I never saw any live ones during the day, but at night they were suddenly everywhere, sitting in the wet grass staring straight ahead. They seemed to be afraid of nothing, hopping languorously if you bumped one with your foot, but otherwise oblivious to any other animals around them.

None of the sanctuary animals seemed to care about the toads, but the very first step in the morning feeding routine was to rinse out the dog bowl that sat outside the barn. The toads would rest in the dog bowl at night, leaving behind enough toxin to sicken the dogs if they drank from it. Because they were so slow and oblivious to things moving around them, one would also accidentally end up under a car tire occasionally. In the morning, while walking up the long driveway to the barn, it wasn't unusual to see a flattened toad stuck to the concrete with its tongue sticking straight out in front of it. Usually the interns would pick the toads up by their tongues and fling them into the bushes. If nobody moved the carcass, though, it would bloat in the morning heat, rerounding out the toad's body like a balloon. Then, if a car happened to drive over it again, it would explode with an audible pop.

The toads are not direct targets of necro-care. Indeed, because they pose no real threat or competition to other animals, killing them could not contribute to the care of sanctuary animals in any meaningful way. Nonetheless, their status as part of the ethical taxonomic category of pest renders them necropolitically vulnerable. There is no reason to actively try to kill them, but neither are they legitimate subjects of life-fostering biopolitical care. Within the sanctuary, toads are neither savable nor sacrificeable—they are instead *bestia sacer.*

## Nidus

Olivia once told me that "the best part of the sanctuary is giving these animals the chance to be happy now. They've been through so much, and it just puts a huge smile on my face to be able to give them the chance to be happy." For a long time, I was not sure how to reconcile this with all the animals who died as a result of being at the sanctuary, like the mice and baby chicks killed for food or the mongooses and mice killed as pests. I was also confused about how the interns felt about killing animals. At times, they expressed ambivalence about it, but at other times, they seemed quite comfortable with it. When first meeting them, I naively assumed aspiring veterinarians would be committed to maximizing animal welfare in all circumstances. I did not anticipate that they would be willing to kill mice, shoot mongooses, and, at least in Kristin's case, work at an animal-testing facility. They revealed that a commitment to animal care can coexist with complex attitudes toward animals that simultaneously allow for compassion, concern, and empathy along with an ethical gradient on which different animal lives have different values in different contexts. Their use of taxonomical ethical categories of sacrificial and saved animals to guide decisions about how to practice necro-care—the use of the deaths of certain animals to facilitate the care of others— illustrated how complex hierarchies of value arise to make killing possible, if not unproblematic, within sanctuaries. The realization that there was a range of complex views and attitudes animal caregivers can simultaneously hold forced me to question my own presuppositions about animal death. I still feel most comfortable at farm sanctuaries where death is simply something to be avoided when possible, but this feeling is a luxury that caregivers at other kinds of sanctuaries do not always have.

Seth was right. It's weird, but sanctuaries are actually full of death. And sometimes, even in sanctuaries, it is necessary to kill animals so that others may live. Death suffuses these life-fostering regimes of care. One day, while we were scrubbing out the large, flexible, rubbery water troughs that the alpacas, llama, and goats drink from, Seth taught me a term from vet school that serves as an apt metaphor for the interpenetration of life and death that occurs in sanctuaries: *nidus.* Derived from the Latin word for "nest," nidus has several meanings, but he defined it as a site or foreign body around which minerals accumulate. A nidus provides the nucleus for formations such as bladder and kidney stones and pearls inside oysters. The inside of each trough was roughly textured from bits of string-like material that were embedded in the rubber. These pieces of fiber provided a perfect nidus for algae growth, requiring us to scrub the troughs several times a week. The conflicting needs of different animals (including humans) both within and around sanctuaries also provide a perfect nidus, in this case, for the accretion of death.

Animals may go to sanctuaries to escape certain deaths, but once there, they often encounter other deaths, because—as any ecosystem across the planet will show—life cannot exist without death, and life-fostering care often depends on necro-care. And as practices of necro-care make the interspecies communities that form within sanctuaries possible, they also require different kinds of sacrifices from both the human and nonhuman citizens of those communities. In the context of necro-care, caregivers may be required to sacrifice the comfort of simple moral convictions for the complex evaluations and decision-making that go into implementing necro-care, but some animals—sanctuary citizens and external animals alike—are required to give their lives for the benefit of other citizens of the community. This may at first seem to be an impossible-to-reconcile contradiction with the mission of many sanctuaries, but it actually reveals precisely how sanctuaries manage to accomplish rescuing and caring for thousands of animals: by balancing the larger goal of creating a better world for animals with responding pragmatically to the daily dilemmas of captive animal care within the political, economic, and social limitations of sanctuary life.

A rescued alpaca. We Animals.

# Conclusion
## Why Do Sanctuaries Matter?

In the contemporary United States, animals who have been entangled in property relations now have at least two possible modes of interfacing with human society: either as living property vulnerable to the deprivations of *bestia sacer* or as improperty suspended within the web of benefits and constraints of sanctuary communities. As zones of exception to the bare life of *bestia sacer*, sanctuaries provide spaces where animals can gain social and political lives as participants in interspecies communities formed around the unmaking of property-based human–animal relations. However, in unmaking these relationships, sanctuaries replace them with "intersubjective relationships of care that are still embedded both in a larger political-economic context fueled by multiple circuits of animal capital and in a larger socio-legal context in which animals remain classified as property."[1] While sanctuary animals cannot be fully unmade as property, within the spaces of sanctuaries, they also do not remain rights-less. Through intersubjective relationships of care, humans afford animals basic rights to life, sustenance, and freedom from harm, although animals often access these rights unevenly and inconsistently.

As I have shown, different kinds of rescue facilities have different approaches to the care of animals that influence this access in different ways. As a model of a No Kill companion animal shelter, Texas Companion Rescue focuses on the *temporary* rescue of companion animals so that they can be adopted out to live with human families in their homes. Because adoptability is central to this mission, animals in these kinds of facilities may face more limited autonomy than animals in other facilities because they must be socialized to humans and refrain from engaging in behavior that would make them less adoptable, even if that behavior is normal for their species (e.g., chasing prey). The primary benefits animals in these facilities receive are an ironclad guarantee that they will not be killed for lack of space (although, as the case of Broxton in chapter 4 illustrates, they may still be killed for other reasons) and that all of their physical needs will be met. Caregivers also work to socialize with the animals as much as possible to provide them with psychological stimulation and help them better adapt to living with humans.

The second kind of facility I examined was a sanctuary for exotic animals, Rainbow Haven. Unlike companion animal shelters, exotic animal sanctuaries provide permanent homes for animals that were purchased as pets or used for entertainment purposes. While facilities like Rainbow Haven try to provide the best lives possible for the animals in their care—meeting all of their physical needs, trying to minimize stress, and providing them with psychological stimulation—the fact that many of the animals in these facilities might hurt each other if they were to interact requires the shelters to segregate the animals and restrict their movement more than facilities without these kinds of animals would. These facilities also must make decisions about which animals are not protected by their commitment of care, since some of their residents eat meat, which thus requires the killing of other animals to feed them.

Finally, farm sanctuaries like Roosevelt Farm Sanctuary focus their efforts on caring for rescued agricultural animals. Unlike the animals at exotic sanctuaries, the species in farm animal sanctuaries are generally either herbivores or capable of thriving on an herbivorous diet (like pigs) and thus do not require the killing of other animals for their food. Because of industrial agricultural practices, though, these animals often develop injuries or illnesses that require invasive veterinary treatment. These kinds of sanctuaries tend to be the most committed to the most expansive liberationist views of human–animal relations, so caregivers are usually vegan or vegetarian and espouse explicit support for animal rights. The necessities of caring for animals in captivity, however, still place restrictions on how much autonomy they can afford the sanctuary animals, and many farm animal sanctuaries choose to privilege safety over freedom of movement in designing sanctuary infrastructure.[2]

By extending limited de facto rights in these various contexts to animals that are still entangled in larger property-based relationships, sanctuaries are in effect affording animals property rights in themselves, creating hybrid property-subjects, or improperty. Furthermore, by relating to animals as rights-bearing subjects, human caregivers essentially transform sanctuary spaces into interspecies communities in which both humans and animals operate as citizens. But sanctuary citizenship comes with costs. Navigating the many postrescue dilemmas of care inflicts costs on both humans and animals. Humans may be expected to sacrifice time (and, by extension, potential wages) and physical and emotional energy, while the potential limitations and costs imposed on animals may be much more significant. In the multispecies citizenship of the sanctuary, inequalities therefore still exist. The costs animal citizens may have to bear that humans do not include limits on bodily autonomy (e.g., the ability to avoid veterinary interventions or reproductive limitation); limits on freedom of movement and association (e.g., spatial confinement and forced proximity to humans or other animals); and sometimes even their lives.

Despite the almost insurmountable odds sanctuaries face in transforming human–animal relations beyond their borders—the number of rescued animals makes up far less than 1 percent of the number killed for various human purposes each year—the sanctuary movement's efforts are not folly. While they provide concrete benefits to many animals, it is true that under current political–economic and social conditions, sanctuaries can only function by excluding most animals from care. Furthermore, while they may hope for a world in which animals are liberated from human control, sanctuary caregivers are currently committed to a course of action in which complete liberation is impossible as long as animals can only be rescued and cared for in captivity. And within those captive spaces, the rights-bearing dimension of animals' subjectivity is drastically curtailed from what many animal rights philosophers and activists have envisioned. Nonetheless, the animal sanctuary movement is doing tremendously important work in creating new possibilities for living with animals as subjects worthy of ethical regard. Yes, the costs, limitations, and constraints imposed on animals play a significant determinative role in these relationships, but as alternatives to relationships in which more totalizing sacrifices are regularly demanded from animals, they also create ethical departure points for further challenging such demands. They do the important symbolic work of prodding people to think seriously about what proper relationships should be, and to ask, as I have throughout this ethnography, who benefits—*cui bono*[3]—in these relationships. Or more specifically, as Lynda Birke asks of those who study human–animal relations, "what's in it for the animals?"[4]

## Animal Futures

Wendy Brown's analysis of the political effects of late global capitalism again provides a useful lens for understanding sanctuaries—this time how they relate to the future rather than how they work in the present. She describes a ubiquitous exhaustion and despair under which most people "have ceased to believe in the human capacity to craft and sustain a world that is humane, free, sustainable, and, above all, modestly under human control," making it almost impossible to develop, "in ideas or institutions, a realizable alternative future trajectory."[5] Describing what she sees as the last vestiges of resistance to this despair, she writes,

> Insistence that "another world is possible" runs opposite to this tide of general despair, this abandoned belief in human capacities to gestate and guide a decent and sustainable order, this capitulation to being playthings of powers that escaped from the bottle in which humans germinated them. The Left alone persists in a belief . . . that all could live well, live free, live together.[6]

Similarly, the animal sanctuary movement persists in a belief that humans and animals could live well and free together (which does not necessarily always mean in proximity). That future remains only a vision at this point and may never be attainable under the political–economic and social conditions that still shape contemporary human–animal relations, but their efforts to reach that future are an insistence that another world is possible. In both ideas and institutions, the animal sanctuary movement provides an alternative future trajectory for a more humane, sustainable world based on the very idea of making human control over that world and the beings in it significantly more modest (if not ending it altogether). This vision for the future is important not just for our relationships with the species we have entangled in human social relations but for all nonhuman species on the planet, particularly in the age of the Anthropocene,[7] as the planet Earth is experiencing its sixth mass extinction (and its first as a result of human activity) or, as some have suggested, its first extermination event, driving the planet toward the Necrocene.[8] In trying to create on a small scale the world they want, sanctuaries do have to make compromises. Despite sanctuary efforts to relate to them as subjects, sanctuary animals still remain entangled in property-based relationships with humans. Despite efforts to respect their autonomy, animals must still endure constraints on their freedom. And despite efforts to give them the best lives possible, animals still remain killable (both generally in the realm of *bestia sacer* and in certain contexts within sanctuaries as well). In accepting these compromises, though, "they also build on the pragmatist tradition in animal activism of seeking to achieve immediate improvements for the animals living now while simultaneously endeavoring to bring about a more fundamental transformation in human–animal relations in the future."[9] As far as these current relationships are from the ones to which sanctuary activists aspire for the future, they are valuable in the present both for the qualitative difference they do make in the lives of animals that have been saved and for the symbolic power these experiments in alternative species relations have in countering the despair that corrodes belief that a better world is possible.[10]

If, in working through the dilemmas of care, humans and animals are cocreating a new ethical praxis of human–animal relations that is adapted to the realities of trying to live differently with other species, then—aside from maintaining hope for a better world—what implications do these new models for living with animals have for the future of animals? More specifically, can the kinds of political subjectivities some animals have accessed in sanctuary spaces continue to expand, moving beyond the zones of exception in sanctuaries to affect the vast majority of animals outside those zones of exception? The animal advocates who run sanctuaries definitely hope so, and there are positive indications of potentially broad social receptivity to rethinking human relations with animals. While animal-based industries produce and commodify more animal bodies than at any other time in human history, public attitudes about the treatment of animals may also reflect more pervasive concern for their well-being than at any other time in history.

The fate of captive chimpanzees used for research is just one example of both potentially positive shifts in the social status of animals more broadly and the still powerful inertia of *bestia sacer*. After years of growing public condemnation of the use of chimpanzees in medical research, the National Institutes of Health (NIH) announced in 2015 that it would stop funding research on chimpanzees and that it would retire the chimpanzees it owned or supported (approximately three hundred) to Chimp Haven, a federally funded chimpanzee sanctuary in Keithville, Louisiana. In fact, a federal law requires the NIH to retire chimps to accredited facilities, of which there is currently only one: Chimp Haven. One problem with this plan was that Chimp Haven was nearly at capacity when it was announced, although they agreed to immediately make space for twenty-five chimps. I had the opportunity to visit Chimp Haven briefly in 2013, and at the time they were constructing a new building to house chimpanzees that had been used in infectious disease research. Since these chimps were infected with potentially communicable diseases, such as HIV, they need to be quarantined from other chimps, which meant any additional capacity afforded by the new facility would not be usable for retiring chimps who were not infectious. Nonetheless, between 2015 and 2017, fifty-one government-owned or government-supported chimps retired to sanctuary.[11] As of October 2019, 178 government-owned or government-supported chimps still lived in biomedical primate facilities, including the Alamogordo Primate Facility in New Mexico; the MD Anderson Cancer Center in Bastrop, Texas; and the Texas Biomedical Research Institute in San Antonio, Texas. Another 190 chimpanzees also still remained at two private facilities: the New Iberia Research Center in Louisiana and Yerkes National Primate Research Center in Atlanta.[12] However, on October 24, 2019, the NIH began backtracking on its pledge to retire all the chimpanzees it owned or supported when it announced that it would not be retiring the forty-four chimps at the Alamogordo Primate Facility because the NIH determined they were too old and frail to move.[13] As of this writing, it was still unclear how many of the other 134 remaining chimps might also fall victim to more NIH broken promises.[14]

Even if the remaining 134 NIH chimps are still allowed to retire, not to mention the 190 chimps in private research facilities, their plight highlights one of the main problems for the future of captive animals. Just as resources and space are limited within sanctuaries, sanctuaries as a collective resource for rescuing animals are even more limited. Following the original decision to retire the NIH chimps, NIH director Francis Collins said that the organization was discussing how to

A rescued chimpanzee. NEAVS.

house the retired chimps in light of the sanctuary space shortage, "especially since the animals' eventual deaths will make sanctuary space unnecessary."[15] In other words, there are two possible outcomes for these chimps: sanctuary or death. While certain companion species, such as the cats and dogs at Texas Companion Rescue, have the possibility of being integrated into private human households, the majority of captive animals caught up in the realm of *bestia sacer* are currently faced with only these two possible exits.

Sanctuary space is no more plentiful for other animals than it is for chimps. And as Susie Coston made clear to the Care Conference attendees in chapter 2, when sanctuaries take on more animals than they can handle, the sacrifices required of the rest of the sanctuary community balloon rapidly. In extreme cases, overburdened organizations implode, leaving behind groups of sanctuary animals with nowhere to go and no one to take care of them. Although he did not run a sanctuary, the case of an exotic animal collector named Terry Thompson in Zanesville, Ohio, illustrates how bad a worst-case scenario can be. In October 2011, Thompson released fifty-six exotic animals from his property—including lions, leopards, tigers, wolves, cougars, and bears—before committing suicide. Police killed all but six of the animals. Less dramatic, but far more common, well-intentioned animal rescue operations that take on more than they can handle often end up in the news as hoarding cases. In August 2015, for example, officers from the Pennsylvania Society for the Prevention of Cruelty to Animals (PSPCA) removed 122 cats from a "filthy, flea-infested" house in Henryville, Pennsylvania.[16] The cats were transported to a facility in North Philadelphia where they could be given medical evaluations and then put up for adoption. The homeowners, who voluntarily surrendered the cats, told authorities they were planning on opening a shelter but were overwhelmed by the cats' swift rate of reproduction. The CEO of the PSPCA, Jerry Buckley, told the media that while it was admirable that these people wanted to help homeless animals, they "were clearly overwhelmed." As these stories suggest, a lack of proper infrastructure and resources can undermine even the best of animal-rescuing intentions, creating conditions for animals that may even be worse than the ones from which they were rescued. When resources are stretched thin, so is the line between a sanctuary and a hoarding case. And as sanctuaries proliferate to expand the possibilities for animals to gain political and social lives outside of the animal-property system, the potential for more failed sanctuaries also increases. My experiences at Quiet Glen Sanctuary, as described in chapter 3, illustrate how precarious the sanctuary vision for animal futures can be.

The Quiet Glen case also points to a related issue affecting animal futures. The fox and the coyotes at Quiet Glen are examples of animals that have lived in the wild and could be feasibly returned to their original habitats. For companion animals, agricultural animals, and exotic animals living far from their original habitats, repatriation to the wild is not a realistic option. Companion animals and agricultural animals could not survive outside of captivity because, in many contexts, they would not be able to meet their own basic needs. Even if they were released in areas where they might be able to care for themselves, they could still pose—or be perceived to pose—a potential safety risk to humans, which could in turn prompt aggressive preemptive action by humans. Exotic animals like the monkeys and birds at Rainbow Haven would face similar challenges, but in addition, they could also negatively impact ecologies to which they are not indigenous. In fact, as mentioned in chapter 4, this has been a significant issue for states, such as Florida and Hawai'i, that have hospitable climates and environments where nonnative species can thrive.

While some formerly wild animals can be released to their native environments,[17] the vast majority of animals entangled in relations with humans—whether they are born into captivity or captured from their native habitats and brought into it—are destined to remain in captivity. The question, then, is what kind of captivity will it be? The bare life of *bestia sacer*, or some form of care-based captivity such as those found in sanctuaries, shelters, and zoos? Since living with humans in some way is a necessity for the majority of animals that do end up in care-based forms of captivity, sanctuaries would ideally extend their approach to animal care over as many animals as possible. But the finite resources of sanctuaries limit this aspiration, while other kinds of care-based facilities have different ways of valuing the animals in their care. In her analysis of the biopolitical governance of captive zoo animal populations, for example, Irus Braverman argues that zoo animals are subjected to a specific form of power theorized by Foucault as pastoral power.[18] Foucault sees pastoral power as a fundamentally beneficent power since its essential objective is the salvation of the flock.[19] Sketching the historical development of zoos as they transformed from exhibitionary institutions to educational institutions and, finally, to conservation-oriented institutions, Braverman argues that the modern manifestation of zoos "as institutions that practice control through care . . . are uniquely grounded in the Western pastoral tradition that Foucault explores."[20] When it comes to the application of this power, Foucault distinguishes between two types of actors: "The bad shepherd only thinks of good pasture for his own profit, for fattening the flock that he will be able to sell and scatter, whereas the good shepherd thinks only of his flock and of nothing else. He does not even consider his own advantage in the well-being of his flock."[21] Like the sanctuaries where I conducted fieldwork, the zoos in Braverman's analysis are arguably closer to the latter category, whereas most sites of animal captivity in the modern animal–industrial complex—the realm of *bestia sacer*—have decidedly more in common with the bad shepherd model. Although it is impossible to care for animals without at least some concern for financial resources, Braverman makes a strong case that for contemporary accredited zoos in the United States, their "extensive power to govern zoo animals is driven by a desire to care for and save animals."[22]

Despite the commonalities in their goals, there are of course significant differences in how sanctuaries and zoos approach their missions. One of the most significant ones is how they approach a central paradox to pastoral power identified by Foucault. "Pastoral power is an individualizing power," he claims.[23] While the shepherd directs the whole flock, Foucault argues that "he can only really direct it insofar as not a single sheep escapes him."[24] The shepherd "does everything for the totality of his flock, but he does everything also for each sheep of the flock," looking "after each of them individually."[25] This is where the paradox arises. By simultaneously looking out for all animals and each individual animal, the shepherd creates a potential dilemma in which it may be necessary to consider the sacrifice of the flock as a whole—"since he must save each of the sheep, will he not find himself in a situation in which he has to neglect the whole of the flock in order to save a single sheep?"[26] For zoos, this pastoral paradox manifests in a range of various everyday conflicts between their concerns for individual captive animals and their conservation-oriented concern for the collective populations of those animals' species.[27] Because modern zoos' primary mission is to foster species conservation, "zoos more readily sacrifice the individual animal for the benefit of the flock, rather than the other way around."[28] However, Braverman notes that "animal activists offer a different balancing scheme, based on the assumption that the individual animal should not be sacrificed in the name of its species."[29] At times this may even lead to potential risk to the flock. Take, for example, a controversy described by Braverman related to the case of Timmy the gorilla, whom activists wanted to remain at the Cleveland Metropark Zoo with his infertile companion Kate. At the same time, "concern for the collective zoo gorilla population dictated and justified the zoo's decision to move Timmy to the Bronx Zoo, with its fertile female gorillas."[30] Foucault, she explains, frames this contention between various groups as the "great battle of pastoralship."[31]

It is true that a significant difference between the zoo-based conservation approach and the sanctuary approach to "good" pastoralship is in how they balance the individual and the flock in navigating the paradox of pastoral power. Sanctuary practices of care are intended to benefit specific individuals. Describing the specific pastoral battle between "the two groups that claim to be the sole expert authorities on the captive animal's well being: zoo people and animal protection activists," Braverman states that this war can be boiled down to the questions "Who cares more, and more properly, about animals? Who is the better pastor?"[32] Based on the range of different ways of caring for and relating to animals that I have encountered across different sanctuaries, I would argue there are almost as many ideas about the most proper way to care for and about animals as there are caregivers trying to implement them. A more useful question, as most—if not all—of these caregivers would agree, is, How can humans help animals in captivity live the best lives possible?[33] As many sanctuary caregivers see it, one important part of the answer is fostering a greater recognition of and concern for animals as relational subjects.

In addition to the many dilemmas and paradoxes sanctuary caregivers try to navigate in pursuing the goals of "good shepherds," there is one final paradox they must confront. In addition to sacrificing the flock for the individual, Foucault also claims that another "form taken by the paradox of the shepherd is the problem of the sacrifice of the shepherd for his flock."[34] Foucault meant that the shepherd's dedication to care is so absolute that even self-sacrifice is possible in service to the flock. He does not refer merely to the kinds of sacrifice related to "sacrificial citizenship" discussed in chapter 3 but to existential sacrifice of shepherds giving their lives for their flocks, if necessary. If sanctuary caregivers were able to follow this logic of pastoral care to its end point, then it could ultimately mean the abolition of sanctuaries. This is because currently, in all their real-world permutations, sanctuaries impose on animals to varying degrees the restraints and costs generated by the dilemmas of captivity, and these limitations are all compromises to the ideal vision of animals as subjects capable of truly acting in their own interests and based on their own desires. As improperty, animals instead remain suspended between property-based relationships and subject-based relationships with humans. They accrue many benefits as members of the sanctuary community, but all those benefits come with the costs described in the previous chapters. Even in Sue Donaldson and Will Kymlicka's animal agency-maximizing "intentional community" sanctuary model discussed in chapter 3, animals cannot escape *all* the restrictions of captivity.[35] Given the variety of caregiver perspectives described in the previous chapters, complete liberation of animal subjects from human control and domination may not be the ideal goal of all sanctuaries. But for the ones that do share this aspiration, then might those sanctuaries, as "good shepherds," need to ultimately sacrifice themselves to fully liberate their animals from the human-imposed obligations of sanctuary life? "To be truly free, must animals be liberated from all forms of control, including the power of care?"[36]

The saliency of this question is further emphasized by Dinesh Wadiwel's identification of a "conceptual gap" related to the role of animals in Foucault's model of pastoral power. As Wadiwel highlights, "through Foucualt's analysis of the pastorate, the question of the pastorate as a model for animal control, instrumentalisation and death is not considered a factor in how it is that we might understand the romantic metaphor of the pastorate."[37] Specifically, he argues,

> What of course lies hidden in the metaphor (and reality) of the pastorate is the inherent violence that encloses and demarcates the relationship between shepherd and animal, a relationship of domination. The human shepherd of an animal flock seeks a relationship of instrumentalisation that maintains as its goal the harvesting of those animals for human benefit: for wool, for milk, for meat and for leather. Even the kindest shepherd, the most beneficent shepherd, maintains some form of instrumentalisation that guides this practice of pastoral power. . . . It is true that

the relationship between shepherd and animals may be rendered benign through a metaphor that assumes a mode of care exists with respect to shepherd and flock. And certainly it is true, that in order for the shepherd to use his or her sheep, then a care must be inculcated in order to maintain the lives of the flock for that use. However, care here is twisted with violence in a particular way to maintain life up until the threshold of slaughter. Care is inscribed in the methods of slaughter and control themselves: thus, as the animal welfare mantra would tell us, humane killing is indeed possible where it limits "unnecessary suffering." This is, after all, a violence that claims to care.[38]

Even though sanctuaries do not share the goal of actual shepherds in their implementation of pastoral care—they are not raising and caring for animals in order to instrumentalize them by consuming their bodies—sanctuaries do instrumentalize animals in their roles as ambassadors, as discussed in chapter 3. Likewise, sanctuary pastoral care can be entangled with violence, as evidenced by the use of necro-care discussed in chapter 4. In fact, many caregivers are acutely aware of the concerns underlying this question. In the words of Olivia, the director of Rainbow Haven, "My ultimate goal is for this place not to exist. But until the world changes, it has to."

Subjecting animals to relationships of care and their related costs in perpetuity must be weighed here against a stark alternative, though: the withholding of such interventions even if this means the death of these animals. Furthermore, aside from the current impossibility of an absolute liberation from human dependency that would not result in death for most sanctuary animals, the question of whether sanctuaries must ultimately sacrifice themselves to achieve their visions for animal futures also assumes the same totalizing schema of human–animal incommensurability at the heart of Agamben's anthropological machine described in chapter 1: two opposing sides, one of which must be sacrificed for the other to thrive.[39] However, the animal sanctuary movement is a counterthesis to this schema. Human and nonhuman animals in sanctuaries form multispecies communities in which they share intersubjective experiences with each other and in which oppositions between human–animal, freedom–captivity, care–control, and subject–property are reconfigured. These alternate zones of exception to the realm of *bestia sacer* in which animals *do* have political lives do not resolve the broader social and political–economic conditions that sanctuary caregivers oppose, but to reiterate, they provide models for alternative ways of living with other species that point toward a future trajectory in which those conditions can be more drastically altered. To borrow a phrase from pattrice jones, one of the cofounders of VINE Sanctuary, they open up other kinds of imaginings.[40] Achieving broader transformations in the way humans treat animals may not be possible at this historical moment, but until it is, sanctuary activists and other animal advocates will continue to work toward a future in which animals' subjectivities are valued in ways that relating to them as property is no longer possible.[41] As Kathryn Gillespie argues, "in a society so dedicated to teaching us that animals are here to be eaten, worn, experimented on, and kept as pets and entertainers, the sanctuary embodies an alternative conceptualization of how animals fit into multispecies social worlds."[42]

Returning to the question of who benefits when it comes to sanctuaries, the answer is all of us, humans and other animals alike. The world would be a worse place without sanctuaries, both because of the animals that could not be rescued and because of the poverty of visions for other possible worlds their absence would deepen. But beyond their symbolic value for inspiring struggle toward better futures, they are also doing the important and necessary task of working through the difficulties and contradictions of realizing those futures—the pragmatic labor that must be done before any sort of liberation is possible. Human–animal relations cannot be radically transformed without a reciprocal radical transformation in a wide array of other social relations, not the least of which is a political–economic system that requires serious sacrifice from any of its subjects. So, if there is going to be change now, it is going to have to be the hard-fought, slow, incremental kind that comes from striving to improve conditions now rather than waiting for the grand rupture of an ever out-of-reach future. But even if the only thing sanctuaries could accomplish was to save a few animals out of the billions that cannot be saved, they would still be a worthwhile endeavor. As jones wrote in a social media post, "I think giving sanctuary is an important form of direct action. It's an action that actually does something about a problem. If there is no direct action of this kind, you get either demoralized doing animal advocacy work, or you become abstract, abstraction as a defense against demoralization. Will our educational efforts make a difference? This is purely speculative, but saving that chicken[43] is saving that chicken."

A rescued battery hen struts on a vet's table. Animal Equality.

For that rescued chicken and other individual animals in sanctuary, a better future is arguably already unfolding.

## Sanctuary as Liberatory Political Action

Jones's comment highlights another important aspect of the sanctuary movement: providing sanctuary is a form of direct political action that makes a real impact on the lives of suffering beings, but as a paradigm of political action, it also has much broader transformative liberatory potential.[44] Sanctuaries' efforts to work through the dilemmas of captive animal care and the small but significant successes that come with saving individual animals, for example, constitute tentative steps beyond the insufficient politics of consumption that characterize many contemporary responses to the Anthropocene. Slow food movements, locavorism, backyard and urban farming, hybrid and electric cars, and venture capitalist start-ups focused on creating plant-based and biotech alternatives to animal products are just some of the many ways people are attempting to contend with global environmental crises. They are to some extent unified in their effort to "reform" consumption practices as the overarching rubric informing political action on behalf of the environment. Yet there are signs as well of frustration with consumption-oriented politics that have been shown to only modestly slow the intensification of some of the myriad crises of life that characterize the Anthropocene. Experiments in moving beyond these politics of consumption have emerged in recent decades, from land rehabilitation and rewilding projects[45] aimed at restoring ecosystems to direct action activism against the poaching of whales and other endangered animals. Rather than just softening the impact of human consumption practices, these efforts seek to actively transform human relationships with other species. Sanctuaries are one such effort. They open the door, however tentatively, to new possibilities for the planetary transformation of contemporary social relations shaped by systems of violence, exploitation, and inequality, especially between humans and other species.

Importantly, sanctuaries are also making pragmatic moves beyond the limits of the rights paradigm in the animal protection movement. The goal of rights for animals can be understood as an example of what Lauren Berlant describes as a cruel optimism. According to Berlant, "a relation of cruel optimism is a double-bind in which your attachment to an object sustains you in life at the same time as that object is actually a threat to your flourishing."[46] Often failing to provide their promised benefits to humans who can make a formal claim to them, rights have in many cases proved to be an illusory goal that nonetheless diverts efforts away from other possible means of fostering human flourishing.[47] Similarly, the ongoing struggle to extend rights to animals has consumed much of the energy and resources of many factions of the animal protection movement while only contributing modestly to the limited flourishing of some animals.[48] As Wadiwel notes, rights can also buttress the broader structure of human–animal inequality. We should be wary, he argues, "of the stratification of rights, status and value between human and non human, and the way in which differential rights might produce inequalities in opportunities and power, and hence re-inscribe the essential right of human domination in animal life; human dignity only experienced through the indignity of other creatures."[49] Like politics of consumption, a rights-based approach to animal protection accepts and reinforces a biopolitical system of social relations that can still demand significant sacrifices from its subjects, including their lives. Beyond the simple practicalities of saving particular animals from death, torture, or suffering (which is no small accomplishment), sanctuaries also point the way toward alternative configurations of human–animal communities that are not rooted in formal investments in rights, property, or ownership as the political or ontological foundation for "protection" or "care." In this sense, they may unsettle conventional political forms that establish human sovereignty over animals as the primary means for saving them even as they rely on this, especially in its property form, as the practical legal basis for establishing zones of protection, care, and mutual flourishing.

Despite this hope for the future, though, sanctuaries also face a significant danger: the possibility that they will become fixed as insular, self-contained enclosures for experiments in alternative ways of cohabitating with other species, functioning as negotiated zones of lived sovereignty for new human–animal communities. This raises the further possibility that they could operate indefinitely more or less as refugee camps for animals who were fortunate enough to escape circuits of animal capital but have no actual home to which to return. The twentieth and twenty-first centuries are marked by perpetual humanitarian crises that have produced permanent human refugee camps around the world, spaces in which children were born and grew into adults without ever knowing a home other than their camps, and where a humanitarian logic enacts divisions between those who "save" and "care" for refugees and those who receive that care.[50] Are sanctuaries rooted in the same humanitarian logic? Are sanctuaries becoming permanent, bounded, and isolated states of exception to the state of exception that is *bestia sacer*? These are questions that could be applied to sanctuary cities or other spatial projects of sanctuary that we can imagine as well, and I raise them as a cautionary consideration, not as an argument against sanctuary as a form of political action. Avoiding this outcome, however, requires that sanctuaries move even further beyond the critique of the politics of consumption and of rights paradigms—hardly an unthinkable possibility for many who are deeply involved in sanctuary work and animal advocacy activism.

To effectively transform the animal–industrial complex as well as other systems of exploitation and inequality, it seems that sanctuary as political action must both transcend spatial barriers and have an inclusive orientation toward the communities it serves. Indeed, a future in which sanctuaries are not permanent refugee camps may be an unlikely possibility, but it is also a necessary (though not sufficient) condition for achieving a radically different world not structured by violent systems of inequality. Another word that shares etymological roots with sanctuary is *sanctum*, for which one of the definitions is "a private place from which most people are excluded." The ultimate goal of the sanctuary movement is the opposite: the extension of its boundaries to the point that it becomes totalizing and paradoxically no longer exists as a space of exception because it has become all places for all people of every species.[51] While sanctuaries reflect a utopic vision for human–animal relations free of the oppression or exploitation of animals, utopias are, in the literal translation of Thomas More's term, "no places."[52] Heterotopias, on the other hand, are real places that exist, as Michel Foucault argues, as "counter-sites, a kind of effectively enacted utopia in which the real sites, all the other real sites that can be found within the culture, are simultaneously represented, contested, and inverted."[53] As models of alternative modes of interspecies engagement, sanctuaries function as heterotopias, countersites to the political–economic arenas of animal use that embody an ethical critique of such use by enacting different ways of living ethically with animals. But the ultimate vision of sanctuary is to be neither "no place" nor a "counter-place" but rather the "all places" of pantopia.[54]

The best strategies for navigating through this current planetary crisis of life[55] are still far from clear, though many movements around the world are struggling against the destructive forces at play in the current conjuncture that have inflicted suffering and violence on the vast majority of the world's human and animal populations, bringing many to the brink of extinction—forces that are intimately tied to, but not exclusively the consequence of, late capitalism and that are rooted in systems of inequality and violence based on race, gender, sexuality, class, and indigeneity as well as species. There are many political paths forward, some easily commensurable with each other, others in seemingly unresolvable tension and antagonism. What is clear, though, is that a concern for the well-being of all kinds of others must be a central element of those strategies.

Political scientist Claire Jean Kim highlights one potential strategy in avoiding the sanctum trap in her work on the intersection between racial politics and conflicts over the treatment of animals. Kim argues that by being attentive to how human–animal inequality synergistically articulates with other forms of domination, social justice activists and animal advocates could together create an "ethics of mutual avowal" that acknowledges the validity of each other's interests and provides a basis for intersectional collaboration and mutual support.[56] By forming such connections, projects of providing sanctuary could help to empower and expand broader social and environmental justice movements. This intersectional or coalitional potential of sanctuary as a form of liberatory political action and transformation could enable it to contribute to a much larger and historically longer, unfinished abolitionist political project that, according to theorist Che Gossett, includes "ending anti-Black racism, racial capitalism, anti-trans, anti-queer, patriarchal policing, colonialism, and caging" of both human and nonhuman animals.[57] Explicitly tying this abolitionist project to ecology, Gossett argues that "abolition is always already about ecology and we continue to need . . . an abolitionist ecology."[58] Political theorist Timothy Pachirat similarly links the future of sanctuary to questions of abolition and intersectional politics, asking:

Is genuine animal liberation possible in a world where other
forms of domination and oppression continue to exist? How
would an authentic grappling with the other faces of oppression
alter, perhaps radically, current conceptions and enactments
of sanctuary? . . . What might it mean to rethink sanctuary
more broadly as a site of resistance in the fight for global social
justice, one that recognizes how the human–nonhuman divide
authorizes violence against *all* who are deemed to be less than
human?[59]

To be clear, in situating the sanctuary movement as a potential component of a broader abolitionist movement, I understand abolition
as an expansive, intersectional, and multioptic[60] political project. As
Pachirat argues, it "is not a matter of superficially or instrumentally
incorporating the rhetoric and symbols of other struggles against oppression, but of asking, at the deepest levels, about how these forms
of oppression are linked to one another."[61] Expanding sanctuary as a
mode of political action has the potential to contribute to an abolitionist ecological politics equipped to address the mutually reinforcing processes of social, environmental, and species inequality that
define and shape the Anthropocene; however, like rights, it also has
the potential to function as merely a cruel optimism. The realization
of that potential will rely, at least in part, on the coalitional bonds it
can foster.[62]

One obvious site for building such bonds is activist opposition to
the hyperexploitative processes of global capitalism, including both
labor activism and other forms of anticapitalist and anticolonial activism. Specifically, Kendra Coulter's concept of interspecies solidarity,
discussed in chapter 3, provides one possible means for forging binds
of mutual avowal. Building on the interspecies solidarity caregivers
are currently creating with animals to varying degrees, sanctuary
as a broader political project could expand its focus on transforming human relations to animals as lively commodities to also include
transforming relations to other humans as exploitable, disposable laborers.[63] In fact, the animal sanctuary ethos is already fundamentally
anticapitalist, premised as it is on directly challenging the commodification and exploitation of living beings by providing them spaces
of care.[64] Of course, not all animal sanctuaries are themselves anticapitalist, and all sanctuaries are still caught in the broader political–

economic web of global capitalism. However, as previous chapters have shown, "sanctuaries are fundamentally spaces for unmaking the property relationships that have afflicted animals for centuries."[65] Extending this ethos to make common cause with movements opposing the same capitalist exploitation of humans would help to build broader coalitional ties for the sanctuary movement in general while also expanding and strengthening the nascent interspecies solidarity within sanctuaries beyond their fences.[66]

At a broader scale, though, the coalitional potential of sanctuary as liberatory political action lies in its challenge to the very idea of human supremacy, or as Syl Ko describes it, "the long project of Western colonialism."[67] Ko argues,

> When we think about our oppressions with respect to their cause—the propping up of "the human" . . . then the fine-grained differences between them start to matter less. Racism, sexism, speciesism, classism, and so on: these are real phenomena, of course. But Sylvia Wynter warns, we should avoid mistaking the "maps" for "the territory." The territory is this massive domain of Others, whose scope can only be grasped when we dig deeper beyond the constraints of the specific "isms" and see ourselves— following Frantz Fanon's words—as *damned* beings by virtue of our lacking the "human" status. The extent of this territory is at once scary but also encouraging. We are a universe of our own—this domain of Others. That means, in spite of our cosmetic differences and situations—our many species, races, genders, belief systems, ways of being, geographic regions of origin—we are kindred spirits in a fight to depose "the human." . . . Let's use our exclusion and invisibility as a power to create impermeable spaces for ourselves, unburdened by the ridiculous biased premises of the dominant class. Let's use our erasure from the rotten-to-the-core Western notions of humanity to build up a different "new world," one that is not defined in terms of dichotomies or hierarchies or emotional death—but centered on love: one in which we accept ambiguity and difference grounded in an expansive, limitless "we."[68]

Building coalitional bonds through a common goal of deposing the human and supplanting it with a love-centric conception of an expansive

and limitless "we" that encompasses all difference would of course require a shared vision between sanctuary activists and other social justice activists, but sanctuaries can at least begin to foster connections
to other abolitionist movements "by continuing to extend their ethics
of avowal beyond the politics of consumption and rights toward the
goals of the larger planetary movement for social and environmental
justice," which has the capacity to make racial, Indigenous, gender,
sexual, disability, class, and species justice (among others) all central
objectives.[69]

The people (both human caregivers and rescued animals) who live
in sanctuary communities—in responding to the many dilemmas of
captive animal care—are cocreating new kinds of human–animal political ecologies that are adapted to the constraints of trying to live
more harmoniously with other species under the material and social
conditions of late global capitalism. In forming these new political
ecologies, sanctuaries also function as a strategy of resistance to more
exploitative human–animal relations, highlighting the liberatory potential for the provisioning of sanctuary as political action in a range
of different but related contexts of social inequality. Indeed, animal
sanctuaries can provide a lens not only for understanding shifting
practices of relating to or caring for other species but also for examining how sanctuary as simultaneously spatial and ideological modes of
being can "provide the basis for a broader counter-hegemonic challenge to violent practices of exploitation targeted at a range of different others."[70] Like Jones said, sanctuaries can open up other imag-
ings. Examining this potential through the lens of queer politics, she
reminds us that as social animals,

> we want relationships more than anything. The same drive for
> queer communion that propelled the Stonewall rebellion can
> power a quest for other kinds of connectedness, bringing us back
> into vibrant relationship with the talking trees, polyamorous
> ducks, and other queer beings who share this queer planet with
> us. In turn, those improved relations can animate our struggles
> for social justice, increasing our ability to think imaginatively
> and act creatively within systems that confound the constraints
> imposed by Eurocentric logic.[71]

At the same time, it is important not to lose sight of the sanctuary project as only a provisional step on the path to achieving the abolition of

structures of inequality that impose bare life on all animals, including humans. After all, saving animals is a project that can only truly be complete when we can save ourselves as well. Circumstances are undoubtedly dire, but sanctuary as a form of liberatory political action provides at least a glimmer of hope that that end is not yet out of reach.

A rescued rooster who has been debeaked. We Animals.

# Acknowledgments

Biology and law (among other fields) share the concepts of proximal and ultimate causation; the proximal cause is the immediate catalyst that gives rise to an event, while the ultimate cause is the greater contextual factors that made the event possible. If I am the proximal cause of this book, then the multispecies community of friends, family, colleagues, and mentors that have nurtured my mind and heart over the past four decades is most certainly the ultimate cause.

Foremost, none of my research would have been possible without the openness and hospitality of all the dedicated caregivers and volunteers at my field sites who allowed me to observe and participate in the incredibly important work they do by rescuing and caring for animals. Although I preserve their anonymity throughout this book, they are an integral part of the animal advocacy movement, and I have profound appreciation and gratitude for everything they accomplish. And a special thank-you to VINE Sanctuary, where pattrice jones, Miriam Jones, and the other human and nonhuman members of the sanctuary kindly welcomed me to their unique and inspiring community on two occasions that will always stand out in my memory as highlights of my journey through the sanctuary world.

Next, this project's incarnation as a book would not have been possible without the generous support and patience of my editor, Jason Weidemann; his assistant, Zenyse Miller; the top-notch editorial, design, and marketing teams at the University of Minnesota Press; and the excellent suggestions of my two peer reviewers, Stephanie Rutherford and Jonathan Clark. They helped me to improve my manuscript tremendously, but of course the arguments in this book are mine and any errors are entirely mine as well.

I am deeply grateful for the many people who have encouraged, challenged, and guided my interests in issues of social justice as it relates to all axes of oppression, but most especially species. Twenty years ago, Delcianna Winders introduced me to the realities of factory farming and the philosophies of veganism and animal rights, steering me toward a path on which this book is, I hope, just one of many milestones to come. Kaja Tretjak spent countless hours over many evenings and glasses of wine helping me strategize all the preliminary elements of this project, from research design and theoretical frameworks to the wording of grant proposals. Jordan Stein, Stephen Lee, Chris Elliott, Gilad Isaacs, Cody Hoesly, Dusty Hoesly, Luke Winders, Shiloh Winders, Sivan Rotholz Teitelman, Ben Dubin-Thaler, Lynn Biderman, Ashley Burczak, Sarah Richardson, Jeff Senter, Sebastian Karcher, Mark Kroncke, Stephen Hicks, Jason Williams, Debbie Williams, Naira Musallam, Rob Robertson, Zackie Achmat, Fatima Hassan, Kabir Bavikatte, Harry Jonas, Holly Shrumm, Johanna Von Braun, Scott Dunlop, Gino Cocchiaro, Ana Tretjak, Dunja Tretjak, Žiga Tretjak, Mirna Lojović, Jasenka Lojović, Mark Padovan, Lydia Wilson, Mark Reed, Carrie Reed, Jackie Ostrem, Sue Davis, Ernest Samudio, Sarah Hooks, Heather Curry, Irene Linares, Mara Kardas-Nelson, Tate Lowrey, Jack Norcross, Heather Pastushok, Anna Norcross, Steve Pilis, Ed Schulz, Ben Varadi, Ben Godwin, Joe Pinto, David Baiz, Darini Nichols, Alan Kornberg, and Amy Trakinski have discussed with me many of the ideas examined in this volume, prodding from different positions and helping me to refine and expand them over the years.

Throughout my ten years at the CUNY Graduate Center, I was incredibly fortunate to share classes, meals, and laughs with a wonderful group of friends whose insights deepened my understanding of anthropological theory in general and the ideas explored here in particular, including Risa Cromer, Nazia Kazi, Mehmet Barış Kuymulu, Yunus Dogan Telliel, Slobodan Mitrovic, Saygun Gokariksel, Ana Vinea, Michael Polson, John Warner, Carwil Bjork-James, Sophie Bjork-James, Shana Lessing, Maggie Clinton, Maria Radeva, Janny Llanos, Chris Grove, Luke Dupre, Lynne Desilva-Johnson, Daisy Deomampo, Jeremy Rayner, Harmony Goldberg, Karen Williams, Preeti Sampat,

Sharon Kelly, Anthony Johnson, Alan Takeall, Jeremy Rayner, and Yoni Reinberg—and the best study buddy east *and* west of the Bosporus, Bahar Aykan.

Equally important in guiding and enriching the intellectual development that made this project possible are the many brilliant professors and mentors with whom I've had the immense pleasure to work. Patrick Skinner taught me how to write and how to think epistemologically, two of the most important skills I ever acquired. Angela Harris, Kathy Abrams, Jonathan Simon, and Ticien Sassoubre helped me to understand the many ways the law shapes and reproduces social inequalities as well as how it can be used to dismantle them. Ananya Roy and Trinh Minh-ha helped me see that a career in academia was my true calling, no matter how much more lucrative practicing law may be. I learned how to think and act like an anthropologist from the excellent faculty at the CUNY Graduate Center, including Louise Lennihan, Don Robotham, Gerald Creed, Michael Blim, Talal Asad, Mandana Limbert, John Collins, David Harvey, and Neil Smith. Ida Susser gave me my first opportunities to conduct fieldwork and introduced me to the rich history of feminist thought within anthropology. And Ellen DeRisso's generous assistance made it possible to navigate the bureaucratic intricacies of the CUNY system; every graduate school program should be lucky enough to have an assistant program officer like Ellen. A wise person once told me that graduate students get the advisors they deserve. If that maxim extends to committee members as well, then I must have done something very right to deserve a dissertation committee like mine. Melissa Checker, Leith Mullings, and Katherine Verdery helped me design bibliographies that made studying for my qualifying exams the most enjoyable and rewarding period of my grad school experience (outside of fieldwork). Katherine and Melissa continued to provide superb feedback and guidance throughout my fieldwork and dissertation drafting, and I remain grateful for their ongoing support.

I am also grateful to the amazing scholars I have had the good fortune of befriending over the past decade as colleagues and as co-panelists and attendees at innumerable anthropology and animal studies conferences, seminars, and workshops, including Katie Gillespie, Fiona Probyn-Rapsey, Jan Dutkiewicz, Dána-Ain Davis, Carol Adams, Nekeisha Alayna Alexis, Dinesh Wadiwel, Yamini Narayan, lynn mowson, Krithika Srinivasan, Anat Pick, Joshua Kercsmar,

Siobahn O'Sullivan, Christiane Bailey, Bénédicte Boisseron, Jessica Eisen, Alex Lockwood, Margo DeMello, Esther Alloun, Guy Scotton, Simon Coghlan, Kat Herrman, Darren Chang, Carrie Freeman, Rod Bennison, Sharri Lembryk, Nikki Savvides, Laura Ogden, Timothy Pachirat, Kenneth Shapiro, Bee Friedlander, Kristin Stewart, John Thompson, Anne Hirky, Petra Pepellashi, Gail Luciani, Ivy Collier, Susan McHugh, Kari Weil, Maya Gupta, Robert Mitchell, jeffrey bussolini, Ananya Mukherjea, Iselin Gambert, Calvin Smiley, Gunnar Theodor Eggertsson, Robert Jones, Deborah Pellow, Sandra Morgan, John Clarke, Catherine Kingfisher, Rudy Gaudio, Denise Lawrence-Zuniga, Molly Mullin, Jessica Lyons, Kris Weller, Mike Anastario, Kyle Ash, Yvette Watt, Avigdor Edminster, Amelia Moore, Hannah Biggs, Gwyneth Talley, Juno Parreñas, Agustín Fuentes, Michał Pręgowski, Claudia Medina, Joseph A. Tuminello III, Jeannette Marie-Therese Vaught, Brett Mizelle, Melissa Boyde, Charlie Jackson-Martin, Stefan Helmreich, Gilberto Rosas, Columba Gonzalez-Duarte, Paul Hansen, Tarry Hum, Catherine Doyle, Lindsay A. Bell, Sarah Osterhoudt, Megan A. Styles, David Kneas, Zipporah Weisberg, Filipe Calvao, Amy Hanes, Justin Marceau, Rosemary Collard, Jane Desmond, Rebecca Winkler, Kate McClellan, Bruce Grant, Kim Stallwood, Kendra Coulter, Hilary Cunningham, Stephen Scharper, Jonathan Clark, Martin Rowe, Mia MacDonald, Ben Wurgaft, Breeana Moore, nico stubler, and Hope Ferdowsian. All these people have influenced my thinking in various ways through thought-provoking conversations or presentations. (And apologies to anyone I forgot—it's a reflection only of my aging mind and not a lack of appreciation.)

A special thanks to the participants at the 2014 "More-than-Human Legalities: Advocating an Animal Turn in Law" conference hosted by SUNY Buffalo Law School. Irus Braverman, Jamie Lorimer, Elizabeth Johnson, Christopher Bear, Adam Reed, Katie Gillespie, Eben Kirksey, Richard Janda, Andreas Philippopoulos-Mihalopoulos, and Krithika Srinivasan provided valuable critiques of theoretical concepts I employ in this book, particularly the idea of *bestia sacer*.

Another special thanks to all the attendees at the 2017 "Sanctuary: Reflecting on Refuge" conference held at Wesleyan University, including Lori Gruen, pattrice jones, Katie Gillespie, Sue Donaldson, Will Kymlicka, Juliana Castañeda Turner, Kellie Heckman, Kathy Keefe, Judy Woods, Melody Martinez, Katie Bartel, Claire Camblain, Susie Coston, Indra Lahiri, Karen Davis, lauren Ornelas, Brenda Sanders,

Elana Santana, and all the other attendees. Lori, pattrice, and Katie created a truly unique space for academics and sanctuary workers to come together to think through the joys, challenges, and heartbreaks of sanctuary work, and I was honored to be able to participate.

Speaking of academic conferences, the anthropology ones are infinitely more fun and hilarious than they otherwise would be thanks to the best conference crew anybody could hope for: Julian Brash, Jeff Maskovsky, Deborah Pellow, and Susan Falls.

And an extra special thanks to the wise editors who have given me immeasurably helpful feedback and advice on smaller publications related to this research, through which I was able to refine the ideas here, including Irus Braverman, Andreas Philippopoulos-Mihalopoulos, Melissa Boyde, Katie Gillespie, Patricia Lopez, Bob Fischer, Marcel LaFlamme, and Alex Blanchette.

If I have learned anything from twelve years of college teaching, it is that the classroom is as powerful a crucible as the field site for the forging of new ideas and insights. Thank you to all the students who have taken courses with me through the Wesleyan University Animal Studies Program and the New York University Animal Studies MA Program—you have all stretched my brain in new directions, and that is reflected in these pages. Thank you also to my colleagues in NYU Animal Studies, including Jeff Sebo, Christopher Schlottman, Jennifer Jacquet, Dale Jamieson, Colin Jerolmack, Matt Hayek, David Kanter, Gernot Wagner, Becca Franks, Tyson-Lord Gray, Nandine Thiyagarajan, Yanoula Athanassakis, Una Chaudhuri, Beau Brammer, Obi Ude, Mari Roberts, and David Wolfson, for so generously and warmly welcoming me into your community.

Thank you to my colleagues at the Harvard Animal Law and Policy Program for their friendship and support during my time as a Farmed Animal Law and Policy Fellow. Chris Green, Jon Lovvorn, Alice DiConcetto, Kristen Stilt, Matt Hayek, Ceallaigh Reddy, Kate Barnekow, Gabriel Wildgen, and Kelley McGill made the commute back and forth between Boston and New York more than worth it.

A gigantic thank-you to Jo-Anne McArthur for her beautiful, essential work on behalf of the animals—and for granting permission to use the phenomenal photographs in this book through the We Animals Archive. All her work is as incredible as these photographs are, so check out weanimalsmedia.org as soon as you get the chance.

Three people deserve more gratitude than I could possibly express here:

Eben Kirksey introduced me to multiple new bodies of literature relevant to this project, provided invaluable advice in crafting grant proposals and designing the research methods for this project, and made it possible for me to begin the first stage of research by generously inviting me to participate in the Silver River monkey research collective. Eben continued to provide outstanding mentorship throughout the fieldwork and writing stages, and his creativity in bridging the worlds of art and multispecies ethnography has been a constant inspiration. Our fellow members in the Silver River collective—Erin Riley, Tiffany Wade, Amanda Concha-Holmes, Bob Gottschalk, and Beatrice Pegard Ferry—also helped to make the early days of my fieldwork a blast (especially the spontaneous birthday party vegan barbeque they threw together on incredibly short notice). Also, Eben recommended this project to Jason Weidemann at the University of Minnesota Press, so, after me, that makes him the next most proximal cause of this book.

As a moral philosopher and ecofeminist scholar, Lori Gruen has provided me the analytical tools through which to clarify my own ethical commitment to animals and to think through many of the issues this book addresses. As a mentor, she provided endless support in navigating the early career path of an animal studies scholar, including the opportunity to teach my first animal studies courses. Most important, Lori has been an incredible friend. She is also the ideal accomplice for hunting down the perfect mezcal.

Jeff Maskovsky was my grad school advisor and is my ongoing mentor. I would add "friend," but Jeff is more than a friend: he's family. I don't know if I deserve him, but I certainly got the advisor I needed in Jeff. I cannot imagine how I could have produced the dissertation on which this book is based without Jeff's advice and insight. Jeff saw the potential in this project from the very beginning and never relented in his efforts to aid me in realizing that potential. He helped me hold myself to a higher standard than I sometimes thought possible. He always encouraged me to push my analyses deeper and think through the more complex implications of my arguments, sending me in fruitful new directions with brilliantly incisive suggestions when I became occasionally bogged down in the data or wandered into theoretical dead ends. Recognizing how maddening the labor of writing can be at times, Jeff also provided the compassion and understanding I needed to buoy my resolve through the rough patches when it seemed like a project this large would never coalesce into a coherent whole. Jeff's influence has transformed the way I think and write in subtle but significant ways that have truly made me a better scholar. I will always be proud and grateful to have been his student. It's also no small thing that Jeff is the best vegan chef I know, and the feasts he lays out are nothing short of feats of culinary ecstasy. If that sounds like hyperbole, then you haven't had Thanksgiving at Jeff's house.

Last, but by no means least, none of this would have been possible, nor would I be the person I am today, without the support of family, human and nonhuman alike. Rick Pugh, Carrie Pugh, Noel Pugh, Clifton Brown, Sidney Donnell, Cheryl Johnson, Kenan Johnson, Brooklyn and Miles Johnson, Scott Ames, Debbie Hochstadt and the rest of my California kin, Rita Ryan and the Ryan-Pilis family, Mike Cohen and the Cohen family, and Gail and Dave and the Norcross clan have all provided astonishing amounts of love and moral support throughout the process of researching and writing, from early drafts to the final product in these pages. But most of all, I owe my deepest gratitude to my partner, Lauren Brown, who has not only continued to love, support, and tolerate me but has also kept our lives infused with laughter and joy and—most important—joined me on the adventure of raising the most perfectly wondrous human being either of us has ever met: our son Niko, whose smiles and giggles have made writing this book specifically and life in general more enjoyable than they had any business being. Finally, it is impossible to overstate the influence of the nonhuman animals I have known in shaping me into a person capable of doing such a project in the first place. Sunny, Thumper, Dot, Snowball, Shortclaw, Flash, Mitts, Jimmie, Nippers, Captain Flint, Violet, Darwin, Togo, Misha, Baron, Denzel, Neal, Zazu, Suzie, Abby, Rhodey, Nia, Hugo, Little Dog, Cosmos, Novak, Sammy, Lulu, Dolly, Lele, Jimi, Sadie, Nattie, Curly, Slippin' Jimmy, Owl, Lola, Shadow, and the extraordinary animal individuals I met through my fieldwork have all helped me appreciate the incalculable value of sharing one's life with other animals. And a very special thanks to Panza, the coolest cat I've ever met and the inspiration for this project.

This material is based on work supported by the National Science Foundation under grant 1322203. Any opinions, findings, and conclusions or recommendations expressed in this material are those of the author and do not necessarily reflect the views of the National Science Foundation.

# Notes

## Introduction

1. The names of informants, primary field sites, and individual animals have been changed to preserve anonymity, with the exception of the names of the speakers at and the site of the Farm Sanctuary Care Conference, described in chapter 3, which was a public event (open to anybody who registered).

2. I use the term *animal* to refer to animals other than humans throughout this book. Although a central focus of the book is the work that sanctuaries do to dismantle the human–animal divide on which human supremacy is built, and that divide is partly constructed and reinforced through linguistic practices that treat humans as separate from or above other animals, I felt the prose would become awkward and unwieldy if I were to consistently use terms like *more-than-human* or *other-than-human* or *nonhuman animal* every time I referred to animals. Furthermore, I often use the term to refer to groups of sanctuary animals that do not include humans, so the clarifying label is implied by context. However, I hope this note can serve as a disclaimer that whenever I refer to animals, it is done so with the implicit acknowledgment that humans are a part of that collective as well.

3. Male cattle are not of much value to the dairy industry since they cannot produce milk, so dairy operations often sell them to veal operations. In fact, veal production is a subsidiary industry to dairy production: cows must be impregnated (through artificial insemination in modern dairy production) to make their bodies produce milk. Female calves can be raised to become future dairy cows, during which time they produce milk for about four years before their production starts to decline. After that, they are typically sent to slaughter. Male calves, on the other hand, are usually slaughtered much sooner, making up the bulk of veal production. See Gillespie, "Sexualized Violence."

4. Many cattle farmers use grain to fatten up cattle, but one of Bob's caregivers explained to me that large amounts of grain can actually cause cramps, bloating, or even death. Cows, like other ruminants, digest plant matter like grass by fermenting it in a chamber of their stomach prior to digestion, regurgitating it as cud to chew it and break it down further, and then swallowing it again. This specialized process is not adapted to grain consumption, so cows can only eat grain sparingly without developing problems.

5. As Donaldson and Kymlicka note, there is a "prevalence of cross-species friendships" at animal sanctuaries "revealing that domesticated animals do not have a fixed pattern of preferring the company of conspecifics." "Farmed Animal Sanctuaries," 57. I encountered this phenomenon of interspecies sociality across my field sites.

6. Abrell, "Sanctuary-Making as Rural Political Action," 109–10.

7. Algar et al., *Bambi.*

8. Griffith, Wolch, and Lassiter, "Animal Practices and the Racialization of Filipinas in Los Angeles"; Kim, *Dangerous Crossings,* 14.

9. Franklin, *Animals and Modern Cultures*; Shukin, *Animal Capital.*

10. See, e.g., Adams, *Sexual Politics of Meat*; Boglioli, *A Matter of Life and Death*; Gillespie, "Sexualized Violence"; Mizelle, *Pig*; Pachirat, *Every 12 Seconds*; Paxson, *Life of Cheese*; Schlottman and Sebo, *Food, Animals, and the Environment*; Striffler, *Chicken*; Tansey and D'Silva, *Meat Business*; Torres, *Making a Killing*; Vialles, *Animal to Edible*; Weiss, "Making Pigs Local."

11. See, e.g., Braverman, *Zooland*; Cassidy, *Horse People*; Chrulew, "Managing Love and Death at the Zoo"; Davis, *Spectacular Nature*; Mullan and Marvin, *Zoo Culture*; Warkentin, "Whale Agency."

12. See, e.g., Alger and Alger, *Cat Cultures*; Arluke and Sanders, *Regarding Animals*; Haraway, *When Species Meet*; Irvine, *If You Tame Me*; Nast, "Pit Bulls, Slavery, and Whiteness"; Serpell, *In the Company of Animals*; Shir-Vertesh, "Flexible Personhood"; Winograd, *Redemption.*

13. Noske, *Humans and Other Animals.*

14. Twine, "Revealing the 'Animal–Industrial Complex,'" 23. See also Sorenson, "Introduction"; Wadiwel, *War against Animals,* 1.

15. Humane Society of the United States, "US Slaughter Totals, by Species (Excluding Chickens) 1960–2013"; Humane Society of the United States, "US Slaughter Totals, Chickens 1960–2013." The USDA does not provide data on other farmed animals, including rabbits, marine animals, and equines (which are not classified as farmed animals but are also slaughtered in large numbers for export outside the United States). If these animals were included, the number would be in the tens of billions, largely due to the number of marine animals killed for food each year. The website Animal-Clock.org, which has a running counter of the animals killed for food in a given year, estimates that approximately 54 billion were killed for food in the United States in 2019, which includes fish and shellfish but not equines (Humane Ventures, "2019 U.S. Animal Kill Clock").

16. U.S. Department of Agriculture, "Farm Income and Wealth Statistics."

17. Statistic Brain Research Institute, "Zoo Statistics."

18. American Society for the Prevention of Cruelty to Animals, "Shelter Intake and Surrender."

19. American Society for the Prevention of Cruelty to Animals.

20. See Winograd, *Redemption*, which traces the history of the humane movement in the United States.

21. See Foer's *Eating Animals* (2009), Pollan's *The Omnivore's Dilemma* (2007), and Schlosser's *Fast Food Nation* (2005) for analyses of how industrial agriculture affects animals.

22. Tail-docking is a dairy industry practice that consists of amputating cows' tails (usually without anesthetic) with the intended purpose of preventing cows from spreading fecal contaminants to their udders.

23. Gestation crates are 6.6 by 2 foot metal enclosures used to keep adult sows immobile in intensive pig farming operations, especially during pregnancy and while they are nursing their young. Since sows used for reproduction are either pregnant or nursing the majority of the time until they are slaughtered, they are essentially kept in these crates for most of their adult lives.

24. Battery cages are small wire cages in which egg-laying hens are kept immobile throughout their lives. Each hen has approximately sixty-seven to seventy-six square inches of space. To illustrate the size, animal welfare advocates often compare battery cages to a standard piece of letter-sized paper (ninety-four square inches) or, more recently, an iPad (approximately seventy-one square inches).

25. Walmart, "Walmart U.S. Announces New Animal Welfare and Antibiotics Positions."

26. Cowperthwaite, *Blackfish*.

27. SeaWorld, "Breaking News: The Last Generation of Orcas at SeaWorld."

28. Many animal advocates criticized these changes as not going far enough since both corporations still planned to keep these animals in captivity, and Ringling Bros. planned to continue its captive elephant breeding program.

29. See Francione, *Introduction to Animal Rights*; Francione, "Animals—Property or Persons?"; Francione, *Animals as Persons*; Francione and Garner, *Animal Rights Debate*.

30. Regan, *Empty Cages*, 78.

31. See Jonathan Safran Foer's interviews with farmers who have adopted these practices out of an expressed desire to minimize animal suffering in *Eating Animals*, 149–99.

32. Gruen, "Samuel Dubose." In her work on the intersection between racial politics and conflicts over the treatment of animals—such as a controversy over the sale of live animals in San Francisco's Chinatown—Claire Jean Kim argues that activists could avoid this kind of counterproductive zero-sum mentality if they were instead attentive to how human–animal inequality

synergistically articulates with other forms of domination, enabling them to embrace an "ethics of mutual avowal" that acknowledges the validity of each other's interests and provides a basis for intersectional collaboration and mutual support. Kim, *Dangerous Crossings*, 20.

33. See Abrell, "Mongoose Trap."

34. In his multisited ethnography *Emergent Ecologies*, Kirksey follows several multispecies communities that have formed in response to different disasters, providing similar models for alternative ways of living together with other species.

35. On feminist politics of citation in general and within the field of animal studies specifically, see Fraiman, "Pussy Panic versus Liking Animals."

36. Noske, *Beyond Boundaries*.

37. Although not receiving as much attention as some of the more recent pioneering work in multispecies ethnography, these pieces from Noske and Mullin can be seen as a turning point in the way anthropologists approach human–animal relations.

38. Kirksey and Helmreich, "Emergence of Multispecies Ethnography," 545.

39. Ogden, Hall, and Tanita, "Animals, Plants, People, and Things," 7. See, e.g., Candea "'I Fell in Love with Carlos the Meerkat'"; Fuentes, "Naturalcultural Encounters in Bali"; Hayward, "Fingeryeyes"; Kirksey, *Multispecies Salon*; Kirksey, *Emergent Ecologies*; Kosek, "Ecologies of Empire"; Lowe, "Viral Clouds"; Ogden, *Swamplife*; Riley, "Contemporary Primatology in Anthropology."

40. Brightman, *Grateful Prey*, 3. See, e.g., Cruikshank, "Glaciers and Climate Change"; Descola, "Constructing Natures"; Kohn, "How Dogs Dream"; Kohn, *How Forests Think*; Nadasdy, "Gift in the Animal."

41. Brightman, *Grateful Prey*, 3.

42. Fausto, "Feasting on People," 497.

43. Fausto, 497. See also Vivieros De Castro, "Cosmological Deixis and Amerindian Perspectivism."

44. Boglioli, *A Matter of Life and Death*, 46.

45. Verdery, *Vanishing Hectare*, 13. See also Hann, *Property Relations*.

46. Verdery, *Vanishing Hectare*, 13.

47. Verdery, 14. See also Grey, "Disintegration of Property."

48. Verdery, *Vanishing Hectare*, 15.

49. Verdery, 16–17. See also Povinelli, *Cunning of Recognition*; Rose, *Wild Dog Dreaming*.

50. Verdery, *Vanishing Hectare*, 16.

51. Verdery, 16.

52. Verdery, 16.

53. Verdery, 16.

54. Delaney, "Making Nature/Marking Humans," 489.

55. Agamben, *Homo Sacer*, 8.

56. See Coulter, *Animals, Work, and the Promise of Interspecies Solidarity*.

57. Kirksey and Helmreich, "Emergence of Multispecies Ethnography"; Kirksey, *Multispecies Salon.*

58. Kirksey, *Multispecies Salon,* 2. This question was first formulated by Susan Leigh Star: "It is both more analytically interesting and more politically just to begin with the question, *cui bono?*, than to begin with a celebration of the fact of human/non-human mingling." Star, "Power, Technologies, and the Phenomenology of Conventions," 43.

## 1. Coming to Sanctuary

1. For a linguistic history of the development of the term *sanctuary* as it came to apply to protected spaces for animals in earlier contexts, see Fusari, "What Is an Animal Sanctuary?"

2. Derby, "PAWS." See also Abrell, "Animal Sanctuaries," 569–70; Doyle, "Captive Elephants"; Doyle, "Captive Wildlife Sanctuaries."

3. Baur, *Farm Sanctuary.* See also Gillespie, *Cow with Ear Tag #1389,* 121–38. Gillespie provides a rich ethnographic description of her visit to Farm Sanctuary's satellite location in Orland, California.

4. Abrell, "Animal Sanctuaries," 570. An earlier model was established in 1979 by author and animal rights advocate Cleveland Amory, who founded a sanctuary in Murchison, Texas, to care for several hundred wild burros that he helped rescue from slaughter by the U.S. National Park Service, though PAWS and Farm Sanctuary were most frequently cited as influential models by my interlocutors. The Cleveland Amory Black Beauty Ranch has since extended its care to a combination of wild animals, formerly farmed animals, and exotic animals.

5. Abrell, 569. As Timothy Pachirat points out, these "categorizations are problematic insofar as they define animals instrumentally according to their usefulness to humans." Pachirat, "Sanctuary," 345n16. As an operational typology of sanctuaries, however, these categories also highlight the different arenas of animal instrumentalization that caregivers seek to dismantle.

6. Abrell.

7. I did not include this kind of sanctuary in my fieldwork since it is the one type of sanctuary that others have already studied in depth. See Ferdowsian, *Phoenix Zones*; Fleury, "Money for Monkeys"; Fultz, "A Guide for Modern Sanctuaries"; Fultz and Spraetz, foreword; Gruen, *Entangled Empathy*; Hua and Ahuja, "Chimpanzee Sanctuary"; Gruen, *Ethics and Animals,* 158–62; Gruen, "Dignity, Captivity, and an Ethics of Sight"; Gruen, "Navigating Difference (Again)"; Ross, "Captive Chimpanzees."

8. See Collard, "Putting Animals Back Together"; Parreñas, "Producing Affect"; Parreñas, *Decolonizing Extinction*; van Dooren, *Flight Ways.*

9. Buckley and Bradshaw, "Art of Cultural Brokerage."

10. Abrell, "Animal Sanctuaries," 570. On the history of zoos, see Alcampora,

*Metamorphoses of the Zoo*; Braverman, *Zooland*; Gruen, "Shifting towards an Ethics of Sanctuary"; Horowitz, "The National Zoological Park"; Jamieson, "Against Zoos"; Jamieson, "Zoos Revisited"; Mullan and Marvin, *Zoo Culture*. See also Winders, "Captive Wildlife at a Crossroads," on the use of the term *sanctuary* by roadside zoos and other facilities to "humane-wash" their exploitative treatment of animals.

11. Hua and Ahuja, "Chimpanzee Sanctuary," 634. Possible exceptions are sanctuaries that focus on particular communal species, such as elephants or chimpanzees. Some of these sanctuaries instead seek to provide spaces in which rescued animals can form social groups with each other without much interference from humans. I would argue that even in these types of sanctuaries, the more limited human–animal interactions that occur are still guided by an ethos that values animals as fellow subjects. Abrell, "Animal Sanctuaries," 570. See, e.g., Buckley and Bradshaw, "Art of Cultural Brokerage," for an analysis of this dynamic in a U.S. elephant sanctuary.

12. Abrell, "Animal Sanctuaries," 570. On the spectacular consumption and commodification of nature, see Bulbeck, *Facing the Wild*; Chris, *Watching Wildlife*; Davis, *Spectacular Nature*; Rutherford, *Governing the Wild*; Vivanco and Gordon, *Tarzan Was an Ecotourist*.

13. Abrell, "Animal Sanctuaries," 571.

14. Winograd, *Redemption*, xvii.

15. Winograd.

16. Humane Society of the United States, "Pets by the Numbers."

17. Humane Society of the United States.

18. See Fawcett, "Euthanasia and Morally Justifiable Killing," for a discussion of the politics of language surrounding the use of the term *euthanasia* in relation to the killing of animals.

19. For an analysis of an alternative early definition of sanctuary as a staging ground for combat strategy, see Pachirat, "Sanctuary."

20. Abrell, "Animal Sanctuaries," 570.

21. See Davidson, "Sanctuary," for a political history of the affording of sanctuary to humans.

22. Abrell, "Animal Sanctuaries," 570. See Cunningham, *God and Caesar at the Rio Grande*. Pachirat notes that when they cofounded Farm Sanctuary, Gene Baur and Lorri Houston were actually directly "influenced by Latin American liberation theology and the 1980s sanctuary movement to shield refugees from war-torn El Salvador, Guatemala, and Nicaragua from US immigration laws." Pachirat, "Sanctuary," 347.

23. Abrell, "Sanctuary-Making as Rural Political Action," 109. See also Butcher, "Small Towns Are the Place to Challenge Immigration Policy."

24. Agamben, *Homo Sacer*, 181.

25. Agamben, 166.

26. Agamben, 8, 15.

27. Agamben, 113.
28. Agamben.
29. Agamben, 8.
30. Agamben, *Open*, 80.
31. Agamben, 92.
32. Wadiwel, *War against Animals*, 84.
33. Wadiwel, 85.
34. Agamben, *Remnants of Auschwitz*, 55; Wadiwel, *War against Animals*, 85–86.
35. Agamben, *Open*, 37–38. See Abrell, "Lively Sanctuaries," 141.
36. Wadiwel, *War against Animals*, 86.
37. Wolfe, "'A New Schema of Politicization,'" 156.
38. Shukin, *Animal Capital*, 10.
39. Political theorist Jan Dutkiewicz similarly argues that the "'living death' of animal subjects is not a state akin to a concentration camp or colony, but one of constant biopolitical intervention aimed at the achievement of a specific type" of value-producing body. Dutkiewicz, "'Post-modernism,' Politics, and Pigs," 303. See also Wadiwel, *War against Animals*, 82.
40. Wolfe, "'A New Schema of Politicization,'" 159.
41. Foucault references this distinction between man and animal in *History of Sexuality*: "for millennia, man remained what he was for Aristotle: a living animal with the additional capacity for a political existence" (134). See Wadiwel, *War against Animals*, 66–70; Wolfe, "'A New Schema of Politicization,'" 152.
42. Wadiwel, *War against Animals*, 83.
43. Although the methods of killing may be restricted by anticruelty laws.
44. Wadiwel, *War against Animals*, 84, quoting Singer, *Animal Liberation*, 16.
45. Abrell, "Lively Sanctuaries," 141. I am grateful to Katherine Verdery for suggesting this more evocative variation on my original neologism, *animal sacer*. For a related but different theorization of *bestia sacer*, see Mackenzie, "Bestia Sacer and Agamben's Anthropological Machine"; Mackenzie, "How the Politics of Inclusion/Exclusion and the Neuroscience of Dehumanization/Rehumanization Can Contribute to Animal Activists' Strategies."
46. Wadiwel, "Three Fragments from a Biopolitical History of Animals," 23.
47. Wadiwel, 29.
48. Nicole Shukin observes that the concentration camp, Agamben's paradigmatic scenario of bare life in modernity, "finds its zoopolitical supplement in Derrida's theorization of the 'non-criminal putting to death' of animals, a related state of exception whose paradigmatic scenario is arguably the modern industrial slaughterhouse." Shukin, *Animal Capital*, 10. I agree that the slaughterhouse is the most apt paradigmatic localized parallel to the concentration camp, but spatialized bare life for animals also extends far beyond the walls of the slaughterhouse throughout and coextensive with the vast spaces of human societies in which animals are entangled in capitalist property systems around the world.

49. See Wadiwel, *War against Animals*, 56.

50. Bolender, "R. A. W. Assmilk Soap," 85.

## 2. Care and Rescue

1. See Puig de la Bellacasa, *Matters of Care*.

2. Foucault, *History of Sexuality, Volume I*.

3. See Donaldson and Kymlicka, "Farmed Animal Sanctuaries," 55. As they note, farm animal sanctuaries "have expanded our understanding of the possibilities for animal wellbeing" (55).

4. See Gillespie, "Sexualized Violence," for nuanced and illuminating analyses of the lives of cows in the U.S. dairy industry.

5. Cows in general, however, are quite capable at overcoming fences. As Kathryn Gillespie notes, "cows are notoriously difficult to keep contained, as they are able—with a little incentive—to leap six foot fences or figure out other creative ways through fencing meant to contain them." Gillespie, *Cow with Ear Tag #1389*, 119.

6. Wadiwel, *War against Animals*, 84; Wolfe, "'A New Schema of Politicization,'" 163. On the animal–industrial complex, see Noske, *Humans and Other Animals*; Sorenson, "Introduction"; Twine, "Revealing the 'Animal–Industrial Complex'"; Wadiwel, *War against Animals*.

7. Taylor, *Beasts of Burden*, 42.

8. Although some sanctuaries, such as VINE Sanctuary, discussed later in this chapter, endeavor to minimize this risk as much as possible. See also Buckley and Bradshaw, "Art of Cultural Brokerage."

9. However, as suggested by the manure trough into which Flower fell when she was born, industrial agriculture's standards for cleanliness are generally much lower than sanctuaries' standards are.

10. Taylor, *Beasts of Burden*, 43. Revealing one of the many ways in which human–animal inequality is socially constructed, thus buttressing the category of *bestia sacer*, Taylor continues, "In the end, it is not only disabled animals who could be called crips. All animals—both those we human beings would call disabled and those we would not—are devalued and abused for many of the same basic reasons disabled people are. They are understood as incapable, as lacking in various abilities and capacities that have long been held to make human lives uniquely valuable and meaningful. They are, in other words, oppressed by ableism. The able body that ableism perpetuates and privileges is always not only able-bodied but human" (43).

11. Gruen, *Ethics and Animals*, 133.

12. Gruen, 159.

13. Gruen, 160.

14. Gruen.

15. Donaldson and Kymlicka, *Zoopolis*, 146–47. See also Donaldson and Kymlicka, "Farmed Animal Sanctuaries," 59. However, Wadiwel argues that

"reproductive control" is a violent form of domination shaping human relationships with other animals and sees "human control over sexuality and
reproduction 'for the good'" of animals as "human sovereign prerogative
play[ed] out to disturbing effect." Wadiwel, *War against Animals*, 56, 62.

16. See Abrell, "Animal Sanctuaries," 572.

17. Regan, *Empty Cages*, 78.

18. Candea, "'I Fell in Love with Carlos the Meerkat,'" 249.

19. Candea, 249.

20. Candea.

21. For another example of animal–researcher interactions that might qualify as interpatience, see Roger Tabor, *Wildlife of the Domestic Cat*, in which he
describes realizing that affecting a disinterest in the feral cats he's studying
while simultaneously reacting as he normally would to the sounds and other
stimuli around him helped him to cultivate a similar dynamic with the cats.

22. Derrida, *Animal That Therefore I Am*, 378–79.

23. Derrida, 416.

24. Abrell, "Interrogating Captive Freedom," 4.

25. Gruen, "Entangled Empathy"; Gruen, "Navigating Difference (Again)."

26. Gruen, "Entangled Empathy," 228.

27. Gruen, 229.

28. Abrell, "Interrogating Captive Freedom," 4.

29. Noske, *Beyond Boundaries*, 169.

30. Abrell, "Interrogating Captive Freedom," 4.

31. See Gillespie, *Cow with Ear Tag #1389*, 119–20.

32. For other descriptions of VINE, see Donaldson and Kymlicka, "Farmed
Animal Sanctuaries"; Gillespie, *Cow with Ear Tag #1389*.

33. Jones, "Captivity in the Context of a Sanctuary," 91. See also Gillespie,
*Cow with Ear Tag #1389*, 137.

34. Jones, "Captivity in the Context of a Sanctuary," 92.

35. Jones.

36. VINE Sanctuary, "About Us." See also jones, *Oxen at the Intersection*.

37. VINE Sanctuary, "About Us."

38. A large portion of the back half of the property is also separated from the
front half, where the sanctuary animals live, to provide a nature preserve for
indigenous wild animals.

39. Donaldson and Kymlicka have also noted the similarity between some
farm animal sanctuary aesthetics and the imagery of farms in children's
books. See their "Farmed Animal Sanctuaries," 54.

40. Donaldson and Kymlicka argue that the aesthetic and architectural similarities between sanctuaries and farms risk inadvertently reinforcing "assumptions about where farmed animals belong, what forms of society and
behavior are 'natural' for them, and their relationship to humans." This is because since "few members of the public have witnessed factory farms or feedlots," what might strike visitors to these sanctuaries "is not how *different*" farm

animal sanctuaries are from factory farms "but rather how *similar*" they are to traditional farms. "And while the informational component of a [farm animal sanctuary] visit may discuss the violence of factory farming, the more visceral experience may reinforce a pre-existing sentimental image of farms and animal husbandry." Donaldson and Kymlicka, "Farmed Animal Sanctuaries," 54. See also Gillespie, *Cow with Ear Tag #1389*, 120; Gillespie, "For a Politicized Multispecies Ethnography," 21; Van Kleek, "The Sanctuary in Your Backyard."

41. Gillespie, "For a Politicized Multispecies Ethnography," 20. See also Donaldson and Kymlicka, "Farmed Animal Sanctuaries"; Buckley and Bradshaw, "Art of Cultural Brokerage."

42. Morris, "Firefighters Eat Sausages Made of Piglets They Saved from Blaze."

43. Morris; Abrell, "Animal Sanctuaries," 573.

44. Morris, "Firefighters Eat Sausages Made of Piglets They Saved from Blaze."

45. Abrell, "Animal Sanctuaries," 573.

46. Verdery, *Vanishing Hectare*, 13.

47. Although see Shir-Vertesh, "Flexible Personhood," for an analysis of human–pet relationships in Israel, where, she argues, pets are sometimes treated as "flexible persons," losing their familial status when human children enter the family.

48. Mullin, "'Shock' and 'Heartbreak' after Adopted Pig Ends Up on Dinner Table."

49. Minder and Belluck, "Spain, amid Protests, Destroys Dog of Ebola-Infected Nurse."

50. Gruen, "Why Euthanizing Ebola Animals Is a Dangerous Road to Go Down."

51. Wadiwel, *War against Animals*, 56.

52. Braverman, *Zooland*, 152 (citing the court's decision in *Animal Protection, Education, and Information Foundation v. Friends of the Zoo for Springfield, Missouri, Inc.*).

53. Braverman, "Animal Mobilegalities," 112.

54. Favre, "Living Property," 1033.

55. Deckha, "Initiating a Non-Anthropocentric Jurisprudence," 813.

56. Francione, *Introduction to Animal Rights*; Francione, "Animals—Property or Persons?"; Francione, *Animals as Persons*; Francione, *Animal Rights Debate*. See also Gillespie, "Nonhuman Animal Resistance," 119.

57. Gillespie, "Nonhuman Animal Resistance," 121.

58. Gillespie.

59. Collard and Dempsey, "Life for Sale?" See also Barua, "Animating Capital"; Collard, "Cougar–Human Entanglements"; Collard, "Putting Animals Back Together"; Collard and Gillespie, "Doing Critical Animal Geographies"; Gillespie, *Cow with Ear Tag #1389*; Whatmore and Thorne, "Wild(er)ness."

60. Gillespie, "Nonhuman Animal Resistance," 121.

61. Barua, "Lively Commodities and Encounter Value." On the commodification of nature and its governmental effects, see Rutherford, *Governing the*

*Wild.* On encounter value, see Haraway, *When Species Meet,* 45. Imagining a modern-day version of Karl Marx writing *Biocapital, Volume I,* Haraway posits that the author "would have to examine a tripartite structure: use value, exchange value, and encounter value. . . . Trans-species encounter value is about relationships among a motley array of lively beings," in which commerce, consciousness, evolution, ethics, and utilities are all in play. Like use and exchange value, encounter value is a name for a relationship (45).

62. Gillespie, "Nonhuman Animal Resistance," 120–21. See also Francione, "Animals—Property or Persons?"; Wolfson, "Beyond the Law"; Wolfson and Sullivan, "Foxes in the Hen House."

63. Wadiwel, *War against Animals,* 83.

64. Engels, *Conditions of the Working Class in England,* 240.

65. Hobsbawm, *Primitive Rebels.*

66. This is an ongoing strategy employed by other animal advocates, though. In 2012, PETA filed a lawsuit against SeaWorld seeking to establish protection for five orcas under the Constitution's Thirteenth Amendment, which prohibits slavery. The presiding judge ruled that the Thirteenth Amendment does not apply to orcas, however. In 2015, the Nonhuman Rights Project (NRP) filed a lawsuit on behalf of Hercules and Leo, two chimpanzees being used for research at Stony Brook University. The lawsuit sought the release of the two chimpanzees based on a right to bodily liberty, though it was unsuccessful. However, both chimps have since been released to the Project Chimps sanctuary in Morgantown, Georgia.

67. Hobsbawm, *Primitive Rebels,* 19.

68. Of course, the individual homes of humans who choose to share their lives with other animals and form subject-based relations with them also may function as small, limited zones of exception to the norm of *bestia sacer,* but I am referring here to both larger social spaces and animals that cannot necessarily live in human domestic spaces.

69. Collard, "Putting Animals Back Together."

70. Collard, 152.

### 3. Creating and Operating Sanctuaries

1. Farm Sanctuary, *How to Start, Operate, and Develop a Farm Animal Sanctuary.*

2. Abrell, "Animal Sanctuaries," 573.

3. Collard and Dempsey, "Life for Sale?"

4. Abrell, "Animal Sanctuaries," 573.

5. Graham, "Hollywood Mogul Simon Buys Fur Farm with Animal Rights Activists."

6. Farm Sanctuary, *How to Start, Operate, and Develop a Farm Animal Sanctuary,* 3.

7. Abrell, "Animal Sanctuaries," 575.

8. Donaldson and Kymlicka, *Zoopolis.*

9. Donaldson and Kymlicka have specifically examined farmed animal sanctuaries as co-citizenship models, which I discuss further in the last section of this chapter. See their "Farmed Animal Sanctuaries."

10. Donaldson and Kymlicka, *Zoopolis*, 101.

11. See Donaldson and Kymlicka, "Farmed Animal Sanctuaries," 55.

12. This economics of rescue is a common line of reasoning in vegan advocacy circles, although critics argue that it would actually take a significant decrease in the consumption rate of any animal product before producers would decrease their output to compensate for the decreased demand. This critique relies on the idea of a triggering event or threshold of a certain amount before demand would impact supply. Shelly Kagan provides an example of how the triggering event would work: "There are, perhaps, 25 chickens in a given crate of chickens. So the butcher looks to see when 25 chickens have been sold, so as to order 25 more. (Perhaps he starts the day with 30 chickens, and when he gets down to only 5 left, he orders another 25—so as never to run out. But he must throw away the excess chickens at the end of the day before they spoil, so he cannot simply start out with thousands of chickens and pay no attention at all to how many are sold.) Here, then, it makes no difference to the butcher whether 7, 13, or 23 chickens have been sold. But when 25 have been sold this triggers the call to the chicken farm, and 25 more chickens are killed, and another 25 eggs are hatched to be raised and tortured. Thus, as a first approximation, we can say that only the 25th purchaser of a chicken makes a difference. It is this purchase that triggers the reaction from the butcher, this purchase that results in more chicken suffering." Kagan, "Do I Make a Difference?," 122. The critique, however, does not contradict the underlying idea that a decrease in demand for animal products can lead to a decrease in animals used for food, but such an effect would be the result of collective action rather than the actions of an individual. Gruen and Jones, "Veganism as an Aspiration." The idea that one person refraining from eating turkey meat is one turkey saved thus functions better as a symbol of vegan advocacy's goals than as an accurate economic calculation.

13. On sanctuary animals as ambassadors, also see Donaldson and Kymlicka, "Farm Animal Sanctuaries."

14. Abrell, "Animal Sanctuaries," 574.

15. Emmerman, "Sanctuary, Not Remedy," 229. See Abrell, "Interrogating Captive Freedom," 3–4. Relatedly, Pachirat notes that sanctuaries risk "becoming victims of their own success, their potential to serve as sites of resistance blunted by an increasing mainstream acceptance, even popularity, that brings with it funding, membership, and attention precisely because it is not perceived as fundamentally threatening to the existing political and economic order. At best, this type of domestication risks turning sanctuary into a politically defanged, libidinal object of escapist desire. . . . At worst,

it risks packaging sanctuary as gift shop merchandise, selling it as lifestyle choice, and branding it as fundraising icon." Pachirat, "Sanctuary," 349–50.

16. Emmerman, "Sanctuary, Not Remedy," 230.

17. Emmerman.

18. Gruen, *Ethics and Animals*, 161–62. See Pachirat, "Sanctuary," 341.

19. Mason, "Stereotypies."

20. See Kirksey, *Emergent Ecologies*, 105–33, and Riley and Wade, "Adapting to Florida's Riverine Woodlands," for ethnographic analyses of the novel ecological entanglements that have formed between the macaques, humans, and other species that live in this riparian region.

21. See Cassidy and Mullin, *Where the Wild Things Are Now*, for explorations of historical and contemporary processes of domestication and how they are continuing to transform relationships between humans and other species.

22. Donaldson and Kymlicka, "Farmed Animal Sanctuaries."

23. Donaldson and Kymlicka, 51.

24. Donaldson and Kymlicka, 62.

25. See also Gillespie, *Cow with Ear Tag #1389*, 125–27.

26. Donaldson and Kymlicka, "Farmed Animal Sanctuaries," 57–62.

27. Donaldson and Kymlicka, 62.

28. Donaldson and Kymlicka.

29. Contrast this with the privileging of freedom and agency over safety (in certain contexts) practiced by Miriam Jones, pattrice jones, and the other caregivers at VINE Sanctuary, described in chapter 2. Donaldson and Kymlicka also cite VINE as an example of an alternative to the "refuge + advocacy" model.

30. Donaldson and Kymlicka, 68.

31. Donaldson and Kymlicka, 62. See Balcombe, "Animal Pleasure and Its Moral Significance," 214.

32. Donaldson and Kymlicka, "Farmed Animal Sanctuaries," 63.

33. Donaldson and Kymlicka.

34. Donaldson and Kymlicka, 66–67. See also Scotton, "Duties to Socialise with Domesticated Animals," on the role of interspecies friendships in realizing the goals of the "intentional community" model.

35. Donaldson and Kymlicka, "Farmed Animal Sanctuaries," 51.

36. Abrell, "Interrogating Captive Freedom," 1.

37. Brown, *Undoing the Demos*, 201–12. See also Brown, "Sacrificial Citizenship." I use the term *neoliberalism* here with caution. Following Catherine Kingfisher and Jeff Maskovsky, I understand neoliberalism as a process "fraught with contradiction and partiality and subject to limitation." Kingfisher and Maskovsky, "Introduction," 115. Brown similarly observes, "'Neoliberalism' . . . is a loose and shifting signifier. It is a scholarly commonplace that neoliberalism has no fixed or settled coordinates, that there is temporal and geographic variety in its discursive formulations, policy entailments, and material

practices. . . . Neoliberalism as economic policy, a modality of governance, and an order of reason is at once a global phenomenon, yet inconsistent, differentiated, unsystematic, impure." Brown, *Undoing the Demos*, 20. In examining neoliberalism's influence on the creation of sacrificial citizenship, she specifically focuses on neoliberal rationality, rather than neoliberalism per se, as a ubiquitous form of governance-shaping ideology that is "converting the distinctly *political* character, meaning, and operation of democracy's constituent elements into *economic* ones" (17, emphasis original). See also Clarke, "Living with/in and without Neo-liberalism," for a critique of neoliberalism's overuse as a theoretical concept and an argument for the need to recognize its contingent and contested nature.

38. Brown, *Undoing the Demos*, 210–11.

39. Coulter, *Animals, Work, and the Promise of Interspecies Solidarity*.

40. Coulter, 152–53.

41. Coulter, 152.

## 4. Animal Death

1. Foucault, *History of Sexuality*, 138.

2. Humane Ventures, "2019 U.S. Animal Kill Clock."

3. Humane Society, "Pets by the Numbers."

4. See Davis, *Holocaust and the Henmaid's Tale*; Patterson, *Eternal Treblinka*; Spiegel, *Dreaded Comparison*.

5. Schnurer, "At the Gates of Hell," 121.

6. Quoted in Davis, *Holocaust and the Henmaid's Tale*, 8.

7. Wolfe, "'A New Schema of Politicization,'" 162.

8. Wolfe, 162–63. See Patterson, *Eternal Treblinka*, 72.

9. Teather, "'Holocaust on a Plate.'" However, addressing the controversies around these analogies, philosopher Syl Ko insightfully argues that people use "crudely drawn and elementary images or analogies of oppression" in an effort to close the theoretical and discursive gap between human and animal oppressions, but "these simplistic characterizations miss the ways in which these struggles and these wounded subjectivities relate to one another. So, although the debate continues to play out in terms of whether or not making these comparisons or connections is offensive, . . . it obscures a far more interesting point we should be discussing: this debate only makes sense on the assumption that we continue to understand speciesism as independent and animal-specific and, as such, a phenomenon that *requires* connection to other struggles. . . . [We] tend to be blind to the fact that in both the narrative of speciesism and the narrative of racism the members of the losing side both fall short of *real* human status, and as a result, their suffering and their deaths are mundane, normal, and expected. In my view of things, the 'humanity' trumped up in one narrative is the same 'humanity' trumped up in the other. If we want to make a connection, *this* is the connection we should

be making. We're really not 'comparing' anything in this type of thinking. We're noting a common source. The connection we make is not found *in* the oppressions themselves or the oppressed bodies. It's about realizing that we're wrong to focus on human bodies or animal bodies or what those bodies and souls face in being oppressed when we want to make 'connections.' All we need to do is focus on and make salient 'the human' in both cases." Ko, "We Can Avoid the Debate," 84–87, emphasis original. See also Kim, "Abolition."

10. Kalechofsky, *Animal Suffering and the Holocaust*, 34.

11. Wadiwel, *War against Animals*, 80–82. Complementing Syl Ko's argument in note 9, he adds, "My view is that we must understand the co-evolution of techniques of violence used by humans against humans and those against animals. This involves understanding the way in which developments in means for killing and containing animals flow to the human sphere, and vice versa. However, describing human violence towards animals as a 'holocaust,' 'genocide,' 'slavery,' or 'colonisation' not only risks emptying examples of mass human violence towards humans of their descriptional specificity and characteristic memory, but simultaneously pretends that what we do to animals can actually be described using existing metaphors of human to human violence" (81n50).

12. Arguing similarly that the act of killing agriculture animals is a "value-creating one rooted in ongoing market processes," Jan Dutkiewicz calls this value "necrovalue." Dutkiewicz, "'Postmodernism,' Politics, and Pigs," 303.

13. With recent breakthroughs in efforts to create cell-cultured meat and genetically modified yeast capable of producing a substance chemically identical to cow's milk, it is even possible to conceive of a future agricultural industry that does not require animal death at all.

14. Wolfe, "'A New Schema of Politicization,'" 163.

15. Mbembe, "Necropolitics," 39.

16. Mbembe, 40, emphasis original.

17. Mbembe, 27.

18. Mbembe, 29.

19. See Dutkiewicz, "'Postmodernism,' Politics, and Pigs," 303.

20. Van Dooren, *Flight Ways*, 116.

21. Van Dooren, 92. For analyses of different practices that might constitute "violent care," see also Collard, "Putting Animals Back Together"; Parreñas, *Decolonizing Extinction*; Srinivasan, "Caring for the Collective."

22. Van Dooren, *Flight Ways*, 91.

23. Van Dooren, 114.

24. Van Dooren, 115.

25. Chrulew, "Managing Love and Death at the Zoo."

26. Van Dooren, *Flight Ways*, 117. See also Haraway, *When Species Meet*, 78.

27. Van Dooren, *Flight Ways*, 216. See also Van Dooren, "Invasive Species in Penguin Worlds."

28. See Van Dooren *Flight Ways*, 159n15.

29. See Plumwood, "Human Vulnerability and the Experience of Being Prey."
30. See also Abrell, "Mongoose Trap."
31. As anthropologist Eben Kirksey notes, environmental humanities scholar "Deborah Bird Rose argues for an ethics of care that does not exclude death. 'An ethical response to the call of others does not hinge on killing or not killing,' she argues. The question becomes what constitutes a good death?" Kirksey, *Emergent Ecologies*, 61. See also Rose, *Wild Dog Dreaming*, 18. Kirksey goes on to describe an ethnographic encounter with a frog biologist in which he mentioned this idea of a "good death" in relation to the systematic "euthanasia" of hundreds of excess tree frogs in a zoo-based conservation program. The biologist told him "that a 'good death' cannot come from euthanasia at the hands of a zookeeper. Amid a sedate and melancholic conversation about biodiversity loss, financial woes, and zoo overcrowding, she suddenly slammed down her glass, spilling margarita on the table. Lifting her hand in a parody of a revolutionary salute, she shouted, 'Live free or die!'" (61). Whether an animal can truly have a "good death" while in captivity is an important question. Assuming the animal's life is significantly negatively impacted by captivity, though, an equally important question is whether the impossibility of being free from captivity could make the prospect of death better than it would otherwise be. Or in other words, at what point does providing death become a more ethical response than providing an impoverished life? See the story of Broxton the dog in this chapter for an example of caregivers' response to this question.
32. See Arluke and Sanders, *Regarding Animals*, 82–106; DeMello, *Animals and Society*, 225–26, for analyses of how caregivers in open-admission shelters use institutional rules and blame-shifting strategies to cope with participating in the euthanasia of dogs and cats.
33. See Gillespie, *Cow with Ear Tag #1389*, 135.
34. Van Dooren, *Flight Ways*, 159n15. See also Fischer and Lindenmayer, "An Assessment of the Published Results of Animal Relocations."
35. Abrell, "Mongoose Trap," 70.
36. Hawaiian Invasive Species Council, "Invasive Species."
37. See Comaroff and Comaroff, "Naturing the Nation"; Kirksey, *Emergent Ecologies*; Probyn-Rapsey, "Dingoes and Dog-Whistling"; Van Dooren, "Invasive Species in Penguin Worlds."
38. Hawaiian Administrative Rules §13-124-2.
39. Abrell, "Mongoose Trap," 71.
40. Hawaiian Penal Code §711-1109(c).
41. Abrell, "Mongoose Trap," 71. Florida, where the Quiet Glen sanctuary described in chapter 3 was located, uses similar categories of foreignness to enforce spatial ideologies that designate certain animals as killable in the wild. A laissez-faire approach to regulating exotic animals, combined with a keen interest in them as pets and exhibits at tourist attractions throughout

Florida, has resulted in a widespread proliferation of exotic species in captivity, creating ideal conditions for their human-assisted or self-initiated repatriation to the wild. According to the Florida Fish and Wildlife Conservation Commission (FWC), "over 500 nonnative fish and wildlife species . . . have been documented in the state." FWC defines "nonnative" or "exotic" species (the terms are used interchangeably) as "animals living outside captivity that did not historically occur in Florida." Florida Fish and Wildlife Conservation Commission, "What Is a Nonnative Species?" According to FWC, most exotics "are introduced species, meaning they have been brought to Florida by humans." However, it notes, "a few of Florida's exotics arrived by natural range expansions, like cattle egrets, which are native to Africa and Asia but flew across the Atlantic Ocean and arrived in Florida in the 1950s. Several common nonnative species, like coyotes, armadillos and red foxes, were not only introduced by humans but also spread into Florida by natural range expansions." Exotic status has repercussions for the future of any animal that finds itself in human captivity because no exotic animal can be legally released back into the wild in Florida, as is the case in many other states as well, including Hawai'i. This is why the coyotes and fox at Quiet Glen will spend the rest of their lives in captivity—not because they could not be safely returned to the wild but because they are legally classified as alien species to Floridian ecologies. The state's real problem, however, is with nonnative species determined to be invasive. Similar to "injurious wildlife" in Hawai'i, these are species deemed to pose an ecological or economic threat. State wildlife management officials and private conservationists are concerned that the ability of certain "exotics" to quickly adapt and thrive in Florida's incredibly hospitable ecologies could pose a danger to indigenous flora and fauna as well as human safety and economic interests. The Cuban tree frog, for example "was introduced in 1931 . . . and has invaded Florida's natural areas, preying on . . . native tree frogs." Green iguanas, on the other hand, do not pose a clear ecological threat but are still considered invasive because they cause "significant economic damage to landscape plants, primarily in Miami-Dade and Broward Counties." Florida Fish and Wildlife Conservation Commission, "Invasive Species." One way the state has tried to ameliorate this problem is with the designation of conditional and prohibited species. People can obtain permits to possess or import conditional or prohibited species, but only for exhibition or research purposes. FWC also issues permits for people to capture and remove conditional exotics from state land. For example, this practice is encouraged with a yearly contest called the Python Challenge. The contest targets the Burmese python, an invasive exotic snake that has gained a bellyhold in the Florida Everglades, posing a risk to native birds, bobcats, foxes, raccoons, and other animals. The 2020 Python Challenge contest offered a $2,000 prize for the largest python and a Tracker 570 Off Road ATV worth approximately $5,000 for the most pythons caught over the seven-day period of the event. Contest participants are encouraged to kill pythons with a bullet, shotgun blast, or captive bolt to the head. Decapitation by blade is considered inhumane because constrictors can survive for several minutes afterward. A less violent and presumably more preferable solution for the animals are the dozens of small private sanctuaries—like Quiet Glen—and private zoos across the state that house and care for exotic animals, which FWC licensing procedures enable.

42. Unless, of course, the rodent has toxoplasmosis, which is caused by a parasite that spends half of its life cycle in cats and half in rodents. It rewires a part of rodents' brains to make them sexually attracted to the smell of cat urine, so that they congregate in places where they are more likely to get eaten, enabling the *Toxoplasma gondii* protozoan to continue its life cycle inside the cats.

## Conclusion

1. Abrell, "Animal Sanctuaries," 573.

2. See Donaldson and Kymlicka, "Farmed Animal Sanctuaries"; Jones, "Captivity in the Context of a Sanctuary."

3. See Star, "Power, Technologies, and the Phenomenology of Conventions." See also Kirksey, Schuetze, and Helmreich, "Introduction."

4. Birke, "Naming Names," 1. See also Coulter, *Animals, Work, and the Promise of Interspecies Solidarity*, 3.

5. Brown, *Undoing the Demos*, 221.

6. Brown, 222.

7. Scientist Paul Crutzen first proposed that this current epoch in human history, in which humans have so drastically altered the global environment (and continue to do so at an accelerating pace), should be called the Anthropocene. Crutzen, "Geology of Mankind."

8. Kolbert, *Sixth Extinction*; McBrien, "Accumulating Extinction"; McBrien, "This Is Not the Sixth Extinction." As pattrice jones notes, "the droughts, floods, and wildfires of recent years are but the tip of the melting iceberg that has already begun to submerge the lands on which we stand under rising tides for which our own reprocentric rapacity is to blame." jones, "Queer Eros in the Enchanted Forest," 81.

9. Abrell, "Animal Sanctuaries," 576.

10. See Kirksey, Shapiro, and Brodine, "Hope in Blasted Landscapes," for an analysis of a similar future-oriented opposition to despair, which they describe as "hope in blasted landscapes." See also Tsing, "Blasted Landscapes."

11. Grimm, "Some of NIH's Chimpanzees Will Not Retire to a Sanctuary."

12. Grimm.

13. Grimm.

14. For more on the chimpanzees who have been used for research in the

United States, see Lori Gruen's "First 100," which memorializes the first one hundred chimps used for laboratory research and provides biographies and photos for each, and her "Last 1000," which documents the last one thousand chimps used in research and whether they have been retired to sanctuary yet.

15. Reardon, "NIH to Retire All Research Chimpanzees."

16. NBC10, "122 Cats Rescued from Pennsylvania Home."

17. See, e.g., Collard, "Putting Animals Back Together."

18. Braverman, *Zooland*. See Foucault, *Security, Territory, Population*.

19. Foucault, *Security, Territory, Population*, 171–72.

20. Braverman, *Zooland*, 36.

21. Foucault, *Security, Territory, Population*, 172.

22. Braverman, *Zooland*, 36. See also Abrell, "Lively Sanctuaries," 144.

23. Foucault, *Security, Territory, Population*, 173.

24. Foucault, 173.

25. Foucault, 173.

26. Foucault, 173.

27. Braverman, *Zooland*, 36.

28. Braverman, 36.

29. Braverman, 36.

30. Braverman, 37.

31. Braverman, 36. See Foucault, *Security, Territory, Population*, 149.

32. Braverman, *Zooland*, 203, 38.

33. Abrell, "Lively Sanctuaries," 148.

34. Foucault, *Security, Territory, Population*, 173.

35. See Donaldson and Kymlicka, "Farmed Animal Sanctuaries."

36. Abrell, "Lively Sanctuaries," 149.

37. Wadiwel, *War against Animals*, 110. See also Cole, "From 'Animal Machines' to 'Happy Meat'?"

38. Wadiwel, *War against Animals*, 112.

39. Abrell, "Lively Sanctuaries," 149.

40. jones, "Derangement and Resistance." See also Gillespie, *Cow with Ear Tag #1389*, 215. On the transformative potential of "reimaginings" for human–nonhuman relations, see Rutherford, *Governing the Wild*, 201–3.

41. Abrell, "Lively Sanctuaries," 150.

42. Gillespie, *Cow with Ear Tag #1389*, 143.

43. Similarly, as Lori Gruen notes, "a common refrain in the sanctuary community is certainly true: 'Saving one animal may not change the world, but for that one animal, the world will change forever.'" Gruen, *Ethics and Animals*, 161.

44. See Abrell, "Sanctuary-Making as Rural Political Action"; Abrell, "Animal Sanctuaries"; Meijer, "Melancholic Animal," 122.

45. See Lorimer, *Wildlife in the Anthropocene*.

46. Berlant and Seitz, "On Citizenship and Optimism." See also Berlant, *Cruel Optimism*.

47. For example, Wendy Brown, examining women's rights, argues, "Rights almost always serve as a mitigation—but not a resolution—of subordinating powers. While rights may attenuate the subordination and violation to which women are vulnerable in a masculinist social, political, and economic regime, they vanquish neither the regime nor its mechanisms of reproduction. They do not eliminate male dominance even as they soften some of its effects. Such softening is not itself a problem: if violence is upon you, almost any means of reducing it is of value. The problem surfaces in the question of when and whether rights for women are formulated in such a way as to enable the escape of the subordinated from the site of that violation, and when and whether they build a fence around us at that site, regulating rather than challenging the conditions within. And the paradox within this problem is this: the more highly specified rights are as rights for women, the more likely they are to build that fence insofar as they are more likely to encode a definition of women premised upon our subordination in the transhistorical discourse of liberal jurisprudence." Brown, "Suffering Rights as Paradoxes," 231. See also Wadiwel, *War against Animals*, 38–39.

48. See Lovvorn, "Animal Law in Action."

49. Wadiwel, *War against Animals*, 39.

50. See Boltanski, *Distant Suffering*; Fassin, "Compassion and Repression"; Fassin, "Inequality of Lives, Hierarchies of Humanity"; Malkki, "Speechless Emissaries"; Redfield, *Life in Crisis*; Ticktin, "Policing and Humanitarianism in France." For contrasts between refugee camps and farmed animal sanctuaries, see also Donaldson and Kymlicka, "Farmed Animal Sanctuaries."

51. See Ferdowsian, *Phoenix Zones*. Conceptualizing spaces of resilience and recovery from trauma as "phoenix zones," medical doctor Hope Ferdowsian identifies sanctuaries as models of such phoenix zones and calls on people to envision the expansion of these spaces to encompass the planet: "Imagine a world that allows for full self-determined potential of every being. Consider what we might learn from each other—as women and men, girls and boys, nonhuman and human animals—and how we could grow together. Envision a Phoenix Zone, truly planetary in scale, replacing what were once conflict zones" (120).

52. Ferdowsian, *Phoenix Zones*.

53. Foucault, "Of Other Spaces," 24. See Abrell, "Interrogating Captive Freedom," 5.

54. Relatedly, Timothy Pachirat argues, "There is an urgency to unimagine sanctuaries as sacred utopias—places that are no places—and instead (re)think them as sites of potential rupture and resistance." Pachirat, "Sanctuary," 351.

55. See Bendell, "Deep Adaptation."

56. Kim, *Dangerous Crossings*, 20; Abrell, "Animal Sanctuaries," 575. On mutual avowal, see also Gruen, "Samuel Dubose."

57. Gossett and Filar, "Cruising in the End Times." See also Gossett, "Blackness, Animality, and the Unsovereign."

58. Gossett and Filar, "Cruising in the End Times." See Abrell, "Animal Sanctuaries," 575.

59. Pachirat, "Sanctuary," 350–51.

60. Kim, *Dangerous Crossings*. See also Pachirat, "Sanctuary," 350. As Kim observes in her incisive critique of the animal abolition movement and its use of the slave/animal analogy, "animal abolition's radical instincts are entirely correct: it is right in its unforgiving critique of welfarism and right to call for revolutionary change. The problem is not, as is sometimes argued, that it is too extreme but rather that it is not extreme enough in its conceptualization of the problem, its sense of what needs to be done and its vision of the future." Kim, "Abolition," 29.

61. Pachirat, "Sanctuary," 350.

62. Abrell, "Animal Sanctuaries," 575.

63. See Joyce, Nevins, and Schneiderman, "Commodification."

64. Abrell, "Sanctuary-Making as Rural Political Action," 110.

65. Abrell.

66. Indeed, mutual aid is a common component of solidarity movements, and given that animals inspired the concept, it's fitting that the principle of mutual aid—helping others as a basis of relating—is reflected in the work of animal sanctuaries today. In the late 1800s, Russian naturalist and anarchist philosopher Petr Kropotkin wrote his influential book *Mutual Aid: A Factor of Evolution* based on his observations of intraspecies and interspecies practices of mutually beneficial cooperation and reciprocity among animals on the Eurasian steppe. He showed that these forms of mutually beneficial interaction played as much (if not more) of a role in animal life as the competition for resources that Charles Darwin saw shaping evolution. His work provided an important corrective to popular social Darwinist theories of the time and helped to inspire generations of anarchist and socialist activists to embrace principles of mutual aid in their lives and activist work.

67. Ko, "Notes from the Border of the Human–Animal Divide," 73.

68. Ko, 73–75.

69. Abrell, "Animal Sanctuaries," 575.

70. Abrell, "Sanctuary-Making as Rural Political Action," 110.

71. jones, "Queer Eros in the Enchanted Forest," 81.

# Bibliography

Abrell, Elan. "Animal Sanctuaries." In *The Routledge Handbook of Animal Ethics*, edited by Bob Fischer, 569–77. New York: Routledge, 2019.

Abrell, Elan. "Interrogating Captive Freedom: The Possibilities and Limits of Animal Sanctuaries." *Animal Studies Journal* 6, no. 2 (2017): 1–8.

Abrell, Elan. "Lively Sanctuaries: A Shabbat of Animal Sacer." In *Animals, Biopolitics, Law: Lively Legalities*, edited by Irus Braverman, 135–54. New York: Routledge, 2016.

Abrell, Elan. "The Mongoose Trap: Grief, Intervention, and the Impossibility of Professional Detachment." In *Grieving Witnesses: The Politics of Grief in the Field*, edited by Kathryn Gillespie and Patricia Lopez, 68–79. Berkeley: University of California Press, 2019.

Abrell, Elan. "Sanctuary-Making as Rural Political Action." *Journal for the Anthropology of North America* 22, no. 2 (2019): 109–11.

Adams, Carol. *The Sexual Politics of Meat: A Feminist-Vegetarian Critical Theory.* New York: Continuum International, 1990.

Agamben, Giorgio. *Homo Sacer: Sovereign Power and Bare Life.* Translated by Daniel Heller-Roazen. Stanford, Calif.: Stanford University Press, 1998.

Agamben, Giorgio. *The Open: Man and Animal.* Translated by Kevin Attell. Stanford, Calif.: Stanford University Press, 2004.

Agamben, Giorgio. *Remnants of Auschwitz: The Witness and the Archive.* New York: Zone Books, 1999.

Alcampora, Ralph, ed. *Metamorphoses of the Zoo: Animal Encounter after Noah.* Lanham, Md.: Lexington Books, 2010.

Algar, James, Samuel Armstrong, David Hand, Graham Heid, Bill

Roberts, Paul Satterfield, and Norman Wright, dirs. *Bambi*. Burbank, Calif.: Walt Disney Studios, 1942.

Alger, Janet M., and Steven F. Alger. *Cat Cultures: The Social World of Cat Shelters*. Philadelphia: Temple University Press, 2003.

American Society for the Prevention of Cruelty to Animals. "Shelter Intake and Surrender." https://www.aspca.org/animal-homelessness /shelter-intake-and-surrender/pet-statistics.

Arluke, Arnold, and Clinton Sanders. *Regarding Animals*. Philadelphia: Temple University Press, 1996.

Balcombe, Jonathan. "Animal Pleasure and Its Moral Significance." *Applied Animal Behaviour Science* 118, no. 3–4 (2009): 208–16.

Barua, Maan. "Animating Capital: Work, Commodities, Circulation." *Progress in Human Geography* 43, no. 4 (2019): 650–69.

Barua, Maan. "Lively Commodities and Encounter Value." *Environment and Planning D* 34, no. 4 (2016): 725–44.

Baur, Gene. *Farm Sanctuary: Changing Hearts and Minds about Animals and Food*. New York: Touchstone, 2008.

Bekoff, Marc. *The Emotional Lives of Animals*. Novato, Calif.: New World Library, 2007.

Bendell, Jem. *Deep Adaptation: A Map for Navigating Climate Tragedy*. Occasional Paper 2. Cambridge: Institute of Leadership and Sustainability, 2018. https://www.lifeworth.com/deepadaptation.pdf.

Berlant, Lauren. *Cruel Optimism*. Durham, N.C.: Duke University Press, 2011.

Berlant, Lauren, and David Seitz. "On Citizenship and Optimism." *Society + Space*, March 22, 2013. https://societyandspace.org/2013/03 /22/on-citizenship-and-optimism/.

Birke, Lynda. "Naming Names; or, What's in It for the Animals?" *Humanimalia* 1, no. 1 (2009): 1–9.

Boglioli, Marc. *A Matter of Life and Death: Hunting in Contemporary Vermont*. Boston: University of Massachusetts Press, 2009.

Bolender, Karen. "R. A. W. Assmilk Soap." In *The Multispecies Salon*, edited by Eben Kirksey, 64–86. Durham, N.C.: Duke University Press, 2014.

Boltanski, Luc. *Distant Suffering: Morality, Media, and Politics*. Translated by Graham Burchell. Cambridge: Cambridge University Press, 1999.

Braverman, Irus. "Animal Mobilegalities: The Regulation of Animal Movement in the American City." *Humanimalia* 5, no. 1 (2013): 104–35.

Braverman, Irus. *Zooland: The Institution of Captivity*. Stanford, Calif.: Stanford University Press, 2013.

Brightman, Robert. *Grateful Prey: Rock Cree Human–Animal Relationships*. Berkeley: University of California Press, 1993.

Brown, Wendy. "Sacrificial Citizenship: Neoliberal Austerity Politics." Roundtable discussion. Spring 2012. http://globalization.gc.cuny .edu/events/sacrificial-citizenship-neoliberal-austerity-politics/.

Brown, Wendy. "Suffering Rights as Paradoxes." *Constellations* 7, no. 2 (2000): 208–29.

Brown, Wendy. *Undoing the Demos: Neoliberalism's Stealth Revolution*. Brooklyn, N.Y.: Zone Press, 2015.

Buckley, Carol, and G. A. Bradshaw. "The Art of Cultural Brokerage: Recreating Elephant–Human Relationship and Community." *Spring* 83 (2010): 37–63.

Bulbeck, Chilla. *Facing the Wild: Ecotourism, Conservation, and Animal Encounters*. Los Angeles, Calif.: Earthscan, 2005.

Butcher, Maddy. "Small Towns Are the Place to Challenge Immigration Policy." *High Country News*, June 30, 2017. https://www.hcn.org /articles/opinion-immigration-why-small-towns-are-the-place -to-challenge-trumps-immigration-policy.

Candea, Matei. "'I Fell in Love with Carlos the Meerkat': Engagement and Detachment in Human–Animal Relations." *American Ethnologist* 37, no. 2 (2010): 241–58.

Cassidy, Rebecca. *Horse People: Thoroughbred Culture in Lexington and Newmarket*. Baltimore: Johns Hopkins University Press, 2007.

Cassidy, Rebecca, and Molly Mullin, eds. *Where the Wild Things Are Now: Domestication Reconsidered*. Oxford: Berg, 2007.

Chris, Cynthia. *Watching Wildlife*. Minneapolis: University of Minnesota Press, 2006.

Chrulew, Matthew. "Managing Love and Death at the Zoo: The Biopolitics of Endangered Species Preservation." *Australian Humanities Review* 50 (May 2011): 137–57.

Clarke, John. "Living with/in and without Neo-liberalism." *Focaal* 51, no. 1 (2008): 135–47.

Cole, Matthew. "From 'Animal Machines' to 'Happy Meat'? Foucault's Ideas of Disciplinary and Pastoral Power Applied to 'Animal-Centred' Welfare Discourse." *Animals* 1 (2011): 83–101.

Collard, Rosemary-Claire. "Cougar–Human Entanglements and the Biopolitical Un/making of Safe Space." *Environment and Planning D* 30, no. 1 (2012): 23–42.

Collard, Rosemary-Claire. "Putting Animals Back Together, Taking

Commodities Apart." *Annals of the Association of American Geographers* 104, no. 1 (2014): 151–65.

Collard, Rosemary-Claire, and Jessica Dempsey. "Life for Sale? The Politics of Lively Commodities." *Environment and Planning A* 45, no. 11 (2013): 2682–99.

Collard, Rosemary-Claire, and Kathryn Gillespie. 2015. "Doing Critical Animal Geographies: Future Directions." In *Critical Animal Geographies: Politics, Intersections, and Hierarchies in a Multispecies World*, edited by Kathryn Gillespie and Rosemary-Claire Collard, 203–12. New York: Routledge, 2015.

Comaroff, Jean, and John L. Comaroff. "Naturing the Nation: Aliens, Apocalypse and the Postcolonial State." *Journal of Southern African Studies* 27, no. 3 (2001): 627–51.

Coulter, Kendra. *Animals, Work, and the Promise of Interspecies Solidarity.* New York: Palgrave Macmillan, 2016.

Cowperthwaite, Gabriela, dir. *Blackfish.* New York: CNN Films, 2013.

Cruikshank, Julie. "Glaciers and Climate Change: Perspectives from Oral Tradition." *Arctic* 54, no. 4 (2001): 377–93.

Crutzen, Paul. "Geology of Mankind." *Nature* 415 (2002): 23.

Cunningham, Hilary. *God and Caesar at the Rio Grande: Sanctuary and the Politics of Religion.* Minneapolis: University of Minnesota Press, 1995.

Davidson, Michael J. "Sanctuary: A Modern Legal Anachronism." *Capital University Law Review* 42, no. 3 (2014): 583–618.

Davis, Karen. *The Holocaust and the Henmaid's Tale.* New York: Lantern Books, 2005.

Davis, Susan G. *Spectacular Nature: Corporate Culture and the Sea World Experience.* Berkeley: University of California Press, 1997.

Deckha, Maneesha. "Initiating a Non-anthropocentric Jurisprudence: The Rule of Law and Animal Vulnerability under a Property Paradigm." *Alberta Law Review* 50, no. 4 (2013): 783–814.

Delaney, David. "Making Nature/Marking Humans: Law as a Site of (Cultural) Production." *Annals of the Association of American Geographers* 91, no. 3 (2001): 487–503.

DeMello, Margo. *Animals and Society: An Introduction to Human–Animal Studies.* New York: Columbia University Press, 2012.

Derby, Pat. "PAWS: An Introduction." https://www.pawsweb.org /documents/PAWS_AN_INTRO.pdf.

Derrida, Jacques. *The Animal That Therefore I Am.* Translated by David Wills. New York: Fordham University Press, 2008.

Descola, Philippe. "Constructing Natures: Symbolic Ecology and Social Practice." In *Nature and Society: Anthropological Perspectives*, edited by Philippe Descola and Gísli Pálsson, 82–102. New York: Routledge, 1996.

Dhont, Kristof, and Gordon Hodson, eds. *Why We Love and Exploit Animals: Bridging Insights from Academia and Advocacy.* New York: Routledge, 2019.

Donaldson, Sue, and Will Kymlicka. "Farmed Animal Sanctuaries: The Heart of the Movement? A Socio-political Perspective." *Politics and Animals* 1 (2015): 50–74.

Donaldson, Sue, and Will Kymlicka. *Zoopolis: A Political Theory of Animal Rights.* Oxford: Oxford University Press, 2011.

Doyle, Catherine. "Captive Elephants." In *The Ethics of Captivity*, edited by Lori Gruen, 38–56. Oxford: Oxford University Press, 2014.

Doyle, Catherine. "Captive Wildlife Sanctuaries: Definition, Ethical Considerations and Public Perception." *Animal Studies Journal* 6, no. 2 (2017): 55–85.

Dutkiewicz, Jan. "'Post-modernism,' Politics, and Pigs." *PhaenEx* 8, no. 2 (2013): 296–307.

Emmerman, Karen S. "Sanctuary, Not Remedy: The Problem of Captivity and the Need for Moral Repair." In *The Ethics of Captivity*, edited by Lori Gruen, 213–30. Oxford: Oxford University Press, 2014.

Engels, Friedrich. *The Conditions of the Working Class in England: From Personal Observations and Authentic Sources.* London: Panther Books, 1969.

Farm Sanctuary. *How to Start, Operate, and Develop a Farm Animal Sanctuary.* Informational binder distributed at Farm Sanctuary Care Conference, 2014.

Fassin, Didier. "Compassion and Repression: The Moral Economy of Immigration Policies in France." *Cultural Anthropology* 20, no. 3 (2005): 362–87.

Fassin, Didier. "Inequality of Lives, Hierarchies of Humanity: Moral Commitments and Ethical Dilemmas of Humanitarianism." In *In the Name of Humanity: The Government of Threat and Care*, edited by Ilana Feldman and Miriam Ticktin, 238–55. Durham, N.C.: Duke University Press, 2010.

Fausto, Carlos. "Feasting on People: Eating Animals and Humans in Amazonia." *Current Anthropology* 48, no. 4 (2007): 497–530.

Favre, David. "Living Property: A New Status for Animals within the Legal System." *Marquette Law Review* 93 (2010): 1021–71.

Fawcett, Anne. "Euthanasia and Morally Justifiable Killing in a Veterinary Clinical Context." In *Animal Death*, edited by Jay Johnston and Fiona Probyn-Rapsey, 205–21. Sydney: Sydney University Press, 2013.

Ferdowsian, Hope. *Phoenix Zones: Where Strength Is Born and Resilience Lives*. Chicago: University of Chicago Press, 2018.

Fischer, J., and D. B. Lindenmayer. "An Assessment of the Published Results of Animal Relocations." *Biological Conservation* 6, no. 1 (2000): 1–11.

Fleury, Erika. "Money for Monkeys, and More: Ensuring Sanctuary Retirement of Nonhuman Primates." *Animal Studies Journal* 6, no. 2 (2017): 30–54.

Florida Fish and Wildlife Conservation Commission. "Invasive Species." http://web.archive.org/web/20120813155646/http://myfwc.com /wildlifehabitats/nonnatives/invasive-species/.

Florida Fish and Wildlife Conservation Commission. "What Is a Nonnative Species?" http://web.archive.org/web/20120414185424/http:// myfwc.com/wildlifehabitats/nonnatives/what-are-nonnatives/.

Foer, Jonathan Safran. *Eating Animals*. New York: Little, Brown, 2009.

Foucault, Michel. *The History of Sexuality, Volume I: An Introduction*. Translated by Robert Hurley. New York: Vintage Books, 1978.

Foucault, Michel. "Of Other Spaces." Translated by Jay Miskowiec. *Diacritics* 16, no. 1 (1986): 22–27.

Foucault, Michel. *Security, Territory Population: Lectures at the Collège de France, 1977–78*. Edited by Michel Senellart. Translated by Graham Burchell. New York: Picador/Palgrave Macmillan, 2009.

Fraiman, Susan. "Pussy Panic versus Liking Animals: Tracking Gender in Animal Studies." *Critical Inquiry* 39, no. 1 (2012): 89–115.

Francione, Gary. *Animals as Persons: Essays on the Abolition of Animal Exploitation*. New York: Columbia University Press.

Francione, Gary. "Animals—Property or Persons?" Faculty Paper 21, Rutgers Law School, Camden, N.J., 2004.

Francione, Gary. *Introduction to Animal Rights: Your Child or the Dog?* Philadelphia: Temple University Press, 2000.

Francione, Gary. *Rain without Thunder: The Ideology of the Animal Rights Movement*. Philadelphia: Temple University Press, 1996.

Francione, Gary, and Robert Garner. *The Animal Rights Debate: Abolition or Regulation*. New York: Columbia University Press, 2010.

Franklin, Adrian. *Animals and Modern Cultures: A Sociology of Human–Animal Relations in Modernity*. London: Sage, 1999.

Fuentes, Agustin. "Naturalcultural Encounters in Bali: Monkeys, Temples, Tourists, and Ethnoprimatology." *Cultural Anthropology* 24, no. 4 (2010): 600–624.

Fultz, Amy. "A Guide for Modern Sanctuaries with Examples from a Captive Chimpanzee Sanctuary." *Animal Studies Journal* 6, no. 2 (2017): 9–29.

Fultz, Amy, and Cathy Willis Spraetz. Foreword to *Entangled Empathy: An Alternative Ethic for Our Relationships with Animals*. New York: Lantern Books, 2015. Kindle.

Fusari, S. "What Is an Animal Sanctuary? Evidence from Applied Linguistics." *Animal Studies Journal* 6, no. 2 (2017): 137–60.

Gillespie, Kathryn. *The Cow with Ear Tag #1389*. Chicago: University of Chicago Press, 2018.

Gillespie, Kathryn. "For a Politicized Multispecies Ethnography: Reflections on a Feminist Geographic Pedagogical Experiment." *Politics and Animals* 5 (2019): 17–32.

Gillespie, Kathryn. "Nonhuman Animal Resistance and the Improprieties of Live Property." In *Animals, Biopolitics, Law: Lively Legalities*, edited by Irus Braverman, 117–34. New York: Routledge, 2016.

Gillespie, Kathryn. "Sexualized Violence and the Gendered Commodification of the Animal Body in Pacific Northwest US Dairy Production." *Gender, Place, and Culture* 21, no. 10 (2014): 1321–37.

Gossett, Che. "Blackness, Animality, and the Unsovereign." *Verso* (blog), September 8, 2015. https://www.versobooks.com/blogs/2228 -che-gossett-blackness-animality-and-the-unsovereign.

Gossett, Che, and Ray Filar. "Cruising in the End Times: An Interview with Che Gossett." *Verso* (blog), December 18, 2016. http://www .versobooks.com/blogs/3016-cruising-in-the-end-times-an-interview -with-che-gossett.

Graham, Marty. "Hollywood Mogul Simon Buys Fur Farm with Animal Rights Activists." Reuters, August 20, 2014. https://web.archive.org /web/20191022100841/https://www.reuters.com/article/us-usa -california-chinchillas/hollywood-mogul-simon-buys-fur-farm -with-animal-rights-activists-idUSKBN0GK1XF20140820.

Grey, Thomas C. "The Disintegration of Property." In *Property*, edited by J. Roland Pennock and John W. Chapman, 69–85. New York: New York University Press, 1980.

Grier, Katherine. *Pets in America: A History*. Chapel Hill: University of North Carolina Press, 2006.

Griffith, Marcie, Jennifer Wolch, and Unna Lassiter. "Animal Practices and the Racialization of Filipinas in Los Angeles." *Society and Animals* 10, no. 3 (2002): 221–48.

Grimm, David. "Some of NIH's Chimpanzees Will Not Retire to a Sanctuary as Planned." *Science,* October 24, 2019. https://www .sciencemag.org/news/2019/10/some-nih-s-chimpanzees-will-not -retire-sanctuary-planned.

Gruen, Lori. "Dignity, Captivity, and an Ethics of Sight." In *The Ethics of Captivity,* edited by Lori Gruen, 242–58. Oxford: Oxford University Press, 2014.

Gruen, Lori. "Entangled Empathy: An Alternative Approach to Animal Ethics." In *The Politics of Species: Reshaping Our Relationship with Other Animals,* edited by Raymond Corbey and Annette Lanjouw, 223–31. Cambridge: Cambridge University Press, 2013.

Gruen, Lori. *Entangled Empathy: An Alternative Ethic for Our Relationships with Animals.* New York: Lantern Books, 2015.

Gruen, Lori. *Ethics and Animals: An Introduction.* Cambridge: Cambridge University Press, 2011.

Gruen, Lori, ed. *The Ethics of Captivity.* New York: Oxford University Press, 2014.

Gruen, Lori. "Navigating Difference (Again): Animal Ethics and Entangled Empathy." In *Animal Subjects 2.0,* edited by Jodey Castricano and Lauren Corman, 213–33. Waterloo, Ont.: Wilfrid Laurier University Press, 2016.

Gruen, Lori. "Samuel Dubose, Cecil the Lion, and the Ethics of Avowal." *Al Jazeera,* July 31, 2015. http://america.aljazeera.com/opinions/2015/7 /samuel-dubose-cecil-the-lion-and-the-ethics-of-avowal.html.

Gruen, Lori. "Shifting towards an Ethics of Sanctuary." June 3, 2016. http://www.humansandnature.org/shifting-toward-an-ethics-of -sanctuary.

Gruen, Lori. "Why Euthanizing Ebola Animals Is a Dangerous Road to Go Down." *Time,* October 14, 2014. https://time.com/3506136/ebola -euthanizing-animals-spain-dog-excalibur/.

Gruen, Lori, and Robert C. Jones. "Veganism as an Aspiration." In *The Moral Complexities of Eating Meat,* edited by Ben Bramble and Bob Fischer, 153–71. Oxford: Oxford University Press, 2015.

Hann, C. M. *Property Relations: Renewing the Anthropological Tradition.* Cambridge: Cambridge University Press, 1998.

Haraway, Donna. *When Species Meet.* Minneapolis: University of Minnesota Press, 2008.

Hawaiian Administrative Rules §13-124-2. http://dlnr.hawaii.gov/dofaw
/files/2013/09/Chap124a.pdf.

Hawaiian Invasive Species Council. "Invasive Species." http://dlnr.hawaii
.gov/hisc/info/.

Hawaiian Penal Code §711-1109(c). http://www.capitol.hawaii.gov
/hrscurrent/Vol14_Ch0701-0853/HRS0711/HRS_0711-1109.htm.

Hayward, Eva. "Fingeryeyes: Impressions of Cup Corals." *Cultural Anthropology* 25, no. 4 (2010): 577–99.

Herzog, Hal. 2011. *Some We Love, Some We Hate, Some We Eat.* New York:
Harper Perennial.

Hobsbawm, Eric J. *Primitive Rebels: Studies in Archaic Forms of Social
Movement in the Nineteenth and Twentieth Centuries.* Manchester, U.K.:
Manchester University Press, 1959.

Horowitz, Helen. "The National Zoological Park: 'City of Refuge' or Zoo?"
*Records of the Columbia Historical Society of Washington, D.C.* 49 (1973):
405–29.

Hua, Julietta, and Neel Ahuja. "Chimpanzee Sanctuary: 'Surplus' Life
and the Politics of Transspecies Care." *American Quarterly* 65, no. 3
(2013): 619–37.

Humane Society of the United States. "Pets by the Numbers." https://
www.humanesociety.org/resources/pets-numbers.

Humane Society of the United States. "US Slaughter Totals, by Species
(Excluding Chickens) 1960–2013." *Farm Animal Data* 1 (2014). https://
animalstudiesrepository.org/hsus_industry_statistics_farming/1.

Humane Society of the United States. "US Slaughter Totals,
Chickens 1960–2013." *Farm Animal Data* 6 (2014). https://
animalstudiesrepository.org/hsus_industry_statistics_farming/6.

Humane Ventures. "2019 U.S. Animal Kill Clock." https://animalclock.org
/#section-considerations.

Irvine, Leslie. *If You Tame Me: Understanding Our Connection with Animals.*
Philadelphia: Temple University Press, 2004.

Jamieson, Dale. "Against Zoos." In *Morality's Progress: Essays on Humans,
Other Animals, and the Rest of Nature,* 166–75. Oxford: Oxford University
Press, 2003.

Jamieson, Dale. "Zoos Revisited." In *Morality's Progress: Essays on Humans,
Other Animals, and the Rest of Nature,* 176–89. Oxford: Oxford University Press, 2003.

Jones, Miriam. "Captivity in the Context of a Sanctuary for Formerly

Farmed Animals." In *The Ethics of Captivity,* edited by Lori Gruen, 90–101. Oxford: Oxford University Press, 2014.

jones, pattrice. "Derangement and Resistance: Reflections from under the Glare of an Angry Emu." Keynote address, Animaladies II Conference, University of Wollongong, Wollongong, Australia, December 13, 2018.

jones, pattrice. *The Oxen at the Intersection: A Collision.* Brooklyn, N.J.: Lantern Books, 2014.

jones, pattrice. "Queer Eros in the Enchanted Forest: The Spirit of Stonewall as Sustainable Energy." *QED: A Journal in GLBTQ Worldmaking* 6, no. 2 (2019): 76–82.

Joy, Melanie. *Why We Love Dogs, Eat Pigs, and Wear Cows: An Introduction to Carnism.* San Francisco: Conari Press, 2010.

Joyce, John, Joseph Nevins, and Jill S. Schneiderman. "Commodification, Violence, and the Making of Workers and Ducks at Hudson Valley Foie Gras." In *Critical Animal Geographies: Politics, Intersections, and Hierarchies in a Multispecies World,* edited by Kathryn Gillespie and Rosemary-Claire Collard, 93–107. New York: Routledge, 2015.

Kagan, Shelly. "Do I Make a Difference?" *Philosophy and Public Affairs* 39, no. 2 (2011): 105–41.

Kalechofsky, Roberta. *Animal Suffering and the Holocaust: The Problem with Comparisons.* New York: Micah, 2003.

Kim, Claire Jean. "Abolition." In *Critical Terms for Animal Studies,* edited by Lori Gruen, 15–32. Chicago: University of Chicago Press, 2018.

Kim, Claire Jean. *Dangerous Crossings: Race, Species, and Nature in Multicultural Age.* New York: Cambridge University Press, 2015.

Kingfisher, Catherine, and Jeff Maskovsky. "Introduction: The Limits of Neoliberalism." *Critique of Anthropology* 28, no. 2 (2008): 115–26.

Kirksey, Eben. *Emergent Ecologies.* Durham, N.C.: Duke University Press, 2015.

Kirksey, Eben, ed. *The Multispecies Salon.* Durham, N.C.: Duke University Press, 2014.

Kirksey, Eben, and Stefan Helmreich. "The Emergence of Multispecies Ethnography." *Cultural Anthropology* 24, no. 4 (2010): 545–76.

Kirksey, Eben, Craig Schuetze, and Stefan Helmreich. "Introduction: Tactics of Multispecies Ethnography." In *The Multispecies Salon,* edited by Eben Kirksey, 1–24. Durham, N.C.: Duke University Press, 2014.

Kirksey, Eben, Nicholas Shapiro, and Maria Brodine. "Hope in Blasted Landscapes." In *The Multispecies Salon,* edited by Eben Kirksey, 29–63. Durham, N.C.: Duke University Press, 2014.

Ko, Syl. "Notes from the Border of the Human-Animal Divide: Thinking and Talking about Animal Oppression When You're Not Quite Human Yourself." In *Aphro-ism*, by Aph Ko and Syl Ko, 70–75. New York: Lantern Books, 2017.

Ko, Syl. "We Can Avoid the Debate about Comparing Human and Animals Oppression, if We Simply Make the Right Connections." In *Aphro-ism*, by Aph Ko and Syl Ko, 82–87. New York: Lantern Books, 2017.

Kohn, Eduardo. "How Dogs Dream: Amazonian Natures and the Politics of Transspecies Engagement." *American Ethnologist* 34, no. 1 (2007): 3–24.

Kohn, Eduardo. *How Forests Think.* Berkeley: University of California Press, 2013.

Kolbert, Elizabeth. *The Sixth Extinction: An Unnatural History.* New York: Henry Holt, 2014.

Kosek, Jake. "Ecologies of Empire: On the New Uses of the Honeybee." *Cultural Anthropology* 25, no. 4 (2010): 650–78.

Kropotkin, Petr Alekseevich. *Mutual Aid: A Factor of Evolution.* New York: Doubleday, Page, 1909.

LaCapra, Dominick. *History and Its Limits: Human, Animal, Violence.* Ithaca, N.Y.: Cornell University Press, 2009.

Lorimer, Jamie. *Wildlife in the Anthropocene: Conservation after Nature.* Minneapolis: University of Minnesota Press, 2015.

Lovvorn, Jonathan R. "Animal Law in Action: The Law, Public Perception, and the Limits of Animal Rights Theory as Basis for Legal Reform." *Animal Law* 12, no. 2 (2006): 133–50.

Lowe, Celia. "Viral Clouds: Becoming H5N1 in Indonesia." *Cultural Anthropology* 25, no. 4 (2010): 625–49.

Mackenzie, Robin. "Bestia Sacer and Agamben's Anthropological Machine: Biomedical/Legal Taxonomies as Somatechnologies of Human and Nonhuman Animals' Ethico-Political Relations." In *Law and Anthropology: Current Legal Issues*, vol. 12, edited by Michael Freeman and David Napier, 484–523. Oxford: Oxford University Press, 2009.

Mackenzie, Robin. "How the Politics of Inclusion/Exclusion and the Neuroscience of Dehumanization/Rehumanization Can Contribute to Animal Activists' Strategies: Bestia Sacer II." *Society and Animals* 19 (2011): 407–24.

Malkki, Liisa. "Speechless Emissaries: Refugees, Humanitarianism, and Dehistoricization." *Cultural Anthropology* 11, no. 3 (1996): 377–404.

Mason, G. J. "Stereotypies: A Critical Review." *Animal Behaviour* 41 (1991): 1015–37.

Mbembe, Achille. "Necropolitics," translated by Libby Meintjes. *Public Culture* 15, no. 1 (2003): 11–40.

McBrien, Justin. "Accumulating Extinction; Planetary Catastrophism in the Necrocene." In *Anthropocene or Capitalocene?*, edited by J. W. Moore, 116–37. Oakland, Calif.: PM Press, 2016.

McBrien, Justin. "This Is Not the Sixth Extinction. It's the First Extermination Event." Truthout.org, September 14, 2019. https://truthout.org/articles/this-is-not-the-sixth-extinction-its-the-first-extermination-event/.

Meijer, Eva. "The Melancholic Animal—on Depression and Animality." *Humanimalia* 11, no. 1 (2019): 109–27.

Minder, Raphael, and Pam Belluck. "Spain, amid Protests, Destroys Dog of Ebola-Infected Nurse." *New York Times*, October 8, 2014. https://www.nytimes.com/2014/10/09/science/ebola-dog-excalibur-nurse-spain.html.

Mizelle, Brett. *Pig*. London: Reaktion Books, 2014.

Morris, Steven. "Firefighters Eat Sausages Made of Piglets They Saved from Blaze." *Guardian*, August 23, 2017. https://www.theguardian.com/environment/2017/aug/23/firefighters-sausages-piglets-saved-blaze-wiltshire.

Mullan, Bob, and Garry Marvin. *Zoo Culture*. London: Weidenfeld and Nicolson, 1999.

Mullin, Malone. "'Shock' and 'Heartbreak' after Adopted Pig Ends Up on Dinner Table." *CBC News*, February 23, 2018. https://www.cbc.ca/news/canada/british-columbia/molly-the-pig-1.4550000.

Mullin, Molly. "Feeding the Animals." In *Where the Wild Things Are Now: Domestication Revisited*, edited by Rebecca Cassidy and Molly Mullin, 277–304. Oxford: Berg, 2007.

Mullin, Molly. "Mirrors and Windows: Sociocultural Studies of Human–Animal Relationships." *Annual Review of Anthropology* 28 (1999): 201–24.

Nadasdy, Paul. "The Gift in the Animal: The Ontology of Hunting and Human-Animal Sociality." *American Ethnologist* 34, no. 1 (2007): 25–43.

Nast, Heidi J. "Pit Bulls, Slavery, and Whiteness in the Mid- to Late-Nineteenth-Century US: Geographical Trajectories." In *Critical Animal Geographies: Politics, Intersections, and Hierarchies in a Multispecies World*, edited by Kathryn Gillespie and Rosemary-Claire Collard, 127–46. New York: Routledge, 2015.

NBC10. "122 Cats Rescued from Pennsylvania Home, Owner Wanted to

Open 'Cat Sanctuary.'" August 14, 2015. http://www.nbcphiladelphia
.com/news/local/122-Cats-Rescued-from-Filthy-Pennsylvania-Home
-321858862.html.

Noske, Barbara. *Beyond Boundaries: Humans and Animals.* Montreal, Ont.:
Black Rose Books, 1997.

Noske, Barbara. *Humans and Other Animals: Beyond the Boundaries of Anthropology.* London: Pluto Press, 1989.

Ogden, Laura A. *Swamplife: People, Gators, and Mangroves Entangled in the
Everglades.* Minneapolis: University of Minnesota Press, 2011.

Ogden, Laura A., Billy Hall, and Kimiko Tanita. "Animals, Plants, People,
and Things: A Review of Multispecies Ethnography." *Environment and
Society: Advances in Research* 4 (2013): 5–24.

Pachirat, Timothy. *Every 12 Seconds.* New Haven, Conn.: Yale University
Press, 2013.

Pachirat, Timothy. "Sanctuary." In *Critical Terms for Animal Studies,* edited
by Lori Gruen, 337–55. Chicago: University of Chicago Press, 2018.

Patterson, Charles. *Eternal Treblinka: Our Treatment of Animals and the
Holocaust.* New York: Lantern Books, 2002.

Parreñas, Juno Salazar. *Decolonizing Extinction: The Work of Care in Orangutan
Rehabilitation.* Durham, N.C.: Duke University Press, 2018.

Parreñas, Juno Salazar. "Producing Affect: Transnational Volunteerism
in Malaysian Orangutan Rehabilitation Center." *American Ethnologist*
39, no. 4 (2012): 673–87.

Paxson, Heather. *The Life of Cheese: Crafting Food and Value in America.*
Berkeley: University of California Press, 2012.

Plumwood, Val. "Human Vulnerability and the Experience of Being Prey."
*Quadrant* 29, no. 3 (1995): 29–34.

Pollan, Michael. *The Omnivore's Dilemma.* New York: Penguin, 2007.

Povinelli, Elizabeth. *The Cunning of Recognition: Indigenous Alterities and the
Making of Australian Multiculturalism.* Durham, N.C.: Duke University
Press, 2002.

Probyn-Rapsey, Fiona. "Dingoes and Dog-Whistling: A Cultural Politics
of Race and Species in Australia." *Animal Studies Journal* 4, no. 2 (2015):
55–77.

Probyn-Rapsey, Fiona. "Hopes of Killing: The Cultural Politics of Eradi-
cation." Unpublished paper presented at Center for the Humanities,
Wesleyan University, Middletown, Conn., October 3, 2016.

Puig de le Bellacasa, María. *Matters of Care: Speculative Ethics in More than
Human Worlds.* Minneapolis: University of Minnesota Press, 2017.

Reardon, Sara. "NIH to Retire All Research Chimpanzees: Fifty Animals Held in 'Reserve' by the US Government Will Be Sent to Sanctuaries." *Nature*, November 18, 2015. http://www.nature.com/news/nih-to -retire-all-research-chimpanzees-1.18817.

Redfield, Peter. *Life in Crisis: The Ethical Journey of Doctors without Borders.* Berkeley: University of California Press, 2013.

Regan, Tom. *Empty Cages: Facing the Challenge of Animal Rights.* Oxford: Rowman and Littlefield, 2004.

Riley, Erin. "Contemporary Primatology in Anthropology: Beyond the Epistemological Abyss." *American Anthropologist* 115, no. 3 (2013): 411–22.

Riley, Erin P., and Tiffany W. Wade. "Adapting to Florida's Riverine Woodlands: The Population Status and Feeding Ecology of the Silver River Rhesus Macaques and Their Interface with Humans." *Primates* 57, no. 2 (2016): 195–210.

Ritvo, Harriet. *The Animal Estate: The English and Other Creatures in the Victorian Age.* Cambridge, Mass.: Harvard University Press, 1989.

Ritvo, Harriet. "The Emergence of Modern Pet-Keeping." *Anthrozoös* 1, no. 3 (1987): 158–65.

Rose, Deborah Bird. *Wild Dog Dreaming: Love and Extinction.* Charlottesville: University of Virginia Press, 2011.

Ross, Stephen R. "Captive Chimpanzees." In *The Ethics of Captivity,* edited by Lori Gruen, 57–76. Oxford: Oxford University Press, 2014.

Rutherford, Stephanie. *Governing the Wild: Ecotours of Power.* Minneapolis: University of Minnesota Press, 2011.

Schlosser, Eric. *Fast Food Nation.* New York: Harper Perennial, 2005.

Schlottman, Christopher, and Jeff Sebo. *Food, Animals, and the Environment.* New York: Routledge, 2019.

Schnurer, Maxwell. "At the Gates of Hell: The ALF and the Legacy of Holocaust Resistance." In *Terrorists or Freedom Fighters? Reflections on the Liberation of Animals,* edited by Steven Best and Anthony J. Nocella II, 107–28. New York: Lantern Books, 2004.

Scotton, Guy. "Duties to Socialise with Domesticated Animals: Farmed Animal Sanctuaries as Frontiers of Friendship." *Animal Studies Journal* 6, no. 2 (2017): 86–108.

SeaWorld. "Breaking News: The Last Generation of Orcas at SeaWorld." *SeaWorld Cares*, March 17, 2016. https://web.archive.org/web /20160317102157/https://seaworldcares.com/2016/03/Breaking-News -The-Last-Generation-of-Orcas-at-SeaWorld/.

Serpell, James. *In the Company of Animals: A Study of Human–Animal Relationships.* Cambridge: Cambridge University Press, 1996.

Shir-Vertesh, Dafna. "'Flexible Personhood': Loving Animals as Family Members in Israel." *American Anthropologist* 114, no. 3 (2012): 420–32.

Shukin, Nicole. *Animal Capital: Rendering Life in Biopolitical Times.* Minneapolis: University of Minnesota Press, 2009.

Singer, Peter. *Animal Liberation.* New York: New York Review of Books, 1975.

Sorenson, John. "Introduction: Thinking the Unthinkable." In *Critical Animal Studies: Thinking the Unthinkable,* edited by John Sorenson, xi–xxxiv. Toronto, Ont.: Canadian Scholars' Press, 2014.

Spiegel, Marjorie. *The Dreaded Comparison: Human and Animal Slavery.* New York: Mirror Books, 1997.

Srinivasan, Krithika. "Caring for the Collective: Biopower and Agential Subjectification in Wildlife Conservation." *Environment and Planning D* 32, no. 3 (2014): 501–17.

Star, Susan Leigh. "Power, Technologies, and the Phenomenology of Conventions: On Being Allergic to Onions." In *A Sociology of Monsters: Essays on Power, Technology, and Domination,* edited by John Law, 26–56. New York: Routledge, 1991.

Statistic Brain Research Institute. "Zoo Statistics." http://www.statisticbrain.com/zoo-statistics/.

Striffler, Steve. *Chicken: The Dangerous Transformation of America's Favorite Food.* New Haven, Conn.: Yale University Press, 2005.

Tabor, Roger. *The Wildlife of the Domestic Cat.* London: Arrow Books, 1983.

Tansey, Geoff, and Joyce DeSilva, eds. *The Meat Business: Devouring a Hungry Planet.* London: Earthscan, 1999.

Taylor, Sunaura. *Beasts of Burden: Animal and Disability Liberation.* New York: New Press, 2017.

Teather, David. "'Holocaust on a Plate' Angers US Jews." *Guardian,* March 3, 3003. https://www.theguardian.com/media/2003/mar/03/advertising.marketingandpr.

Ticktin, Miriam. *Casualties of Care.* Berkeley: University of California Press, 2011.

Ticktin, Miriam. "Policing and Humanitarianism in France: Immigration and the Turn to Law as State of Exception." *Interventions* 7, no. 3 (2005): 347–68.

Torres, Bob. *Making a Killing: The Political Economy of Animal Rights.* Oakland, Calif.: AK Press, 2007.

Tsing, Anna. "Blasted Landscapes (and the Gentle Arts of Mushroom Picking)." In *The Multispecies Salon*, edited by Eben Kirksey, 87–110. Durham, N.C.: Duke University Press, 2014.

Twine, Richard. "Revealing the 'Animal–Industrial Complex'—a Concept and Method for Critical Animal Studies?" *Journal for Critical Animal Studies* 10, no. 1 (2012): 12–39.

U.S. Department of Agriculture. "Farm Income and Wealth Statistics: Annual Cash Receipts by Commodity." https://data.ers.usda.gov /reports.aspx?ID=17832.

van Dooren, Thom. *Flight Ways: Life and Loss at the Edge of Extinction*. New York: Columbia University Press, 2014.

van Dooren, Thom. "Invasive Species in Penguin Worlds: An Ethical Taxonomy of Killing for Conservation." *Conservation and Society* 9, no. 4 (2011): 286–98.

Van Kleek, Justin. "The Sanctuary in Your Backyard: A New Model for Rescuing Farmed Animals." *Our Henhouse*, June 24, 2014. http://www .ourhenhouse.org/2014/06/the-sanctuary-in-your-backyard-a-new -model-for-rescuing-farmed-animals/.

Verdery, Katherine. *The Vanishing Hectare: Property and Value in Postsocialist Transylvania*. Ithaca, N.Y.: Cornell University Press, 2003.

Vialles, Noilie. *Animal to Edible*. Translated by J. A. Underwood. Cambridge: Cambridge University Press, 1994.

VINE Sanctuary. "About Us." http://vine.bravebirds.org/about-us/.

Vivanco, Luis A., and Robert J. Gordon, eds. *Tarzan Was an Ecotourist . . . and Other Tales in the Anthropology of Adventure*. New York: Berghahn Books, 2006.

Vivieros de Castro, Eduardo. "Cosmological Deixis and Amerindian Perspectivism." *Journal of the Royal Anthropological Institute* 4, no. 3 (1998): 469–88.

Wadiwel, Dinesh. "Three Fragments from a Biopolitical History of Animals: Questions of Body, Soul, and the Body Politic in Homer, Plato, and Aristotle." *Journal for Critical Animal Studies* 7, no. 1 (2008): 17–31.

Wadiwel, Dinesh. *The War against Animals*. Leiden, Netherlands: Koninklijke Brill, 2015.

Walmart. "Walmart U.S. Announces New Animal Welfare and Antibiotics Positions." May 22, 2015. https://corporate.walmart.com/newsroom /2015/05/22/walmart-u-s-announces-new-animal-welfare-and -antibiotics-positions.

Warkentin, Traci. "Whale Agency: Affordances and Acts of Resistance in Captive Environments." In *Animals and Agency,* edited by Sarah E. McFarland and Ryan Hediger, 23–44. Leiden, Netherlands: Koninklijke Brill, 2009.

Weiss, Brad. "Making Pigs Local: Discerning the Sensory Character of Place." *Cultural Anthropology* 26, no. 3 (2011): 438–61.

Weiss, Brad. *Real Pigs: Shifting Values in the Field of Local Pork.* Durham, N.C.: Duke University Press, 2016.

Whatmore, Sarah, and Lorraine Thorne. "Wild(er)ness: Reconfiguring the Geographies of Wildlife." *Transactions of the Institute of British Geographers* 23, no. 4 (1998): 435–54.

Winders, Delcianna. "Captive Wildlife at a Crossroads—Sanctuaries, Accreditation, and Humane-Washing." *Animal Studies Journal* 6, no. 2 (2017): 161–78.

Winograd, Nathan. *Redemption: The Myth of Pet Overpopulation and the No Kill Revolution in America.* Los Angeles, Calif.: Almaden Books, 2007.

Wolfe, Cary. "'A New Schema of Politicization': Thinking Humans, Animals, and Biopolitics with Foucault." In *Foucault Now: Current Perspectives in Foucault Studies,* edited by James D. Faubion, 152–67. Cambridge, Mass.: Polity, 2014.

Wolfson, David. "Beyond the Law: Agribusiness and the Systemic Abuse of Animals Raise for Food or Food Production." *Lewis and Clark Animal Law* 2 (1996): 123–54.

Wolfson, David, and Mariann Sullivan. "Foxes in the Hen House: Animals, Agribusiness, and the Law—a Modern American Fable." In *Animal Rights: Current Debates and New Directions,* edited by Cass R. Sunstein and Martha C. Nussbaum, 205–33. Oxford: Oxford University Press, 2004.

# Index

**Elan Abrell** is visiting assistant professor of environmental studies at Wesleyan University, adjunct instructor of animal studies and anthropology at New York University, and adjunct assistant professor of anthropology at Western Connecticut State University.